P9-DUX-772

The New Screenwriter Looks at the New Screenwriter

THE NEW SCREENWRITER LOOKS AT THE NEW SCREENWRITER

by William Froug

SILMAN-JAMES PRESS
Los Angeles

Copyright © 1991 by William Froug

All rights reserved. No part of this book may be used or reproduced
in any manner whatsoever without written permission from
the publisher, except in the case of brief quotations
embodied in critical articles and reviews.

First Edition 1992

Library of Congress Cataloging-in-Publication Data

Froug, William.
The new screenwriter looks at the new screenwriter/by William Froug.
p.   cm.
1. Motion picture authorship. 2. Screenwriters—Interviews.
I. Title. II. Title: New screen writer looks at the new screen writer.
PN1996.F77   1991   808.2'3—dc20   91-48355

ISBN: 1-879505-04-5

The credits listed at the beginning of each chapter reflect
those provided by the Writers Guild of America
at the time this book was in production.

Cover design by Heidi Frieder

Printed and bound in the United States of America

SILMAN-JAMES PRESS
distributed by Samuel French Trade
7623 Sunset Blvd., Hollywood, CA 90046

For Christine Michaels, best friend, lover, wife, editor,
and partner, a woman for all reasons.

And for Hopi Hall, Ashley Hirano, Andrew and Emily Froug,
who make a grandpa very proud and happy.

And, foremost, to the screenwriters,
without whom our films and these pages would be blank.

Contents

Acknowledgments

Jim Fox, a writer's dream editor; Gwen Feldman, Godmother of this project; Grace Reiner, indispensable advisor, superstar WGA staffer, lawyer, mom, wonderwoman; Roger Ebert, thumbs-up friend and human being, creator of the invaluable *Movie Home Companion—my* constant companion; UCLA Professor Lewis Ray Hunter, esteemed colleague, the man who gave Writer's Block a new and positive meaning for student writers; and Michelle Lemmers, unflappable and nearly perfect typist. Suzy, Nancy, Lisa, and Jonathan, always there when you need them, my four Lifetime Achievement Awards.

Introduction

It is not unusual for a writer to begin a project with a clear vision of what it will be about only to discover in the writing process that his characters and his story take him in a new and surprising direction. This happened to me while working on this book.

When the good folk at Silman-James Press asked me to submit a proposal for a follow-up to my first book, *The Screenwriter Looks at the Screenwriter* (initially published in 1971 and reprinted by Silman-James in 1991), I knew or thought I knew exactly how these new interviews would unfold. If anybody knew up front the answers to these screenwriting questions, I certainly thought I did. After all, I'd spent forty years of my life as an active writer-producer in Hollywood, active in the Writers Guild of America, west, a founding member and former chairman of the Caucus for Producers, Writers and Directors, and a twelve-year member of the Board of Directors of the Producers Guild of America.

I was wrong.

I selected the outstanding screenwriters for this book because they are among the most successful of the new generation of writers who've come up in the past twenty years and they represent an excellent cross section of what is happening today in the Hollywood writing community. Some of them are my former students, either at the University of Southern California's excellent School of Cinema-Television where I taught from the mid to late seventies or at the University of California at Los Angeles's equally excellent School of Theatre Arts, Film, and Television. I was eager to interview my former students who had fulfilled their wildest dreams of becoming superstar writers in the Hollywood mainstream. How did their dreams work out? Is it what they imagined it would be? Was film school worthwhile? How do they pursue their craft? What lessons have they learned?

Circumstances would not allow me to travel to New York to interview East Coast writers as well as Los Angeles to interview Hollywood writers. In addition, almost all of my students set working in the Hollywood mainstream as their goal. So, I decided to go west.

As my first interview, I chose Jeffrey Boam. His rapid success in Hollywood is nothing less than phenomenal. He wrote screenplays for *two* of the top ten grossing movies of 1989, *Lethal Weapon II* and *Indiana Jones and the Last Crusade*. It must be noted that the second *Lethal* not only garnered excellent reviews but almost doubled the gross of the first *Lethal Weapon*. The public liked it so much that Jeff is now working on *Lethal III*. In addition, Jeff has written *Funny Farm*, *The Lost Boys*, and *The Dead Zone*, among others. Any way you look at it, Jeff is riding high. He's probably the highest paid contract screenwriter in the history of the movies. When I recently checked in with Jeff, he was still writing *Lethal III* at a furious pace, though they are in the *third month* of shooting! Alas, this is not unheard of for a Hollywood screenwriter.

I had never met Joe Eszterhas, but I knew from the start I wanted him in this book. Joe is a flamboyant character who always manages to find himself in the center of controversy. He is also a leading and most outspoken defender of the rights of screenwriters to protect their material. That is one of the reasons many screenwriters look on him as a leader in their battle for recognition. Joe also happens to be the highest paid *freelance* screenwriter in the history of motion pictures. This past year he sold his original screenplay *Basic Instinct* for *three million dollars*, the highest price ever paid for a screenplay, and, in that same year, sold another of his original screenplays for *1.5 million dollars*. As Joe said to me, laughing, "I had a good year."

I chose Anna Hamilton Phelan, an actress turned screenwriter, not only because she wrote a movie I much admired, *Gorillas in the Mist*, but because she wrote another original screenplay, *Mask*, knowing that the chances of selling it were close to zero. Anna is a writer who writes from her *instincts*, her intuition, a quality I much admire in a screenwriter. Anna offers wannabe screenwriters one line of advice that is surely the best I have ever heard. If you pay heed, it will stand you in good stead.

Following your bliss has been the screenwriter's wisest choice since long before we all heard of Joseph Campbell. It is surely one of the important themes that runs through all these interviews. When I first contacted Diane Frolov, fifteen years after our UCLA graduate seminar together, she reminded me that I told my students back then not to try to second-guess the marketplace, but to write their own vision. In the final analysis of our lives, as well as our writing, what else do we really have to listen to but the messages from our own souls, psyches, guts, instincts, muses, whatever you call it? That is where our personal truth, our themes, our creativity lies. The writers who fearlessly kept writing what they truly believed, in my experience, are the ones who have gone on to the greater glory—not merely money or fame but something far more basic: inner-peace and genuine fulfillment.

The elegant and the ageless Fay Kanin, a screenwriter of long standing, was the last interview in my first book. I had to find out what had happened to her in the twenty years since then. What Fay did is go out and knock them dead, that's all. She wrote two of the best television movies ever made:

Friendly Fire, a true classic, and *Tell Me Where It Hurts*, a fine piece of writing that earned her *two* Emmy Awards—Best Original Teleplay and Writer of the Year. She has been seen on TV at the Oscar ceremonies as President of the Motion Picture Academy of Arts and Sciences for *four years running*, making her probably the most *seen* screenwriter in the history of the movies.

My friend at Samuel French Trade, Gwen Feldman, suggested, and I coincidentally planned, to interview agents who understood both writers and the writers' marketplace. I immediately knew the two agents I wanted in the book: Bill Haber and Rowland Perkins, two of the five co-founders of Creative Artists Agency. CAA is currently the most powerful talent agency in Hollywood. Bill and Rowland have been my good friends for many years. They were also my agents for about five years. Together, we lunched many times, socialized with our wives, and even managed a few grotesque tennis games. The one thing I knew about these guys, besides their now being superagents, was that they would be absolutely straight with me, no twists and turns, no dipsy-doodles. I knew they would tell me the way it is now, concisely and without frills. That's what you've got in their interview: the way it really is today for screenwriters in Hollywood. When they say that there are writing jobs to be had, an open market waiting for material, it takes on added meaning.

The former student of mine who opened up new doors for me as I developed this book is Dan Pyne. Dan is one of today's hottest screenwriters. Coming off his rewrite for this summer's hit *Doc Hollywood*, Dan has far more offers than he can handle but still clings to his television work, keeping an eye on his series "The Antagonists," for which he is executive producer.

Why would these hotshot new kids on the Hollywood block waste their time working in TV? The reason is so simple that it amazes me I did not think of it. In television the writer enjoys a level of respect not accorded him or her in movieland. Furthermore, in television what you write today you may very well see on the tube six weeks from now. No such opportunity exists for writers of movies. Most spec filmscripts never get made. And in today's television there is the possibility that you may do your best work *and* get recognition.

The impact of TV on these screenwriters' careers was a total surprise to me. During all my years of teaching, I cannot recall a single writing student who wanted to write television! Yet here they are, screenwriter after screenwriter finding new and different rewards from the home screen.

When Anna Hamilton Phelan found no big-studio buyers for her spec screenplay *Into the Homeland*, she sold it to HBO where its controversial subject matter was acceptable. That unique story is in her interview.

Diane Frolov showed outstanding promise during our graduate seminar together in the late seventies. Though, at that time, I felt her future in Hollywood was uncertain because her talent was far off the beaten path—her characters were fey and delightfully original. I still remember her poignant screenplay *Come Get Maggie,* which I much enjoyed but did not feel stood a chance in the marketplace. She taught me a lesson. *Maggie* became her "show script;" it got her writing jobs and recognition as an outstanding writer. You can see Diane's talent on display in the outstanding television comedy hit of the '90-91 season "Northern Exposure." Diane's writing was custom made for this highly intelligent, off-the-wall comedy series.

Today all the stigma once associated with working for the boob tube is gone, and a curious thing is happening because of it. Writers sick and tired of being treated like serfs in features now find new and even better careers in television. Bill Bryan's interview is a solid and straightforward account of what it's like to have a Hollywood "development" deal. Nothing like that happens to a TV writer. In TV, writers don't work for the director; it's the other way around. No wonder even Jeffrey Boam has tried his hand at working in TV and intends to do more of it.

In 1971, when *The Screenwriter Looks at the Screenwriter*

was first published, the Writers Guild of America, west had 3,000 members. Today, in 1991, that membership stands at 8,000, and the majority of those members presently employed are working in television.

Bill Bryan is one of the two best comedy writers I encountered during my fifteen years at UCLA. After getting a belly full of the humiliation and indignities that are often the price of Hollywood screenwriting, he took his extraordinary talent to TV sitcoms, where they welcomed him with open arms. You can see Bill's latest efforts on the new ABC comedy "Good & Evil." Bill's interview is a must for all wannabe screenwriters who find themselves involved in the seemingly infinite number of development deals the Hollywood studios toss out like bird seed.

Gregory Widen, a fireman-turned-screenwriter who travels his own road and makes a success of it, wrote this summer's megahit *Backdraft* and is now working on a new screenplay for director Ron Howard, with whom he had a very felicitous relationship on *Backdraft*. Yet Greg says he very much enjoyed writing and producing his own TV movie a while back and plans to do more television.

How do you crack the Hollywood market? Follow the example of Jim Cash and Jack Epps, Jr. These top-gun screenwriters wrote spec screenplay after spec screenplay, honing their crafts, developing their talents before becoming one of the hottest writing teams in Hollywood. Among the notches on their guns: *Top Gun, Secret of My Success, Dick Tracy, Turner & Hooch*, and several others. Jack and Jim have not seen each other for five years. They are truly 21st century writers. They do it with modems, fax machines, word processors, speaker phones, and whatever technological whiz-bang turns up next. Jim Cash is also a teacher at Michigan State University, where Jack Epps, Jr. was once his student. Jack likes the *Sturm und Drang* of Hollywood. Jim likes the laid-back life of his East Lansing campus. Who says writers have to meet face-to-face to collaborate? Theirs is a remarkable story.

One of the lessons of these interviews is that writers who are determined to become screenwriters will go to any length to achieve their goal. For a wonderful example, I give you Dr. Laurence Dworet, emergency-room surgeon and screenwriter of enormous talent and incredible determination. Dr. Dworet, a former writing student in one of my UCLA graduate screenwriting seminars, tells us how he became a doctor in order to support himself so one day he could become a screenwriter! His is a remarkably funny and yet cautionary tale. Laury's comic-horror story is all too common an experience for the new screenwriter in Hollywood.

The good news is that you don't have to own anything more than a typewriter to write screenplays. As I've always told my students, the key to writing screenplays is *the seat of the pants to the seat of the chair.* There is no substitute for hard work. There are basically two kinds of writers: writers who *talk* about being writers and writers who *write.* Decide for yourself which kind you are.

Ron Bass was an entertainment lawyer who went home from the office at night and quietly pursued writing. He wrote and sold three novels before he decided it was time to try screenwriting. Like Laury Dworet, Ron always knew he wanted to be a writer but pursued his law career to support his family while he was a closet novelist. Now, when it's writing time, Ron strolls across the street from his office, settles on a park bench, and, pad and pencil in hand, writes his screenplays.

Lawyer, doctor, fireman, actress, you name it, these are the screenwriters who knew what they wanted and gave of themselves completely to get it. Nobody was out there spreading a welcome mat for these folks. Nobody ever has for any writer. Writers since the dawn of time have created their own market and their own income. Nobody ever promised them anything if they'd sit in that lonely room and put words on paper. Those of us who have done it to keep a roof over our heads know there is no substitute for hard work. There are no easy ways, no shortcuts. Seat of the pants to the seat of the chair.

What I came to see and understand while working on this book was that this is a new breed of writer. They not only have their own vision but they have their own medium—film—and they understand it better than any generation of filmwriters since the medium was invented. They pursue it with a relentless determination that is awesome. They have what I will label Passion, Persistence, and Patience. It takes all three to hang in there, fighting rejection, as you struggle to fulfill your dream.

Of all the dedicated young screenwriters I have met in my classrooms over the years, none has so impressed me with their grit and single-minded determination as my former USC student and no doubt lifelong friend Dan O'Bannon. His is a story of the Grail pursued and maybe won. It is unlike any other I have ever known.

When I first met Dan back in the seventies, he was a USC film student and he was close to starving. I kid you not. This pale, wan, undernourished young man had not eaten in days because he did not have money to buy food. He was also developing his chronic inflammatory bowel disease that would keep him in and out of hospitals all of his adult life. Yet he had another kind of fire in his belly. He was *going to be a filmmaker*, starting as a screenwriter, and *nothing was going to stand in his way.* I knew that from our very first meeting.

Though he was not my writing student, Dan gave me his first screenplay to read. It was over two hundred pages long (at least eighty pages too long), but I took it home and read it carefully. It was verbose, the plotting was clumsy, and one of the two major characters, Pancho Villa, was written as a stereotypical Hollywood idea of a Mexican. Everything was wrong with the script except for one feature that overwhelmed all the defects: the writing was brilliant. It was a masterful piece of work. I met with Dan several times to discuss this screenplay, *The Devil in Mexico.* What I came away with was this incredible character—Dan—who would follow his vision and fight for his dream in spite of serious illness, near starvation, and a lot of rejection. I knew beyond a shadow of a doubt that this young man would realize his dreams if his health held out.

Over the next decade, we kept in contact and I hired him to write a television script for a series Bill Bowers and I were struggling to make work, but Dan's mind was not on TV. He was going to make his mark on the big screen and make it big. Which he has. I knew from the git-go that I had to interview Dan for this book. I met him in his hospital room and we talked as he paced about, his hand connected to various IV tubes on a rolling rack. Surely it was one of the most bizarre setups for an interview ever encountered.

Dan O'Bannon is the ultimate extension of all the new screenwriters you will find in this book, some of them my former students, a few my lifelong friends, all of them full of an almost overwhelming determination to follow their vision and to put that vision on film.

Nothing I have ever done in my long life and long career has ever so informed me about film being this generation's medium as has working on this book.

It's true, there are hundreds and hundreds of writing jobs now available in Hollywood. Cable television and home video have opened up new and rich markets. Who twenty years ago could have dreamed that almost the entire world would own VCRs and build their evenings at home around movies on videotape? Reliable reports say that the videotape-market income is bigger than the domestic box-office income. Apparently it will only grow. America and much of the world have gone movie-mad. And the movies they all seem to want are *American* movies. Why? I am now writing a new book about it.

This work is dedicated to all writers, young or old, black or white, male or female—all writers everywhere who dream of becoming screenwriters and who have the courage to follow their dreams.

W.F.
Ponte Vedra Beach, Fl
October 3, 1991

Anna Hamilton Phelan

1985 MASK *(Writer)*

1987 INTO THE HOMELAND [HBO Movie]
  (Writer)

1988 GORILLAS IN THE MIST *(Shared Story and
  Sole Screenplay)*, WGA and Academy
  Award Nominee

#02165

*Because of what I felt might
be the audience's reaction to seeing Rocky Dennis' face
the first time I decided to handle this
moment in a very specific way.
Let the audience
enter Rocky's world
slowly... have them
get to know him
through the music
he was listening to.
By seeing his base-
ball card collection,
his posters on his
walls. Then using
quick glimpses of
the boys face
in a mirror...
until slowly they
see his face
fully... but
still in the mirror
I wanted to give
each person some
time alone with
this boy & his
beyond face...
before beginning to
tell his story.*

FADE IN

1   EXT. MOUNTAIN FOOTHILLS - MORNING   1

The foothill communities lie in a trench at the bottom of
the San Gabriel Mountains: towns given birth by subdividers
after World War II that now fold into one another.

BEGIN CREDITS

The sound of Bruce Springsteen's "Badlands" is faintly heard
as we see the results of the Planning Department of the City
of Azusa. The seventy-five square miles of streets are
crisscrossed in perfect pattern.

A series of shots brings us in closer as the music becomes
slowly, but increasingly, louder.

EXT. AZUSA STREET - MORNING   -

The street is lined with small tract homes built in the
1950s. Pickup trucks and American-made cars sit in drive-
ways. Several of these cars are propped up on cinder blocks.

3   EXT./INT. ROCKY DENNIS' ROOM - MORNING   3

We are now close in on a bedroom window of one of the houses.
Through the window we see a back view of fifteen-year-old
Rocky Dennis. His movements, as he rushes around his room,
are typical of the average hurried teenager. The room is
also representative of a young American male in the year 1977.
The walls are covered: a Bruce Springsteen poster, a   (X)
Beatles poster, pictures of Harley Davidson motorcycles and
a cork bulletin board partially covered with baseball trading
cards. "The 1955 BROOKLYN DODGERS" printed on cardboard.

4   INT. ROCKY'S ROOM - MORNING   4

The music is now at a level only a fifteen-year-old can
love. Half-opened cardboard boxes tell us Rocky is in the

process of moving into this room in his new house. We see (X)
quick glimpses of him in the mirror. A jacket is pulled
from the closet and, with his back still to us, he shoves
his arms into the sleeves. He checks out his image in
the mirror. For the first time we see, in the mirror, the
face of Rocky Dennis. Small eyes are extremely wide-set
on his enormous face. The bridge of his nose is nonexistent.
It looks like he's wearing a bizarre mask. He ruffles his
hair, hikes up his collar, and assumes a "rock star with
guitar" pose and does a little pantomime to the music. He
checks the image again. He likes it. Turning from the mirror,
he sees something out the window. Then it's one more look in
the more mirror and a push on the stop button of his tape
machine. The music cuts off midnote. He's out the door.

> *"Write with no attachment to outcome."*

I lived for more than a dozen years in Santa Monica, California, overlooking Santa Monica Canyon, a beautiful, wooded area populated with more than its share of artists, writers, and all sorts of creative folks.

Yet when I went searching for Anna Hamilton Phelan (yes, she uses all three names though none of them are her married name), I soon found myself hopelessly lost. Knowing that I was within walking distance, I nonetheless had to phone for directions.

Within minutes a gracious, friendly, beautiful woman, tall, with blond tresses, was at the curb to greet me as I parked my car. It would be reasonable to suppose that more than one man has fallen in love with this screenwriter on first sight.

But mine was another mission. Last year my wife embarked on an African safari that included a trek up into the mountains of Rwanda to visit the great apes, nose-to-nose. I have been fascinated by the photographs on her office walls ever since. I had to meet the woman who wrote the movie *Gorillas in the Mist* about the pioneer researcher of the great apes, Dian Fossey.

Ms. Phelan lives in a frame house that began life as a typical Southern California beach shack and has, over the years, been upgraded several times to a comfortable, two-story, rambling epitome of casual California living.

As we settled in to talk, I noted several African art pieces scattered about. I asked Ms. Phelan about them, since my wife and I also collect primitive art. And she replied, "They just seem to have settled in here."

Though we had never met, I felt immediately as though I was revisiting an old friend. This is our conversation, which happens to include the best single sentence of advice for the new screenwriter that I have ever heard.

FROUG: Let's start with *Gorillas in the Mist.* Tell me about it. Did you go up to the mountains of Rwanda?

PHELAN: I did when I took the assignment from Universal, who had purchased Dian Fossey's book called *Gorillas in the Mist.* I think it was 1987. When Dian Fossey was still living, they had bought that book from her and offered the project to me. I read the book. It was mostly Dian's research with the gorillas. Chapter after chapter on gorilla dung and things; there was no story. So I said, "Thank you very much, but no thank you." Subsequently, about a year after that, Fossey was murdered. And then I thought, "Well, what is this about? What is this?" Now there was something more going on here than just a woman going up there and researching.

FROUG: There was a line of dramatic tension to say the least, right?

PHELAN: You bet. Exactly. It was right there for me. So I started asking around and made some phone calls, and someone told me in New York that they knew a saleswoman at Bergdorf Goodman who knew Dian Fossey and who twice a year sent evening gowns to Dian Fossey's research camp. And I thought, "This is very interesting that this woman, who's up there mucking around in the mud with the gorillas, orders these fancy ballgowns." I had visions of Blanche DuBois, you know. It was just wonderful.

FROUG: In the mist.

PHELAN: Yeah, Blanche in the Mist.

FROUG: Streetcars in the Mist.

PHELAN: Right. So after snooping around a little bit more and finding out this was a very interesting woman, aside from her involvement with the gorillas, I thought, "There may be something to this. This is something I'm interested in." So I called Universal and said, "Remember that book you offered me, that project? I'm interested now." They said, "Great. We'd love for you to do it." And at that point in time I went to Rwanda, Africa, before I started writing it. I went there to really find out what the story was on this woman. I spent a month in Rwanda, part of it talking to people who knew her—everyone, I think, that knew her I was able to get to—and the other part of it, going up to her research center, which is up ten thousand feet.

FROUG: You made that climb?

PHELAN: Yes. It was interesting because our guide walked a lot faster than I did and we left too late, so we ended up getting to that research center after dark, which was really something. I had never seen dark like that. Deepest, darkest Africa was deepest, darkest, Africa. This was only a month and a half after her murder. So everyone in the camp—there were two student researchers and some of the trackers—was a little bit leery of me. They knew I was there to research this woman's life.

FROUG: Did they think they were getting another Dian Fossey?

PHELAN: No, they thought they were getting someone who was investigating the murder. They were worried, because after she was murdered, the Rwanda government did arrest several of the trackers, and they were never heard from again. Rwanda's one of the seven countries in the world that's still on Amnesty International's list. It's real bad there. But, yes, I did spend time with the gorillas. I went out the next day after I arrived and didn't have any sightings, went out with one of Dian's trackers and one of the researchers, a young American man. The second day we went out—we were out for only an hour and a half—and came upon a gorilla family and spent the day kind of just sitting there looking at each other. It's a very strange experience to look into their eyes, because you feel this kind of connection. It's very bizarre. You keep saying, "This is a gorilla. This is an animal." It's a very strange kind of thing. These were habituated families, because Dian had done that with them. She made them pretty comfortable. She made the animals very comfortable around humans, which in some ways was not good, because you can *tell* a tourist, "Don't ever touch one; don't get close." But it's real hard for people not to. Gorillas don't have our viruses. They have different kinds of viruses. The gorillas become ill from the humans. But it was an extraordinary experience, getting to know her world. I interviewed thirty-six people and I couldn't find anyone who liked her.

FROUG: I've heard that, too, by the way. My wife read her book and said that she concluded Dian probably was an alcoholic.

PHELAN: That's right. She was.

FROUG: No doubt she was a totally unlikable person, as a zealot is, who is just determined, "Nobody will stand in my way." It makes for a great character in a film, doesn't it?

PHELAN: It does, except that I think it would have made for a better character in this particular film if the scenes that had been written to give us some insight into her childhood would have been in the film. They unfortunately were cut for time reasons.

FROUG: They were filmed but cut?

PHELAN: Yes. There's one scene in the screenplay where she tells this man that she's in love with, this photographer named Bob Campbell, a little bit about her background. Dian's father was an alcoholic who committed suicide. You get kind of an idea of what kind of childhood she had. She was a very big-boned girl, the daughter of a very tiny, little bird-like mother. So Dian must have looked like her biological father. Anyway, the mother, after Dian's father died, remarried, and something happened there. The stepfather didn't like Dian; she spent most of her time by herself; she always ate alone. She was a loner from the get-go. She was an only child. Even in college she insisted on her own room. There were certain personal things that were established a long, long time ago. People were going to disappoint her, so I think she felt more comfortable with the gorillas. As I said, that scene was cut. I think the studio felt that vistas of the geographic location were more important than the character scenes that I, of course, would want. Let's know a bit more about the character.

FROUG: The character scenes, it seems to me, are the first to go in most screenplays.

PHELAN: Always. But, yes, she was fascinating, but quite unlikable. As she got older and ill, the fact that she was a three-pack-a-day smoker plus the lack of oxygen up there—ten thousand feet up, very thin air—eventually got her. She couldn't go out with the gorillas anymore. She just couldn't breathe.

FROUG: When she was murdered, was she in failing health?

PHELAN: She was in failing health. I think if Dian Fossey could have arranged her death, this is exactly the death she would have arranged.

FROUG: A martyr's death. Did you get any sense of who might have killed her while you were there?

PHELAN: Many people in Rwanda felt that the government had her killed because she was becoming such a pain in the rear for the government. It was "her" mountain and "her" gorillas and she didn't want the tourists. But the government was finding that there was an income (they're a very poor nation) coming from the tourists. They wanted the tourists in there. So she was fighting them on that. And the poaching, she was just so crazy on that. She was on the government all the time about getting her more policemen out there to try to catch these poachers. She was just becoming a pain to them, I think. Some people think they may have arranged her murder.

FROUG: I heard a story—I don't know if it's true or not—that

Jon Peters and Peter Guber made a deal with the government to lease the use of the gorillas. True?

PHELAN: That's what I've been led to believe.

FROUG: Universal wanted to do the story, but Peters and Guber, working with Warner Bros., in effect, tied up the rights by buying the gorillas.

PHELAN: They bought the gorillas. I said to Peter, "You know you did the smartest thing." But I hated it because I did the screenplay for Universal.

FROUG: But they didn't have the gorillas.

PHELAN: They didn't have the gorillas. As soon as Dian was murdered, very smart businessmen across town—the two Peters—said, "You know, there's something here. We don't have a script, but we do have the money to get on an airplane, fly to Rwanda, and buy up the rights to that mountain." Get those gorillas and make sure nobody else can photograph them. And what that did was force Universal into bed with Warner Bros.

FROUG: How did they happen to come to you in the first place?

PHELAN: Probably because I had written *Mask,* and that was a Universal picture. I had a good relationship with the people at Universal.

FROUG: You'd had a good start, so they wanted to get another film from you?

PHELAN: I guess so, yes.

FROUG: I understand you knew the mother of the kid in *Mask,* Rusty Dennis.

PHELAN: Yes. In fact, I spoke to her yesterday.

FROUG: How's she doing?

PHELAN: She's doing fine. She lives in North Hollywood. She is now a telephone psychic. Only in Los Angeles.

FROUG: Only in Los Angeles indeed. [*Laughter*] That's marvelous. I love that.

PHELAN: I'm not sure exactly how it works, but, anyway, she's doing it. I forget how much she gets—twelve dollars an hour or something. She was quite excited about that.

She's done well. She's clean and sober. Her life is a bit bizarre by conventional standards, but . . .

FROUG: Was she happy with Cher's portrayal of her?

PHELAN: Oh, very much so.

FROUG: She was on the set?

PHELAN: She was not on the set, but she spent some time with Cher. I'll never forget the first day they met each other. It was before the shooting started. Cher was set to play the part, and I remember sitting in Cher's kitchen and watching these two women kind of walk around each other. They were very, very similar in temperament and the way they raised their children. Loose, but not loose. Very protective in many ways. Not a conventional kind of mom thing. You wouldn't give a Mother of the Year Award to either of these women, yet they should get it. It's that kind of thing. They're both very honest with their children, and if anybody threatens their children in any way, you can really see the mother lioness coming out. So they had some qualities that were similar, these two women. Cher was perfect. In fact, I wrote it for Cher.

FROUG: You had hoped they'd cast her or you knew they'd cast her?

PHELAN: No, I wrote it as a spec script. There was nobody who would have ever paid me to write it.

FROUG: How did it get made? Did Bogdanovich see it or what?

PHELAN: Well, no, I saw Rusty with her son Rocky in a hospital corridor when I was doing some work in a pediatric ward as an actress. I was doing a course for young doctors in how to take histories. I would pretend I was a parent of a child on the ward, and they'd learn how to ask the proper kinds of questions. Anyway, I saw this boy one day in the corridor of the hospital, and I was just amazed.

FROUG: Did he look like the character in the film?

PHELAN: He did. [*Anna shows me photographs of the real Rocky.*] Westmore won an Academy Award for the makeup that he created for Eric Stoltz, the actor who played the part. But anyway, I saw this boy and his mother in this hospital corridor, and I was so taken with just the whole package, the whole biker thing. This kid was in a lot of pain, but he took time with the other little kids who were afraid of him at first. There was something about him. I approached him and said, "You know, you really must have a story to tell. Would you ever be interested in talking to me?" And he said, "Sure. That'd be fine."

FROUG: Remarkable that he had that kind of poise.

PHELAN: Yeah. He was really something. But I think that had a lot to do with his mother. She threw him out the door and said, "You don't have to be beautiful to play baseball. Get out there." And that kind of thing.

FROUG: Marvelous.

PHELAN: But he subsequently died before I got a chance to ever really talk to him. But a few years later, after I had taken Al Brenner's writing course at UCLA, my children said, "Why don't you write a movie about the boy that you saw that day?" I used to tell my children about him, about this boy I'd seen in the hospital. And I said, "Oh, nobody'd ever do a movie like that." And they said, "Yeah, but, mom, you have to write it." So I tracked down Rusty and got her rights. And I wrote the screenplay as a spec screenplay. I entered into an agreement with Rusty that the first-year option was a hundred dollars. The second-year option, I think, was two hundred dollars. And the deal was, if the movie ever got made (well, the chances of this movie getting made were about one in four zillion), she would get fifteen thousand. The lawyer who had arranged the rights agreement with Rusty, a young lawyer in town named David Colden, was with the Weissmann Wolff law firm. I sent the script to him (I didn't have an agent), and he read it and said, "Well, I can't imagine anyone making this movie because it's kind of dark. But it's a good writing sample. Is it okay if I send it to Marty Starger? We also represent him." I said, "Yes, that would be great." He did, and Marty Starger read it. Somehow, I don't know how, it got to the top of the pile on his desk—he always has fifteen or twenty scripts that he's reading. Anyway, Marty happened to read it. He also happened to have dinner that night with Sid Sheinberg [the head of Universal]. Marty said to him, "You know, Sid, I read this script. It's kind of strange, but there's something about it. I happen to have it in the trunk of my car." And so that's how it got set up.

FROUG: Was Fay Kanin working for Marty?

PHELAN: No, not at the time.

FROUG: Do you know Fay?

PHELAN: Yes. I adore her. Fay and I are on a committee together at the Writers Guild for the professional status of writers.

FROUG: Let's talk about that. Tell me about the committee's function and purpose.

PHELAN: Well, this committee was born out of the 1988 strike. Somebody said, "One of the things we could do if this strike ever gets settled is get a committee together of maybe eight or ten screenwriters and the studio heads." So we get together about every three months. We've put together some guidelines that aren't finalized yet. One of the things we're going to try to do is to get the original writer to be able to stay on the project longer, things like that.

FROUG: Good. I asked Jeff Boam a question, and I was surprised by the neutrality of his answer. I saw everybody's films that I'm interviewing, including yours—and I said to him that I'd seen *The Dead Zone*. It was based on a novel by Stephen King with a screenplay by Jeffrey Boam and starred Christopher Walken, who was in every scene. Yet it's labeled "A David Cronenberg Film." I said to Jeff, "How does that become a David Cronenberg film?" He said, "Well, he's the director. I guess he deserves it." I think that's nonsense.

PHELAN: I do, too. This possessory credit (I don't know if

I'm saying it correctly), many directors won't do it. Michael Apted, on *Gorillas in the Mist,* said, "I would never take that kind of credit, it's ridiculous." For one person to take credit like it's their possession, like they've done it all, doesn't seem to make any sense to me either.

FROUG: That reminds me of a funny story. Bill Bowers was driving along in Brentwood with a screenwriter friend. He said, "Look, there's Bob Aldrich's house. Or should I have said, that's a house by Bob Aldrich." [*Laughter*]

PHELAN: That's the whole thing. Some deserve it—I think Woody Allen deserves it.

FROUG: He writes, directs, and stars in some of his films. Yes, he deserves that kind of credit.

PHELAN: That makes sense to me. And there are more directors than you think who will not take a possessory credit because they think it's strange, too. At least they're open enough to realize that there's a writer, there's a director of cinematography, there're all these people.

FROUG: A whole army of assistants.

PHELAN: Talk about collaborative art, I mean, this seems to be it. Possessory credit doesn't make any sense whatsoever.

FROUG: But that's something that the Directors Guild won in their negotiations. What can we in the Writers Guild do to stop it in our negotiations?

PHELAN: I think we need to negotiate with the Directors Guild on that.

FROUG: You can't go through the AMPTP [Association of Motion Picture and Television Producers] people?

PHELAN: I don't think so. I think it's the directors and the writers who have to do something.

FROUG: Do you think we will take a stand on it?

PHELAN: I don't know. To some writers, it doesn't seem to be important enough. I think it's wrong, but I don't know if I'd be willing to fight to the death for it. I think there are other things that are better to fight for. For instance, the idea that something goes wrong in the developing process of a screenplay and the first thing they do is bring on another writer is just crazy. I've never been rewritten, [*knocks on wood*] but I'm sure it will happen. It must be somewhat different than it used to be.

FROUG: No. You'd think so, but here's Laury Dworet, an emergency-room surgeon, who sold a screenplay to Disney for three hundred thousand dollars. Disney assigns it to a producer who's not happy with the screenplay, of course. And the producer brings in other writers to rewrite, pays them another three hundred thousand, and Dworet's left out in the cold.

PHELAN: That's one of the things the committee's going to try to get changed. On *Mask,* for instance, I was a new writer. I'd written a screenplay and the producer liked it. He optioned it for three months or so and we did some minor changes and then gave it to Universal. Universal optioned it, and the first thing they said was, "All right, fine, we own it. Let's bring on a real writer." [*Laughter*] And I didn't know this at the time. I'm glad I didn't.

FROUG: Because you'd have been out of there, right?

PHELAN: Well, I would have been, but Marty Starger went to bat for me. I found out later through somebody else that he said, "Look, this is hers; it was a spec script. Let's give her a shot at the first rewrite."

FROUG: First set of revisions.

PHELAN: First set of revisions. Let's give her that. They did, and they were pleased with what I did. That's why I was able to stay on. But I was only able to stay on because the producer fought for me. One of the things we hope to do with this status of writers committee is get into an agreement with the studios that the original writer at least gets to stay on for maybe one or two sets of revisions.

FROUG: There was another writer credit on *Gorillas in the Mist.* Who is Tab Murphy?

PHELAN: After Dian Fossey was murdered, Guber-Peters jumped on the train and did two things. They went to Africa and tied up the rights to the gorillas, and they hired a young screenwriter to write a screenplay as quickly as possible. That was Tab Murphy. I think he wrote one in about two weeks. I've not read it but, when the studios got married, they decided to use my screenplay. And it did seem fair to give this kid some kind of credit. I was more than willing to share story credit. He had gone into his agreement with Guber-Peters in good faith, and he didn't know about Universal

FROUG: That they already had a screenplay.

PHELAN: Exactly.

FROUG: I loved the device you used in *Gorillas* of the cross-narrations; it works wonderfully. You have Louis Leakey talking and it overlays with Dian reporting, reporting back and forth. That was a wonderful device, months and months and years pass by, but you manage to keep a kind of continuous thread.

PHELAN: Narrations are sometimes real cheats, you know. If it works, it seems to be good. But so many times it doesn't work. I think in this case, it did. I think it was luck more than anything. The thing with writing these darn lifetime biographies is, and this is somewhat interesting, people always say, "Well, you do biographies." And I always think, "Well, not necessarily." I went to my hometown two summers ago, a little town in Pennsylvania called Lock Haven. The librarian was still there from when I was in second grade, and she said, "Oh, yes. I remember you. You checked out *Clara Barton, Army Nurse* seventeen times." She said, "You always went to the biography section." And I said, "I did?" She said, "Oh yes, all you ever read was *Florence Nightingale*," and so on. So I think I am kind of drawn to biographies, although I never thought I was.

FROUG: They make wonderful movies if you find a character who has a driven situation, where they must take action. Is that a key to it?

PHELAN: I think so. And I think that cross-narration kind of helps solve some of the problems with these things that span fifteen years. But, you know, I have the desire to do a twenty-four hour something, a screenplay where everything happens in twenty-four hours.

FROUG: In order to get a built-in line of dramatic tension.

PHELAN: Exactly.

FROUG: In *Mask,* did you have a problem finding a built-in spine?

PHELAN: That was the easiest screenplay to write because the built-in spine was this kid's face. He carried the tension with him. So everywhere you went you had conflict, because of the way people perceived him, and, boy, that was easy compared to others.

FROUG: Also, early on you tell us that he has been doomed to die very soon.

PHELAN: Pretty quickly.

FROUG: So your protagonist is dealing with a life-and-death situation, even as he's trying to cope with a society that rejects him. It was built-in. I just saw *Into the Homeland* and thought it was a wonderful piece of work. You were the executive producer *and* the writer. How did you happen to sell it to television?

PHELAN: Well, I wrote it as a spec script after *Mask* was made. It was an area I was interested in—the area of the white-supremacist movement. It wasn't anything that anyone seemed to be interested in having me write, so I decided to write it as a spec script. The most interesting thing about this piece, for me, was that to get this story—to understand these people—I went to Coeur d' Alene in the northern part of Idaho, where the Aryan Nations compound is located. I infiltrated. I felt like an undercover CIA agent or something. I spent three days and three nights at the Aryan Nations compound as a person who was sympathetic to their cause and was able to get dialogue and to observe families—these very all-American families—mothers making gingerbread in the kitchen and fathers playing baseball with their sons. Picture-perfect families. And then this stuff would spew out of their mouths.

FROUG: Wasn't it frightening?

PHELAN: It really wasn't. No. It was frightening making the decision to go up there. My husband was not thrilled.

FROUG: I wouldn't blame him.

PHELAN: But once I was there, the old actress stuff came into play. I felt very comfortable and was able to absorb into the way they were living there. I never had a feeling that anyone was wondering who I was. I told them that I was visiting my sister in Spokane and that I had come up from Los Angeles, where I kept seeing all these mixed relationships, mixed marriages—black and white. They really took me to their bosoms. They desperately wanted converts. When people want converts very desperately, they believe.

FROUG: They overlook.

PHELAN: You bet. It was fascinating. I came back with a lot of good information about them. I'd also been interested in writing about a policeman who had kind of lost his will to go on. I thought I could couple those stories, and that's what I did.

FROUG: You did it beautifully.

PHELAN: Thank you. And then HBO . . .

FROUG: Yeah, I want to hear about that.

PHELAN: Well, the studios were not interested in it. They said it was too political. They didn't believe it. They thought it was so far-fetched. This was *before* all this stuff came out of the closet. These last few years there've been some trials with a man named Tom Metzger and his son who were exactly like the father and son in *Into the Homeland.* The studios thought it was kind of science-fiction.

FROUG: Would you look forward to working in television again?

PHELAN: Well, HBO is kind of a hybrid. It's kind of television, but it's not television. It's weird. I'd never worked in television. We had a three-million-dollar budget, which is not large even for television, but it felt like a smaller-scale feature film. It was certainly handled that way by HBO. I liked the HBO people a lot. I had a good experience with them.

FROUG: Would you do more television? Do you look forward to it?

PHELAN: Network television is tough because of the commercials and all that business. Let's say cable television, yes. I don't know about network. Cable is somewhat different.

FROUG: Did you have creative control of the project as executive producer?

PHELAN: I had more control than I would have had as just the writer. Ultimately, HBO had control of it.

FROUG: Did they make changes? Ask for changes in the script?

PHELAN: They asked for changes in the script, which I did after a little bit of a battle and deciding that it was worth it to get this project on the screen. I felt the subject was that important. I did change a major facet. In my original draft, the main character was the product of a white mother and a black father—a black jazz player who played in the bands in Los Angeles in the forties.

FROUG: They wouldn't let you do that?

PHELAN: They didn't like that. And they never really gave a reason. In the original draft, the main character played by Powers Boothe had, as he was growing up, pretended that he didn't have this black father. He, himself, had turned away from his heritage.

FROUG: I see. He passed.

PHELAN: And he accepts his heritage. In the original, in the end he seeks out his father, Honey—the black trombone player. And his whole family reunites.

FROUG: That's a pretty big change, don't you think?

PHELAN: It was a huge change, but I was willing at the time to make that change to get the story about the white supremacists on the tube.

FROUG: You did, and you did it well. How was the pay?

PHELAN: I can't remember what it was. It's much less than features. But there's an avenue in television. Television, particularly cable, seems to be much more willing to deal with controversial subjects than the feature-film studios.

FROUG: That's a very important point.

PHELAN: Yeah. It's just amazing—AIDS, racism, all that.

FROUG: They've done those things wonderfully, haven't they?

PHELAN: Absolutely. I think some of the writing in television is some of the best writing ever. Even some of the things like "thirtysomething."

FROUG: I have some general craft questions. One thing I liked particularly about *Gorillas* is that, because I'm an Aristotelian, I always tell my students they must read Aristotle's *Poetics*. Aristotle says, "The beginning is that which nothing need come before." And you did it so beautifully in *Gorillas*. You start with Leakey's lecture and Dian rushing to class—she's late. You set it up immediately—nothing need be known before that. The story's starting on page one, scene one. Do you always do that when you're writing?

PHELAN: I try, but that is one of the most difficult things to do.

FROUG: Yeah, I always say to my students, "Page one is the toughest page you'll ever write."

PHELAN: Absolutely. Probably your students have the same thing, that page one feeling. You want to do a backstory.

FROUG: You want to tell a lot of stuff we don't want to know yet.

PHELAN: Exactly. So you have this tendency to write the first scene and then, you know, "Well, I'll put a scene in front of that and in front . . ." and then all of a sudden your first scene is four scenes ahead of your original first scene. I think that's a real trap. But I think you're right about page one as the place to start your story.

FROUG: In *Gorillas,* that particularly struck me. The story starts immediately, and you're right into it.

PHELAN: It has to be that way or I think the whole thing doesn't work. It just kind of . . .

FROUG: Lies there. The backstory can come much later, if at all.

PHELAN: Yeah.

FROUG: Hitchcock said, "A person who tells you everything right away is a bore." I think that's true. I think you start a character in motion and you slowly unpeel the onion and gradually reveal information only when you have to, on a need-to-know basis. That's what you did in *Gorillas*. It works great.

PHELAN: It's a difficult thing to do, an expository kind of writing—you want to stay away from getting all that information out in dialogue. And if you can find some creative ways to do it, where people see it rather than hear it, that always seems to feel better. I structure my screenplays in three acts.

FROUG: Do you follow a general paradigm? Do you say to yourself, "I need to have a first-act curtain around page twenty or twenty-five"?

PHELAN: I do. I think for me it's from coming out of the theater and writing in acts. I wrote plays before I wrote screenplays. I try to find a dramatic event to bring in around page twenty, twenty-five—twenty minutes into the movie—that hooks into the action and swings it around.

FROUG: Tell me about your playwriting background.

PHELAN: Well, when I was an actress in New York, I wrote two plays that were done off-off-off-off-off-Broadway. In church basements. I started by writing monologues for other actors to audition with. My background is in theater arts; I was a theater-arts major at Emerson College in Boston. They taught no screenwriting then. I think now they have a screenwriting course. But I just learned from plays. I learned dialogue. I think that I've a tendency to have somebody "enter a scene." You know, I keep thinking, "No, wait a minute. This isn't a play. Someone's not entering stage left. Get them in there and then start the scene." But that old stuff keeps coming back.

FROUG: I noticed that you're billed as the "Puppy Lady" in *Mask,* so you're still being an actress.

PHELAN: That's true. I have a very small part in a black wig and black leather. That was kind of a joke. It was fun.

FROUG: Do you still do any acting?

PHELAN: I don't, now. But, I'm working on a one-woman show that, if I get it into shape, I'm going to take it out and maybe do it around town in Equity. You know, Equity waiver stuff, but I'm not sure.

FROUG: Do you think, speaking of one-woman shows, that women writers are discriminated against in this town?

PHELAN: Well, it would seem so in that they are paid sixty-three cents to the dollar for their work, for their screenplays. So that would indicate that they are. That's from the Writers Guild Bielby Report that came out about a year ago, where they gave all the various numbers on what women make and . . .

FROUG: What older writers and black writers and minority writers make.

PHELAN: That's the real discrimination for older writers; I think it's worse for them than for anybody else. And an older writer, you know, is forty. It's very strange. Apparently, there was a memo that was circulated about six months ago. Peter Rainer, who's a critic for the *L.A. Times,* said there was a memo that was circulated (and I don't know what studio sent it out) that said, "Don't even bring us projects that are female-driven. We just will not do them." Now that was before Julia Roberts opened with *Sleeping with the Enemy,* so it's the first time a female-driven movie has what they call "opened," you know, has done a good first weekend. So I hope it will change.

FROUG: Also *Pretty Woman* was a big hit. That was the other turnaround.

PHELAN: Yes, that was Julia Roberts. That was still more of

his story than her story, I think. Or that's what I understand. This other one is strictly females. She gets top billing. It's been a long time since a woman could carry a film. I guess Barbra Streisand can still do it, but other than that, it's pretty rough. They say that nobody wants to see movies about women. I was advised to stop writing them. But, you know, I think I can't really do that. If I do that, then I'm part of the problem. So I will always continue to write about women and about men, but I'll continue to write about women because I think if we as writers, female writers or male writers, stop writing about fifty-two percent of the population (and women are fifty-two percent of the population), then, as Meryl Streep said, "In the year 2000, there won't be any on the screen." It just seems crazy.

FROUG: We were talking about a kind of self-censorship. I mean, for example, do you think you can sell a story about people over forty?

PHELAN: Much more difficult. I think that the studios seem to be frightened of taking a chance on it, because they have this demographic group, boys eighteen to twenty-six, that they think buy the theater tickets, and maybe they do. But I seem to remember as a kid that you went to the movies and you learned. You learned watching Barbara Stanwyck and David Niven. I had a friend, a boyfriend in high school, who learned how to tip from watching movies. I mean, a small town in Pennsylvania, the only thing you know is the coal mines. We learned how to do certain things from the movies. Well, today that's all gone. Here's a quote on that: "In 1987, women writers for television and film earned sixty-three cents for every dollar that a white male writer earned." That was a drop from seventy-three cents. We earned seventy-three cents in 1982, and it's dropped to sixty-three. It's going backwards.

FROUG: Well, regarding this frantic search for a certain hit, I like William Goldman's statement, "Nobody knows anything." As to what will be a hit movie, nobody knows in advance. I was on the Age Discrimination Committee of the Writers Guild for some years, and we initiated that study you quoted. I can tell you it's horrendous. We were shocked. We did the computer study of how many older writers were working, how many women were working, how many blacks were working, and the result was that it was all tilted to the white, male Caucasian. But since the study was released, I don't know if it's helped anything.

PHELAN: The only thing that would help, I guess, is everybody boycotting, if everybody stopped writing or started striking or something. But people don't seem to want to do that anymore. So I don't know what can be done. I was on a panel the other day, and Marilyn Bergman, the songwriter, said, "People can't like what they don't ever see." Somebody said, "Well, the public doesn't want to see stories about old people who are fifty." [*Laughter*] She said, "Well, how do you know? Why don't we make a few and see?" But I don't know what can really be done about it. I don't think it's a conscious thing with the studio heads. God, I hope it isn't. I think they just kind of subconsciously feel that only one age and one color and one sex can write. I mean, what else is there?

FROUG: Or pays money to see themselves, right?

PHELAN: Yeah, maybe.

FROUG: It's fear of failure that drives the industry.

PHELAN: Yeah. Their jobs are so tenuous all the time that they don't take risks. However, I say that and then I have to say I've been trying to set up a story for three years about a man named John Spain, who was the product of a white mother and black father, born in Mississippi in 1949, and was taken at age six by his white mother and put on a train to Los Angeles to be raised by a black family out here. When he was born he looked like a white baby. And as he got older, three, four, five, his features started to change and his skin started to darken, which is common among mixed-race babies. The Klan was snooping around and saying, you know, "That baby's not a white baby," and so on. His mother became frightened, and she put this child on a train and arranged for him to be raised by a family in Compton. So Johnny Spain got on a train at age five, a little white boy, and got off a little black boy.

FROUG: Marvelous story.

PHELAN: I thought so, too. I'd go around town and I'd say, "Listen to this story." Subsequently, this boy, very angry, committed a crime when he was seventeen. It was a street altercation that resulted in his murdering someone. He was sent to prison and this is him. [*She shows me a picture of Johnny Spain today.*]

FROUG: That's with you?

PHELAN: Yeah. And Johnny's spent twenty-one years in San Quentin. In prison, he became a protege of a man named George Jackson, who was a Black Panther and who was part of the prison revolutionary movement in the seventies. He's been out for three years. Anyway, it's a fascinating story. It really traces racism through one man's life. He got to see racism from both sides, as a white man and a black man. We'll also go through those revolutionary years of the sixties and the seventies. Anyway, I've been carting this story around for three years, and finally, a month ago, Columbia Studios said, "Okay, write it." So I'll be starting in about a month. So here's a story—who knows? It's a story that doesn't have any of the earmarks of a commercial success.

FROUG: But you believe in it.

PHELAN: I do, yeah.

FROUG: You know, I was talking to my friends and former agents, Bill Haber and Rowland Perkins, yesterday at CAA. And Haber said something very interesting at the close of our discussion. "Tell your students, if they're only writing for the money, they shouldn't bother."

PHELAN: I agree. Absolutely. It's amazing that he would say that, because I know so many young agents at other

agencies (at all agencies) who counsel exactly the opposite. They say, "You write a certain thing. If you want to
get it made, you gotta write it this way, and you gotta
write it for that age group." I think it's crazy to do it that
way. I'm pleased that Bill Haber said that.

FROUG: Even though you didn't go to film school you
obviously have a good background in drama.

PHELAN: Emerson College is a liberal-arts college in Boston.
I majored in theater arts. You come out with a degree and
twenty-five cents. It will get you what, a cup of coffee?
With no skills whatsoever, except that I must have learned
something, because . . .

FROUG: An understanding of drama.

PHELAN: Exactly. And it served me, but not right away. I was
an actress for years, doing things off-Broadway, little
things in television. Later, when I started to write seriously, a lot of things that I was taught in school came
back.

FROUG: How did you get an agent?

PHELAN: Well, in my case, because I had written a spec
screenplay that a studio had optioned, they came out of
the woodwork. See, I went in the back way. I had a script
that sold without an agent, and then, suddenly, agents
were everywhere.

FROUG: You got started because Marty Starger had your
script in the trunk of his car?

PHELAN: Exactly. Marty Starger had the script in his trunk,
gave it to Universal, and when they said yes, we're going
to option this, then agents were all over the place.

FROUG: Swarming?

PHELAN: Yes. I will share with you an agent story that I
always tell young writers—not necessarily *young* people,
new writers are not necessarily young (I didn't start
writing until I was thirty-five, thirty-six)—but writers who
don't have agents. When I first went to New York after
college, to be an actress, I made the rounds of the various
agencies in New York. I went into this major agency in

New York City to leave my 8 x 10 glossy. As I'm there at the front desk, the head agent walks by, looks at me, stops for a minute and says, "Are you an actress?" I said, "Yes, I am." He said, "Come on in." So I walked into this office with him, and he said, "How long have you been doing acting work?" I said, "Well, I just got here from college. I graduated three months ago, and I'm trying to get an agent." "Sylvia," he yelled to his secretary, "bring in the agency contracts. We're signing this gal, this girl." So I signed that day and he gave me the best advice an agent had ever given me. He said, "I represent a lot of big people. I'm going to forget about you unless you bug me. You have to call me. You have to call me three, four times a week, and you have to make me crazy. Make me hate you. If you don't, I'm going to forget about you, and this is not going to go anywhere." That was wonderful advice that man gave me. I did bug him and he did get me work. I became a friend of his, a friend of his wife's, a friend of his daughter's. I was invited to his grandson's bar mitzvah. At this bar mitzvah, he'd had a couple of drinks and came over to me and we talked. By then I had been doing some work, some television. He had indeed gotten work for me, and it was a good relationship. I said to him, "You know, I've always wanted to ask you, what in God's name possessed you to sign me like that?" Because I remember asking when I'd first gone in to see him, "Do you want me to read for you or anything?" He had said, "No, no, you don't have to read anything." And at this bar mitzvah (this is after a few drinks) he said, "Well, I'll tell you why. When I saw you that day in my office, you looked like a former girlfriend of mine who was the first girl I ever schtupped when I came to this country." And I said, "And that's why you signed me?" He said, "Yes. You looked like this Irish girl I knew in North Bronx," or wherever he was raised. "You looked so much like her it just took me back in my memory." And that's why he signed me. Because I looked like the first girl he'd ever gone to bed with. I think in many ways it's that simple. Something happens, something in somebody's mind clicks, you know, actors will go into auditions and the director will hate them. It will be because they remind them of somebody else, which is crazy. So the point is, if you get rejected, you have to persist. Don't give up. It was the best advice I ever got.

FROUG: I wrote a screenplay very loosely based on my experiences as skipper of a subchaser in World War II, and I gave it to Frank Cooper, my agent at the time. He shopped it around from studio to studio, and it was turned down as fast as they got it. After about nineteen rejects, I said, "Frank, let's forget the whole thing." He said, "No. One thing you gotta always remember, Bill: It only takes one buyer." Frank gave it to Walter Mirisch, and he bought it. And I learned forever that you can be rejected by almost everybody, but if *one* person likes your work, it's all you need.

PHELAN: It's so true.

FROUG: The Navy wouldn't rent us a subchaser, so the film was never made.

PHELAN: But it only takes one. That's hard to remember when you're getting all those "no"s.

FROUG: Who's the screenwriter you most admire?

PHELAN: Well, nobody remembers Frances Marion. Years ago, I was able to dig up some of her screenplays. *Dark Star*. She was a wonderful screenwriter. So I would say Frances Marion was somebody that I greatly admire. I also like William Goldman's work a lot.

FROUG: Do you read screenplays?

PHELAN: No. I hate to read them because of the form they use. It seems very awkward to me.

FROUG: Would you recommend that new screenwriters make up their own form? Goldman kind of did with *Butch Cassidy and the Sundance Kid*.

PHELAN: Yes. I think if you have a piece that you're doing and you really feel that the conventional form doesn't represent that work well, I'd say absolutely. Go for it. I know Goldman writes little things in the margins and stuff for the readers.

FROUG: Yeah. Something to make 'em read it.

PHELAN: William Goldman's screenplays are a lot of fun to read.

FROUG: He makes sure it's an entertaining experience.

PHELAN: He's a novelist, so it may come from that.

FROUG: Did you read Goldman's *Adventures in the Screen Trade*?

PHELAN: Yes, of course.

FROUG: Like it?

PHELAN: Yes, I loved it. And then I had the pleasure of spending some time with Mr. Goldman on a trip that eight screenwriters took to the Soviet Union. What a learning experience for me. Not only did I learn about the Soviet Union, but being on a bus with this crew, you know, and me being the newest of them, just sitting there with my ears open, listening to William Goldman. We were sometimes stuck for hours on this bus, so you can imagine. William Goldman, Paul Schrader, Frank Pierson, Ernie Lehman, Mel Shavelson . . .

FROUG: Two former presidents of the Writers Guild.

PHELAN: For want of a better word, the "older" writers, and then you had John Patrick Shanley, Larry Kasdan. I was the only female writer. The rest of them were males. And it was just wild. I learned so much, because you don't think that these really, really topnotch writers have the same problems you do. But they do. We all have the same problems, you know. We all have the same struggles, so that was great.

FROUG: What is your current price per screenplay? About what ballpark are you in these days?

PHELAN: This is a really bad thing for women, that I don't even know what I make.

FROUG: Oh, that's good that it elicited that answer. That's interesting.

PHELAN: I really don't—you know . . .

FROUG: That's why I was asking.

PHELAN: I'm terrible that way. How do the ballparks go?

FROUG: Some of the guys are getting three hundred thousand for a rewrite. For a brand new writer, three hundred thousand for an original is not unusual. A couple of my former students are now getting millions. Jeff Boam signed a three-year deal with Warners for four and a half million dollars. Joe Eszterhas got three million for *Basic Instinct*. I asked CAA agents Haber and Perkins yesterday, "What can a new writer expect on a spec screenplay?" They said, "Anything. The sky's the limit. We never know."

PHELAN: Well, my contracts are set up so that I get so much for the first draft. I'll have to check my things and then I'll call you.

FROUG: It's not important. It's just interesting whether you are below the price men get.

PHELAN: Oh, I'm sure I am. I'm sure I'm below the men. Usually I am. Sixty-three cents to the dollar is what we women average.

FROUG: Do you think there's any hope of changing that?

PHELAN: I don't know. Is there any hope for change across the board for women in every other job? It's about the same for women who are in any profession. I think it's a little worse as a screenwriter; I'm not sure. I think of how Jeffrey got started—that you put him in touch with somebody. It's easy to forget those things because there are certain people like you, Bill, who have a reputation for helping people. And you've probably done that so many times that you do forget. It's a wonderful example of how networking works.

FROUG: Let's discuss networking.

PHELAN: Unfortunately, in the beginning, you have to be in Los Angeles to do that. It's real hard to network from Scranton, you know. I think a new writer has to be in either New York or Los Angeles. And unfortunately it's probably Los Angeles. It could be anyone that you meet (you just have no idea), be it a teacher or a next-door neighbor who happens to know the boyfriend of so-and-so, who knows the something of so-and-so. That's how it works. And it's really so important in this business, particularly for writers. We don't get the exposure. A young actor can be in a play and an agent can go in and see them, but what do we writers do? Stand on the corner and read our scripts? So networking is very important.

FROUG: Haber and Perkins said, "All they have to do is get in a network where they know somebody who knows somebody who knows somebody." Even if you only know the guard at the gate, you've already got a foot in.

PHELAN: Absolutely. No question about it. So I think that's a great story.

FROUG: Do you see a trend toward smaller, more intimate films?

PHELAN: The small pictures that have done well last year— like *Ghost* and *Pretty Woman*—will hopefully help us get away from the hardware pictures.

FROUG: The crash and bash pictures?

PHELAN: Yeah. I hope that happens. There's certainly a place for them, but it would be nice if there would be a little bit of a selection. One of the reasons that I think this has happened is because the foreign market is so big and so much of the profits now come from there. So you have a motion picture that opens in Bangkok and that audience does not speak the English language. What they can understand is explosions.

FROUG: Right. Car chases they can understand. Good point.

PHELAN: So I think that's a problem. That may be the problem for women—screenplays or movies about women, the protagonist being a woman. Perhaps that's been a reason women aren't getting their movies made. Because so many cultures of the world don't want to see women, I guess, in motion pictures, or they're more sexist societies, or something. I don't know. One of the criticisms I get in my work all the time is that if I do write a female character, she's not sympathetic enough. And I always think, what if I went to a studio to pitch a story, and said I wanted to write a story about this female character. I'm going to describe her to you: she's very beautiful—that's a plus, okay?—she's very manipulative—that's a minus. Just to give you some idea of what she does through this story, she loves a man who is married to another woman, and she constantly tries to take this man away from the other woman. And the other woman is very, very lovely and a very good friend to her, but she wants to break up this marriage. She wants this man very badly. Because he doesn't feel the same way about her, she marries someone else. That someone gets killed in a war, and she's really happy that he gets killed . . .

FROUG: Scarlett. [*Laughter*]

PHELAN: Scarlett O'Hara! There you are, Bill. You describe that character, and you'd have executives with their eyes rolling back in their heads. She's the most unsympathetic character. Well, it's the most wonderful character in the world.

FROUG: She is really kind of the ultimate symbol of the liberated woman. I don't think any film has ever shown a totally liberated woman better than Scarlett O'Hara in *Gone With the Wind.*

PHELAN: I mean, she raises that fist, you know, and says, "This will never happen to me again." So I think that you just have to write from your heart, though many people and your friends and your family will tell you it's not commercial, and the agents will tell you it's not commercial, but you just have to go ahead and write it if you want to write it. It has to come from your heart, because if you write it from your head or from your wallet . . .

FROUG: Forget it.

PHELAN: Forget it.

FROUG: I tell my students to write what they feel about. If you don't write from what you feel, from your passion or from your instincts—follow your bliss, as Joseph Campbell said—you're out of luck.

PHELAN: I think so. And I think for new writers, if you can't think of anything to write about, just look in your family. Just think about Uncle Harry, because it's pretty amazing what's happening right near you. You can fictionalize so that nobody gets upset or, if you want to, you can do what I do—get the rights. You don't have to pay a fortune. I paid Rusty a hundred dollars. You get those rights and write about somebody in your home town. Fascinating stories are happening right next door to you. You don't need to write about someone famous, or you don't need to write, you know, John Rambo. Right down the street there's that old woman who lives in that house and nobody ever sees her. She's back in there. I would just love to know what's going on, or what happened in the past, or . . .

FROUG: People stories. I think, from what I'm hearing, maybe we're going to get more and more into people stories. I interviewed Dan Pyne, whose interview was wonderful because he was exploring character. He says he starts from character. Well, you do, too, don't you?

PHELAN: I have, actually, in both of the pictures that I've had made, *Mask* and *Gorillas*. I did start from character in those. It's the character that usually grabs me. My downfall always is the plot. That's the hardest part for me, plot. I can steal Alvin Sargent's great line. Alvin Sargent said, and this is the same way I feel, when he dies and is buried, he's going to have written on his tombstone, "Finally, a plot." [*Laughter*]

FROUG: Great line. Do you use scene cards when you're developing your plot?

PHELAN: I used to use index cards. Now I use legal pads, large legal pads.

FROUG: Do you write longhand or are you a computer person?

PHELAN: I do write longhand. I've never learned how to

type. It's really awful. I've tried. I've taken various courses on how not to be afraid of your machine, but I still go back to a pad and pencil.

FROUG: I'm terrified of computers. If it's good enough for Eugene O'Neill, it's good enough for me.

PHELAN: It's all right with me. I also do something that you might find interesting. I'll show it to you and then you can describe it. It's like newsprint. And I write out stories on it. When I pitch a story, I show them the story. I'll show you this.

FROUG: I'd like to see that. [*We walked upstairs to Anna's book-lined office where a large roll of thick cream-colored paper covered with large black handwritten notes was open on the floor.*] You've just shown me a unique style of laying out a story. Would you tell me about it, please?

PHELAN: Well, rather than using index cards . . . I used to use index cards, but now I buy a roll of butcher paper. It's about two feet wide, and it's in a long roll, like a scroll. And I write the story out on that. (Talk about linear!) I'll have a scroll twenty, thirty, forty feet long. And I just wind it around my walls so, as I look up, I can really see the whole movie that way, the whole screenplay. I used this method when I pitched this story about a man named Johnny Spain, the Black Panther, which I knew was a difficult subject. I thought I've got to have all the advantages I can have, so I thought maybe I could use visual aids. I took this long scroll as a visual aid. I had the whole story mapped out on it, and I unscrolled it down this long conference table. One of the scenes is the Watts riot that this little boy named John Spain happens to witness. So I drew in the flames; it was almost like third grade. But it did seem to work, because they were able to see my screenplay.

FROUG: The studio executives could walk around the room?

PHELAN: They could walk around it, and they did, and they could ask the questions. I think you have to give them as much help as you can, because, you know, these people move their lips when they read. [*Laughter*]. So, it has helped me. I just put it on the wall. I don't stick to it all the time; I move things around, but it gives me a feeling of security.

FROUG: I like your term—it's kind of a ladder that you cling to. I believe you have to be a little loose in outlines.

PHELAN: Oh, absolutely.

FROUG: So that you can improvise if something good comes up.

PHELAN: Because your characters take you in the direction they want to take you, and you can always come back and cut and rearrange and cut the fat out and all that stuff that sometimes happens when you take off. But I think a good solid structure when you start is not only helpful, it's not so terrifying.

FROUG: How many pages do you go for when you're writing your first draft?

PHELAN: My first go-round is usually about a hundred and thirty-five, and then I cut. I try to cut it down to around a hundred and twenty.

FROUG: And when you turn in that script, it's not really your first draft.

PHELAN: Oh, no.

FROUG: About how many drafts before you show it to somebody?

PHELAN: About two and a half, between two and three. I'll try to get that first draft down on paper as fast as possible.

FROUG: You don't look back.

PHELAN: Boy, I try not to, and that is the most difficult thing.

FROUG: Sure.

PHELAN: If I could say anything to your readers, it is keep going. Don't go back and fix that first scene. Don't go back and fix that dialogue. Write yourself a little note saying, "Put in first scene such-and-such," if you happen to think of something, then get a little stickum and stick that somewhere on the wall. But don't go back, because going back is a trap. It keeps you from going forward. It keeps you from going ahead. Your first enemy, of course, is yourself. Yourself is also that little critic that sits on your shoulder that says, "This is terrible."

FROUG: My wife and I call it the little fucker.

PHELAN: Yes, he or she certainly is. You have to wipe him off your shoulders and keep going. He's the one who says, "Go back. Go back."

FROUG: I tell my students never, never, never go back.

PHELAN: No. It's a killer. Because you don't go forward. You must get it down on paper. The thing that I do more than anything, the one thing I'd like to get in this interview is that you must sit down and write with no attachment to outcome. Try to distance yourself from what's going to happen to this.

FROUG: That's excellent advice.

PHELAN: Write it and try to get your mind to say, "I'm going to write this and then I'm going to put it in a drawer and nobody's ever going to see it." If you can get your head in that place, you'll free up such great stuff that's in your subconscious mind. It will be so wonderful if you can do that. Write it like you're going to give it to nobody. You're going to put it in a drawer. That's hard to do, because we're raised to do x, y, z in class to get a grade. We're raised for the outcome.

FROUG: That's the best advice I've ever heard.

PHELAN: No attachment to outcome. I don't know where I ever heard it, but I put it on a little piece of paper, and I had it framed. I have it right in front of me. When I get bogged down I say, "No attachment to outcome. Don't worry about what's going to happen to this. Just write the next word."

FROUG: Great. If you think about the money, you're lost.

PHELAN: Finished.

Dan O'Bannon

1975   DARK STAR *(Shared Writer)*

1979   ALIEN *(Shared Story and Sole Screenplay)*

1981   HEAVY METAL *(Shared Story)*

1982   BLUE THUNDER *(Shared Writer)*

1983   BLUE THUNDER *(Shared Credit, two TV
            episodes)*

1985   LIFEFORCE *(Shared Screenplay)*
            RETURN OF THE LIVING DEAD *(Screenplay
            and Directed)*

1986   ALIENS *(Sequel, based on characters by
            O'Bannon)*

1986   INVADERS FROM MARS *(Shared Screenplay)*

1990   TOTAL RECALL *(Shared Story and Screenplay)*

Dear Bill —
I wrote "ALIEN" to introduce a new
demon into the public consciousness
In retrospect, this may not have been
a very nice ambition, but it does
accurately represent my frame
of mind at the time (1976-
1978)
— Dan B

FADE IN:

EXTREME CLOSEUPS OF FLICKERING INSTRUMENT PANELS.
Readouts and digital displays pulse eerily with the
technology of the distant future.

Wherever we are, it seems to be chill, dark, and sterile.
Electronic machinery chuckles softly to itself.

Abruptly we hear a BEEPING SIGNAL, and the machinery
begins to awaken. Circuits close, lights blink on.

CAMERA ANGLES GRADUALLY WIDEN, revealing more and more
of the machinery, banks of panels, fluttering gauges,
until we reveal:

INTERIOR - HYPERSLEEP VAULT

A stainless steel room with no windows, the walls packed
with instrumentation. The lights are dim and the air is
frigid.

Occupying most of the floor space are rows of horizontal
FREEZER COMPARTMENTS, looking for all the world like meat
lockers.

FOOM! FOOM! FOOM! With explosions of escaping gas,
the lids on the freezers pop open.

Slowly, groggily, six nude men sit up.

                    ROBY
          Oh...God...am I cold...

                    BROUSSARD
          Is that you, Roby?

                    ROBY
          I feel like shit...

                    BROUSSARD
          Yeah, it's you all right.

Now they are yawning, stretching, and shivering.

1

"How did he do that?"

Looking back over twenty years of teaching at both USC and UCLA, I single out Dan O'Bannon as the most original, unique student I encountered. Dan was a quiet, modest young man, quite a bit undernourished, gentle, and soft-spoken. Dan was also something of a loner. It was clear he had his own vision, and it was the vision of an iconoclast. I was fond of him from the first time we met in one of my non-writing classes.

Twenty years later I discovered him in St. John's Hospital in Santa Monica, California, suffering from the inflammatory bowel disease that has plagued him much of his adult life. When his wife told me he had been hospitalized two days before our scheduled interview, I suggested a delay, but she told me Dan insisted he would do the interview there.

A smiling Dan O'Bannon, in hospital gown and robe, greeted me at the door to his room with a warm embrace. The back of his hand was connected by an IV tube to a tall stainless-steel rack, from which hung inverted bottles and a small measuring instrument.

"Don't worry," Dan reassured me, glancing at the rack, "it's on wheels. So, if you don't mind, I'll keep moving around while we talk."

Dan looked startlingly different from when I knew him during his college years. Instead of the lean, haggard face of the kid who was so poor he couldn't eat for days at a stretch, here was a moon-faced man with graying blond hair and an inverted halo of chin whiskers. All in all he looked like a slightly rotund Santa Claus. We laughed about the time he hadn't eaten for three days and came to my house and consumed a pound of hot dogs right out of my fridge, too hungry to pause to cook them. And how ten years later Dan picked me up in his brand-new Cadillac and took me to a lobster and champagne lunch. Whatever Dan did, he did with style.

I asked him for a picture to include in this book. I got a quintessential Dan O'Bannon reply:

"I'd rather not, Bill," he said, "let's just keep a little air of mystery about it, shall we?" His eyes were twinkling.

For almost two hours Dan and I conducted what surely must be one of the most bizarre interviews on record. He rapidly wheeled his IV rack about the small hospital room, weaving around the bed and furniture like an unsteady Fred Astaire, never missing a beat or a question. Dan is a showman to the core.

This is the record of that unique encounter.

FROUG: Dan, the first question I want to ask you is, now that you've gotten fame and fortune and yet find yourself in the hospital with your usual stomach trouble, is this what you meant on the phone when you said God has ambiguous feelings toward you?

O'BANNON: Yeah. Although I have only a small driblet of fame and fortune, it's enough. My life has gone very well in all spheres except for my physical health. I have an inflammatory bowel.

FROUG: This you inherited from your father?

O'BANNON: I think so.

FROUG: Dan, let's go back to the beginning, because we've known each other since you were at USC. So we've been friends since somewhere back in '68 or '69. I'm thinking about the first script you brought to me when I was a part-time teacher at USC, a script called *The Devil in Mexico.*

O'BANNON: Oh, yes.

FROUG: One of the outstanding student screenplays I've ever read.

O'BANNON: Thank you.

FROUG: That was the script about Ambrose Bierce going into Mexico to look for Pancho Villa.

O'BANNON: It was indeed.

FROUG: And it was about a hundred and eighty or two hundred pages long, wasn't it?

O'BANNON: The first draft was long. It was like two fifteen or something.

FROUG: Yeah, extremely long. You'd shown that around, and people said it showed a writer with great promise, but nobody had picked it up, right?

O'BANNON: Right.

FROUG: It's interesting that in 1984, some fifteen years later, Carlos Fuentes wrote the novel *The Old Gringo*, which is based on Ambrose Bierce going into Mexico to find Pancho Villa.

O'BANNON: Wait, wait. He wrote it after?

FROUG: He wrote it in 1984.

O'BANNON: He did?

FROUG: He wrote it sixteen years after you.

O'BANNON: How interesting. If he did steal it, it's too late. There's a pretty tight statute of limitations on plagiarism. Anyway, I'm not big on suing people. He probably didn't steal it. It was probably creative parallelism.

FROUG: I'm not big on suing people either, but William Morris gave that screenplay to several major stars they represented.

O'BANNON: I'd wondered why I hadn't read it, how Carlos Fuentes' book had escaped my attention when I was doing *Devil in Mexico*. I thought, "Well, I'm such an illiterate boor; I obviously didn't do my homework." It turns out he wrote his later?

FROUG: '84, and yours you wrote in '68 or '69.

O'BANNON: Tsk, tsk, Carlos. Tsk, tsk.

FROUG: Well, the only thing that's kind of coincidental, I would say, is that Peter Ustinov read the screenplay in Mexico while he was shooting a film, and he loved it. He gave it to Beau Bridges to read, or vice versa, and Beau Bridges dropped by to see me on the set when I was working at Fox and said, "This is one of the best screenplays we ever read, and Peter wants to do it." Peter was in Mexico at the time. The screenplay was widely circulated, including in Mexico. Very interesting coincidence.

O'BANNON: Well, I've had the experience of seeing some of my work come back to me from odd directions. When *Alien* was made, for example, I went into a Thrifty Drug and there was a little Alien doll in the toy stand. When your work begins to become somewhat influential like that, you do see pieces of yourself come floating back in the oddest places. I guess there are all kinds of different attitudes a person could take; some of them are probably not very wholesome. I just prefer to think, "Well." I prefer to feel empowered rather than get all agitated about "where's my nickel?".

FROUG: Very good. You know, I remember a time after *The Devil in Mexico* when you were dirt poor. All of us agreed it was a beautifully written screenplay, but it wasn't moving. You didn't have enough money for food.

O'BANNON: No, I had no money.

FROUG: You said to me at one time somewhere in there, "I'm working on a piece of shit that's going to make me some money." That was *Alien?*

O'BANNON: I don't remember, because I don't recall thinking of it as a piece of shit. It may have been something else. I have worked on some true pieces of shit.

FROUG: You also told me something else that's fascinated me ever since. You told me you knew the formula, after these long years of trying to get something launched, of how to write for success. The formula, you told me, was to find a genre that had already been worked out, been well-mined, and then come back and write some more of it.

O'BANNON: This was a joke, okay? When I said the formula of success, what I was referring to was a fast sale. The idea being that I came up with the notion that they just keep buying the same thing over and over again, especially when it's been made recently and is really tired. And at the same time I was trying to formulate a true formula for success in a screenplay, and it's something that, no matter how many times I repeat it to people, nobody seems able to learn it.

FROUG: What is the true formula for success in a screenplay?

O'BANNON: Three acts and a conflict.

FROUG: Three acts and a conflict. How true. You and John Carpenter, who were both students of mine in a non-writing class, did a screenplay and a student film called *Dark Star,* which was astonishing. You expanded it later and made it into a theatrical release, right?

O'BANNON: Yeah.

FROUG: You did the thing on like a two dollar budget, didn't you?

O'BANNON: It was about fifty-sixty grand when all the tickets came in at the end.

FROUG: It was just excellent. Did you ever get the money back?

O'BANNON: I myself saw about five grand off that picture, which was more money than I'd ever seen in one place at one time.

[At this point in the interview, Dan's various IV tubes were becoming entangled and we had to take a pause. I suggested we continue the interview at another time and place, but Dan wouldn't hear of it. After only a few minutes delay, we continued.]

FROUG: How long have you had this disease now?

O'BANNON: It's been active for about fifteen years. Off and on.

FROUG: And you've been working all through that. You've turned out a lot of wonderful movies since then.

O'BANNON: Thanks. You should see the volume of work I would have turned out by now if I hadn't gotten sick.

FROUG: How many times have you been in and out of the hospital, do you reckon?

O'BANNON: Oh, I have no idea. I couldn't possibly count. How many times has Warren Beatty been to bed?

FROUG: *Alien* was your first big smash hit in '79, yes? Were you happy with the production?

O'BANNON: Oh, in some ways I was ecstatic and in some ways I was disappointed. I think it's a universal experience for screenwriters. What I'm looking forward to is the day when the mistakes are mine.

FROUG: Right. Well, that's your new role as a director, yes?

O'BANNON: Yeah, but you still have to get final cut before

the mistakes are truly yours.

FROUG: Right. You haven't gotten that yet.

O'BANNON: No.

FROUG: I was fascinated by seeing *Invaders from Mars* and found that you did it in '86.

O'BANNON: I'm glad somebody was.

FROUG: Yeah, well, I was fascinated. I thought it was damn good.

O'BANNON: The original was better, though.

FROUG: Was it? What happened to it?

O'BANNON: What happened to it? It was just the wrong combination of people making the movie. Same thing that's always wrong with movies that don't work.

FROUG: I thought what was interesting about it is that the set for the Martians looked strangely like the *Alien* set. Did you design that?

O'BANNON: Not at all, and I wouldn't ever copy anything of mine that way. It's just simply that the *Alien* set was very influential. I mean, I would stay away from something like that, because then you look like you're imitating yourself—or, in this case, imitating Giger. But, in any case, no writer has enough influence to write a design on the page and have them do it. In fact, there's one way to guarantee something won't be in the movie: put it in the screenplay.

FROUG: Marvelous.

O'BANNON: I'm not being a hundred percent serious with that remark, but I'm trying to give you the tone of what goes on. Which you know well enough.

FROUG: I know you well enough to know when you're kidding and when you're not.

O'BANNON: Well, I've learned that you have to say, "I'm kidding," or people don't understand. That was one of my mistakes in the old days. I would make jokes and not say, "It's a joke," and people'd take me seriously.

FROUG: One great joke you sprung on me that I've never forgotten . . .

O'BANNON: Something horrible, I'll bet.

FROUG: No, it was wonderful. I was in the USC auditorium. I was an adjunct professor at the time. There were about five or six hundred students there for the premiere of *Dark Star*. And in the middle of the movie—you were playing one of the astronauts—you walk up to the screen, in close-up, face directly to the camera.

O'BANNON: Oh!

FROUG: You remember this?

O'BANNON: Of course.

FROUG: And you say, "My name is not really Sergeant Pinback; it's Bill Froug."

O'BANNON: Yes.

FROUG: The crowd laughed themselves silly and I nearly fell out of my chair. You always seem to choose a collaborator. Is that because it's easier work, or what?

O'BANNON: No, it's because until recently I didn't have the self-confidence to stand out and represent my own self. I felt that I needed to be the power behind some throne.

FROUG: Well, I notice that you have a lot of credits, even though you jump around from Don Jakoby to Ron Shusett and back.

O'BANNON: Talented people, all of them.

FROUG: Very talented people, no doubt. But the one continuing character through all these films is Dan O'Bannon.

O'BANNON: Thank you.

FROUG: It's true. *Blue Thunder* was a big hit, wasn't it?

O'BANNON: Yeah, it did well.

FROUG: And then it inspired a television series.

O'BANNON: It did.

FROUG: And you got a royalty off that, yes?

O'BANNON: Yes.

FROUG: You own a piece of the "Blue Thunder" series?

O'BANNON: Yeah.

FROUG: You ever see any money from it?

O'BANNON: Well, no, because it doesn't make any money anymore. It only made money on its first run. They didn't get enough episodes to syndicate it.

FROUG: You didn't write any episodes, though, did you?

O'BANNON: I did. I wrote a few scripts, but then they rewrote them so drastically that I quit.

FROUG: That's the story of television writing, believe me.

O'BANNON: I thought, "What am I doing? I'm spinning my wheels."

FROUG: Did you see *Aliens*, the sequel? What'd you think?

O'BANNON: It had its virtues.

FROUG: You thought it was as good as, or . . .

O'BANNON: Oh, I would never draw that kind of comparison in a public interview between my own work and someone else's. Not unless I want some very angry people. *Aliens* was a good film. But, in general, I think it's a mistake to quickly remake somebody else's contemporary film.

FROUG: Unless it makes money for everybody involved, right?

O'BANNON: No. I think it's an even worse mistake if you're making a lot of money off the imitation. It's even a worse mistake to do it because money clouds your mind.

FROUG: That's a very interesting conclusion. Money does cloud your mind. It also clouded your mind when you didn't have any.

O'BANNON: Yeah.

FROUG: So somewhere there's a happy balance. But today, at last, you don't have to worry about money. Only about health.

O'BANNON: Yeah. See, you can move from one kind of sickness to the other, from being broke to having money and being obsessed with it. And both of them are bad attitudes. Money, in and of itself, is unattractive, dirty green paper. But the symbolic power it has is so forceful that many people get lost in it as soon as they get near large columns of numbers.

FROUG: But you haven't, I know. You don't live in the style of a man who has millions of bucks.

O'BANNON: I don't have millions of bucks. I would if I'd
played the cards differently. But, in order to have done
that, I would have had to make the most humongous crap
to put on the screen. I'm just not willing to do that. They'll
pay you big in this town for garbage. And it's hard to fight
them off. Once you get across a certain threshold, they're
willing to offer you all the crap in the universe to write for
huge amounts of money. It's still almost just as hard to
keep making the good things.

FROUG: So you fight to hold on to your integrity.

O'BANNON: I fight to hold on to my balls.

FROUG: *Total Recall* has so many credits in it that it's hard to
decipher who did what.

O'BANNON: Philip Dick wrote a wonderful short story, and
then Ronnie and I did a screenplay. The other names are
these peripheral writers who come and go on a long,
time-consuming project.

FROUG: Were you happy with the result?

O'BANNON: Mixed, as always.

FROUG: Dan, my wife would not go see *Total Recall* because
she read there was so much violence in it. A lot of critics
said the same thing.

O'BANNON: Yeah, well, they have a very good point. The
way the violence plays in the film—in *Total Recall* on the
screen—is as though there wasn't enough there to support the excitement without it. And I feel that there was. I
don't think it needed that level of violence, and I think
that, in order to make the time and space for the violence,
they lost some good things in the way of humor and
surprise and character.

FROUG: Was the violence in the screenplay?

O'BANNON: Of course there was violence.

FROUG: No, I mean as much violence.

O'BANNON: It wasn't as exaggerated or baroque. There was
certainly violence; you can't have an action-thriller, a
James Bond-ish type of spy thriller, without having people
killed and violence and blood. But I was surprised at the

extent to which it was carried. It was as though the director had no confidence in the script. It had much more violence than *Alien*, for example, when *Alien* was intended to be horrible and violent.

FROUG: Well, *Alien* did what I like so much: it suggested the violence without showing it. The terror was in what's going to happen.

O'BANNON: In *Total Recall*, there was just wall-to-wall violence all the way to the door. I was surprised. And then, of course, Verhoeven came out and made public announcements that because he was brutalized as a child, violence on the screen meant nothing to him. To him it was all a big joke.

FROUG: The director said this?

O'BANNON: Yes. He said that because he had to witness Nazi atrocities as a child in Holland that he doesn't take it seriously on the screen.

FROUG: What do you say to that?

O'BANNON: Well, I say it doesn't matter what he thinks. It's a question of what the audience thinks. They weren't there in Holland. He has experienced psychic numbing without realizing that the audience hasn't experienced it as well. In other words, he's not audience-attuned. The more a picture costs, the more audience-attuned I am.

FROUG: The more you feel your responsibility is to make back the studio investment?

O'BANNON: Yeah, right. I mean, if I ever do a picture that's genuinely low-budget, as a writer-director, I might give myself the liberty to do it entirely personally. But, generally, the types of films I like to do are a little more expensive than that, and I rigorously adhere to the idea that this is for us, not me.

FROUG: You and the audience, you mean.

O'BANNON: Yeah. This is not made just for my pleasure. It's made for the pleasure of everyone, and I think we can all meet on a common ground. I think there's plenty of good creative ideas and material out there that can please, not just one.

FROUG: There is an awful lot of violence in contemporary films. Personally, I'm sick of it.

O'BANNON: It's just a shorthand for creativity.

FROUG: It's a way of avoiding the hard choices?

O'BANNON: That's all. In films per se it's not a sinister trend. It simply reflects what's going on in the world. Movies don't cause violence. Mostly, as I say, it's just a shorthand for any real creative effort. It stands in the place of creativity because it has high impact. It's easy to do.

FROUG: Immediate impact.

O'BANNON: Yeah. It's sons, grandsons of Peckinpah.

FROUG: Oh yeah, I used to know Sam, and he was a man with a lot of problems, a lot of personal problems, which I think he put on the screen.

O'BANNON: Often, if a person has inner turmoil, it can be very powerful to express it on the screen, but you do have to find the appropriate mode. That is where the power of a film comes from, from the filmmaker's own inner obsessive experiences. But he does have to find the format to express it that will speak to the larger audience. In the case of Peckinpah, he was pretty disciplined, I think.

FROUG: *The Wild Bunch*. That was excessive violence, I thought.

O'BANNON: Yeah, but it was appropriate to the thing he was trying to achieve, which is still a bit queasy when you see it. It's an amoral universe; that's what is reflected in that film. He's not grafting it onto a script that is aiming for something different. I mean, this was obviously what was set out to be done from the beginning. It is the theme of the picture.

FROUG: One of the special effects men told me, "We measure a Sam Peckinpah film in terms of how many gallons of blood we're going to use." They use artificial blood, of course.

O'BANNON: He did invent that approach to film. It didn't

exist prior to *The Wild Bunch*. And it was so readily imitable that we're still doing it today. *Total Recall*, in that respect, is an obvious direct descendant of *The Wild Bunch*.

FROUG: You think so?

O'BANNON: The squibs—there were no blood squibs before *Wild Bunch*.

FROUG: I didn't know that it was invented for that picture. So, are you looking for violence to attract an audience?

O'BANNON: To attract them? No. Violence is just part of the stew. It's one of the many ingredients of the recipe. But I have not yet made, I think, a picture in which the single foremost attractive thrust was to violence. The violence was always reflective of another theme.

FROUG: How many years were you at USC film school?

O'BANNON: As a student I was only there about two years. But I hung out for a while helping John with *Dark Star*.

FROUG: Did you take Irwin Blacker's writing course?

O'BANNON: Certainly did.

FROUG: Could you describe it a little bit? I thought it was impressive.

O'BANNON: Well, he was a structure man, and, although I've come to differ with him about the specifics of story structure, the basic approach, the structural approach, is the one I came to adopt. I'm a structuralist myself. We believe in discipline, hard work, and architecture. Writing a script is like carpentry.

FROUG: I remember he locked the door of his class.

O'BANNON: Yeah, if people were late.

FROUG: Blacker turned out a lot of good writers, didn't he? You and John Carpenter both were in his class, weren't you?

O'BANNON: I don't know if John had him. I had him. Good old Irwin, yeah. I remember Irwin. The students who didn't like Irwin were the students who didn't like work.

FROUG: Exactly. Those students came to me and asked me if I would take over Irwin Blacker's class. I said, "No chance, because I would do the same thing he's doing.

You'd have to write scripts." I think those were students who didn't want to bother to write scripts.

O'BANNON: One student was very angry at Irwin during the time I took his course. He stood up in class and said, "Why do we have to learn all these methods? Why can't we just do our own thing?" I don't remember what Irwin said, but if I'd been answering, I'd have said, "You don't need to come to this class to do your own thing. Just go do your own thing. You came here to learn something. That's why you have to work to write, in order to learn." Otherwise you don't need the class.

FROUG: When I first came to UCLA, there were some production professors who would say, "Take the camera and shoot anything, and it will be beautiful because you are beautiful." That was sixties' mentality.

O'BANNON: No comment. What if you're ugly? Then you're screwed. Then you'll have to work. [*Laughter*]

FROUG: Now, there's a story here that might be good for every student who reads this, every aspiring screenwriter. That was the story of the law student who came to you at USC and got you to sign a contract to give him fifty percent of all your income for life in exchange for his forming a corporation with you as a partner. Do you remember that case?

O'BANNON: The O'Bannon-Varzeas Production Company, Incorporated. Boy, was I a sucker.

FROUG: I know. I took you up to my attorney and business manager David Licht, and he took one look at the contract and said, "Forget it." You know, it's a cautionary tale, really, for new writers. Don't sign anything with anybody.

O'BANNON: But it doesn't matter, because it was an illegal contract. He couldn't enforce it. It was not a lesson in how I got financially or legally screwed; it was a lesson in human gullibility and disappointment. It was a lesson in how few of the people out there who say that they can deliver something actually can. How much hot air there is wallowing around in this business. And this business includes not only "this business" but also its limbs, like film schools. One of the things I found to my great disappointment when I arrived in L.A. way back then was that every guy pumping gas had a deal in the works. It felt hopeless, because the industry saturates every aspect of this town. And if you really do have some kind of ideas or ambition, your voice is lost in the many teeming other voices who aren't as serious as you are. So you look around for some way to get started, and there are plenty of people out there willing to lie to you and massage you in the hopes that you may . . .

FROUG: They can feed off you.

O'BANNON: Yeah, feed off you. Creative parasitism.

FROUG: I saw *Life Force*, and I have to tell you that girl was the most beautiful creature that ever walked the face of the earth. Who was that girl?

O'BANNON: She's a French model, and I don't know her name.

FROUG: Were you as struck by her as I was?

O'BANNON: Well, it said in the script that she should be perfect. She was. She was *fleshly* perfect. I was picturing somebody who was so perfect as to look synthetic. And Tobe cast a girl who was unquestionably real. I thought she was so attractive as to undermine the point of it, which is that this is a synthetic creation.

FROUG: *Life Force* looked to me like a kind of retelling of Ulysses in space, outer space. The three women were the three sirens. Did you stay close to the book, a novel by Colin Wilson?

O'BANNON: Yeah. I worked from the novel.

FROUG: One of the funniest things you ever did was *Return of the Living Dead*. It's just so full of marvelous humor. You directed that one as well as wrote it, yes?

O'BANNON: It was my first directorial effort.

FROUG: You did a delightful job. Wild and funny. Was it well received?

O'BANNON: Yeah. Better than it had any right to be.

FROUG: Because?

O'BANNON: Very minor effort, but, well, you've got to admit.

FROUG: Well, it was a comedy.

O'BANNON: The one thing I knew going into that was does the world need this movie? The world didn't need this movie, and so it could have definitely done worse than it did.

FROUG: Let me go back to your reference to film schools. Do you think it's advisable for young writers, new screenwriters to go to film school?

O'BANNON: I don't know. Things have changed.

FROUG: How do you see them in comparison to what they were twenty years ago when we first met each other? The theme of this book is what has happened in the twenty years since *The Screenwriter Looks at the Screenwriter* was published in 1971. We're exactly twenty years from that publication. So what has changed since you were a student then?

O'BANNON: Well, the other day I was talking to a couple of young fellows who were recently students at USC film school. I asked them what it was like. And from what I could gather, things have gotten more depersonalized, with less of an emphasis on production at SC, and that's bad. So, in offering advice, I'll have to give it in the most general sense, and the reader will have to apply it to the real situation, which seems to keep fluctuating. And you had asked specifically . . .

FROUG: How is it different? I don't mean the school, I mean the industry itself.

O'BANNON: Oh, a lot more work.

FROUG: There's more work?

O'BANNON: Oh, yeah. For an ambitious young writer, I think it's really important that they should place themselves physically in the midst of the industry they want to work in. I think that to learn how to do it properly at long distance is just insuperable. How you do that? And I think you have to play it as it lays on the given day you want to start.

FROUG: Any job they can get in Hollywood, in other words.

O'BANNON: If you want to work in movies, get yourself physically to L.A. If you want to be a novelist, I suppose you should live in New York. To try to do either of those from Kansas, I think, is insuperable. You have to have your finger on the pulse of the industry you want to work in, unless your goal as a writer is so pure that you're not interested in worldly success. But I don't think that applies to many people. Of course, they could sit in Kansas and write screenplays, but I don't think they'd get very far professionally. They might get good, but they would be writing screenplays unlike anything anybody was making at the time. And they wouldn't know anybody to show them to and they wouldn't have any mentors to guide them.

FROUG: Do you think it's impossible or extremely difficult for a young writer to get an agent? How did you finally get an agent after parading around with *The Devil in Mexico* all that time?

O'BANNON: I got an agent after *Alien* was green-lighted.

FROUG: Not till *Alien* was scheduled for production?

O'BANNON: That should be an indication for you.

FROUG: Amazing. Then they came for you, yes?

O'BANNON: Not in droves, no. They came to me in droves after . . .

FROUG: *Blue Thunder?*

O'BANNON: Some time after *Blue Thunder* they started coming in in more reasonable numbers. That'll give you an indication of how hard it is to get an agent. Basically, there aren't any of those agents out there who build up callow young men to success. They don't exist. Make it for yourself first, and then go pick from among those who are there to service the professionals.

FROUG: How would you advise a new screenwriter to choose an agent? In other words, suppose they have a script sold—I've had this with some students—and now how do they decide which agent to pick?

O'BANNON: Find somebody honest.

FROUG: Is that easy?

O'BANNON: No. But it's more important than anything else. It's more important than their taste or judgment or their contacts. Find somebody honest. When they're not honest, it doesn't matter.

FROUG: How do you determine if they're honest?

O'BANNON: Ah, you're asking me the most important question in life, to determine the character of another human being. Their character's more important than their talent. Character *is* a talent.

FROUG: So you feel that first you get to be a success and then you get an agent.

O'BANNON: Yes.

FROUG: Now that you are a success by any standard imaginable, you don't have to look for jobs; they come to you.

O'BANNON: That's correct. When I do look for jobs, it's because the ones that I really want don't come to me. What comes to me are opportunities to support myself. What doesn't come to me very often, at least, are those glittering creative challenges that we all . . .

FROUG: That you want.

O'BANNON: Yeah. The ones we really want to do. Those you have to work for.

FROUG: That leads into my next question perfectly. Are you eager to break out of the science-fiction mold, which you've been in almost since the beginning?

O'BANNON: I'm eager to expand out of it, not to escape it. There's a difference. I want to utilize my full palette. I don't want to just keep painting the color blue.

FROUG: Do you think that's only going to come when you write a spec script that's out of the new color set?

O'BANNON: Oh, I'm not a prophet. I have no idea how it will happen. I've learned that I can't predict the future. How it will happen. It'll happen just because I sort of keep pounding away at it, but the specifics—who knows? The next project is always a blank till it happens. You make every plan in the world, and then it's not the one you do next.

FROUG: Do you still write screenplays on spec?

O'BANNON: Of course.

FROUG: So you're writing all the time. You used to have a thirty-five gallon wastebasket in your living room, next to the typewriter, into which you kept throwing crumpled up pages.

O'BANNON: It's not in the living room anymore.

FROUG: You're married. Where do you have it now?

O'BANNON: In a bedroom turned into an office.

FROUG: And you still fill it up with pages you're rewriting and reworking?

O'BANNON: Yeah, and I'm very careful not to throw any food garbage into the can, in case I have to go back and salvage a piece of paper.

FROUG: Do you sometimes find you've left something there you wanted?

O'BANNON: Absolutely. That's why it is literally a circular file, and that's why I don't throw any dirty garbage in there. Anything that's thrown in there is probably thrown away, but if not, I can go back in there and find the last several months of work.

FROUG: How long do you figure it takes you to write a screenplay, an original?

O'BANNON: Completely dependent on the script. Every one's different.

FROUG: How do you know when you have an idea that's worth putting in some months on writing a screenplay?

O'BANNON: When the idea proves fruitful. That is to say, it generates enough material. You have an idea and it's neat. But that's not enough in itself. It has to be a neat idea that sparks an entire chain of other neat ideas. That's what I call a fruitful idea.

FROUG: Good definition. Do you lay out some kind of

paradigm before you start? Like first act should occur . . .

O'BANNON: Yeah.

FROUG: You do that?

O'BANNON: In my early days of writing, I was afraid that working it all out in advance would destroy the creative impulse. Now I don't even start seriously writing until it's all worked out on paper first.

FROUG: Do you use index cards?

O'BANNON: No.

FROUG: What do you use?

O'BANNON: Typing paper. I keep retyping from the beginning. I list all my scenes. Then I rearrange them into three acts. I just keep working on it until I run dry of stuff that should go into an outline, and then I start on the script. I don't start writing the script until it's completely working in an outline. Until all the pieces are there.

FROUG: So the longer time, perhaps, is spent making the outline than it is writing the script?

O'BANNON: Yeah.

FROUG: The script goes pretty fast, if I remember.

O'BANNON: Because you've already made up the story. It doesn't take long to write it.

FROUG: So the big thrust is to get the structure first and then the script goes fairly quickly.

O'BANNON: Try to tell that to anybody else in this town.

FROUG: No, some people agree with that. You're not alone in that. I don't know that everybody does.

O'BANNON: Oh, because now . . . that guy wrote that book.

FROUG: What book?

O'BANNON: Oh, it's so famous now . . . Syd Field. Because of Syd Field's book, now people are taking it seriously. I wouldn't write such a book. To me, that's giving away the bacon.

FROUG: [Laughing] You think so?

O'BANNON: Yes. It's a professional secret.

FROUG: So you won't write a book on how to write screenplays?

O'BANNON: No, not until I'm old and retiring. Because it's a professional secret that's lying behind the magician's curtain, and it's showing the other magicians, for only the price of the book, how to do the trick.

FROUG: Well, since we're not giving away secrets, there are probably no other particular books that you would recommend.

O'BANNON: On how to write a screenplay?

FROUG: Yeah.

O'BANNON: No. Not because I don't want to give away secrets, you know. If it was out there, I'd tell you. What there is out there is usually how to do the format. Most of what is written on how to write a screenplay is written by people who don't know how.

FROUG: Or haven't done it.

O'BANNON: The equivalent of those real estate courses. There aren't that many who do know how, and those who do know how tend not to tell. For the very obvious reason: they don't want to train their own competition. These are not unknowns, but it's on the level of the mortuary trade—it's passed on by word of mouth.

FROUG: I like that; it's a nice turn of phrase. What propelled you into directing?

O'BANNON: Well, I always wanted to do it. Writing was a means to that end.

FROUG: And what about the stamina, the physical stamina it takes to direct?

O'BANNON: Delegate. Study Reagan.

FROUG: You have to choose marvelous people to delegate to. That seems to me the first move in order to be confident of what you've delegated. At one time you were your own set decorator, weren't you?

O'BANNON: On *Dark Star.* I wasn't mine; I was John's.

FROUG: You and John Carpenter . . .

O'BANNON: No, he was the director, and I did the dirty work, like make the film.

FROUG: [*Laughing*] Yeah. Well, let me ask you this. Years

ago, you flew over to France to meet on doing *Dune*. Weren't you going to do it?

O'BANNON: I was going to direct the special effects on Jodorowsky's *Dune* production. So, yeah, it was always my desire to learn to do as many of the important things on a film as possible, so that as a director I'd have these tools at my command and not be in the dark.

FROUG: Did you do a lot of those visual effects on *Alien?*

O'BANNON: Well, in the back end of *Alien* I get a design consultant credit. And what that reflects is the fact that I originally wrote *Alien* to be directed by myself. When Ridley came on board as the director, he basically absorbed all of my visual ideas as part of his own visual conception.

FROUG: As an old friend and an old informed character about Dan O'Bannon, I recognized in the film that a lot of that was Dan O'Bannon. Very clearly, you have a signature, my friend. A clear and distinct signature on everything you do.

O'BANNON: Thank you.

FROUG: Tell me about this new film you just finished.

O'BANNON: Well, we think we're calling it *The Resurrected*. Sort of a bastard noun made from an adjective.

FROUG: Is this your own screenplay?

O'BANNON: No, this was written by a new, young writer named Brent Friedman.

FROUG: How come you didn't write it?

O'BANNON: I want to direct.

FROUG: Did Brent Friedman bring you this screenplay?

O'BANNON: The producers brought it to me. It's based on an H. P. Lovecraft novel. I happened to know that H. P. Lovecraft novel; I'd been attracted to it for many years, partly because it represents such a difficult challenge. For me as a filmmaker, the kind of projects I want to do are the ones that appear to be impossible, that are hard to do. It's part of what tickles my fancy. So I had been toying with the Lovecraft story for many years, trying to figure out how to crack the problems of making it into a movie. I was about halfway through with it when the producers came to me with Brent Friedman's script. I was, you know, surprised and delighted, delighted to see this same idea. I looked at it and I saw that, what I hadn't solved, he had. So we got together and I asked the writer and producers to be receptive to my original ideas, and they were. Brent Friedman then did some additional drafts.

FROUG: So you have a film that you're satisfied with.

O'BANNON: Yes.

FROUG: That's good. When will it be released?

O'BANNON: They're trying to get it out as soon as August. I don't know if they can make it.

FROUG: But you're sitting in the hospital room and the film's not at final cut yet, right?

O'BANNON: That's their problem.

FROUG: Well, it's your problem, too. You want to be sure you've got a good film.

O'BANNON: It'll be fine. Panic is not a useful emotion in this industry. And I always think that people would have learned that by now, if they've made a few pictures. Typically, filmmaking resembles a slow-motion emergency. But, the films get finished. The films come out. If you want an opportunity to panic, you'll find plenty of them in the movie industry.

FROUG: Do you project ahead as a writer, like the step after this movie, or do you just wait and see what happens?

O'BANNON: Oh, I project like crazy, but I don't make the next deal right away. I plan and then I see what I'm presented with.

FROUG: When you came to the hospital, you were finishing cutting *The Resurrected* and also writing another screenplay?

O'BANNON: For Universal.

FROUG: I read in *American Film* that you were doing a rewrite of a film.

O'BANNON: That was the one for Universal. It was called

The Tourist. It was a dark and moody kind of science-fiction film noir. And it had a lot of merit to it. It was a reversal for me. What we had here was a script in which all of the original elements, the evocative elements, were already there. But structurally it was incomplete. So I saw my job not as being creative, but as being a structuralist—to build the cake under the frosting.

FROUG: The frosting was there.

O'BANNON: Yeah. But then *The Resurrected* came along and I asked Universal for a leave of absence.

FROUG: You're now at a point where you're sought after, that's for sure.

O'BANNON: That's nice; it's always nice to know you can pay the rent.

FROUG: What would you most like to be remembered for as a screenwriter-director? What do you think is the most important work you've done?

O'BANNON: I'd like my epitaph to read, "How did he do that?"

Joe Eszterhas

1978   F.I.S.T. *(Story and Shared Screenplay)*

1983   FLASHDANCE *(Shared Screenplay)*

1985   JAGGED EDGE *(Writer)*

1987   BIG SHOTS *(Writer)*

1988   HEARTS OF FIRE *(Shared Writer)*
         BETRAYED *(Writer)*

1989   CHECKING OUT *(Writer)*
         MUSIC BOX *(Writer)*

1991   BASIC INSTINCT *(Writer)*

INT. A BEDROOM--NIGHT

It is dark; we don't see clearly.

A man and woman make love on a brass bed. There are mirrors
on the walls and ceiling. On a side-table, atop a small
mirror, lines of cocaine. A tape deck plays the Stones:
"Sympathy For The Devil."

Atop him...she straddles his chest...her breasts in his
face. He cups her breasts. She leans down, kisses him....

Johnny Boz is in his late 40's, slim, good-looking. We don't
see the woman's face. She has long blonde hair. The camera
stays behind and to the side of them.

She leans close over his face, her tongue in his mouth...she
kisses him...she moves her hands up, holds both of his arms
above his head.

She moves higher atop him...she reaches to the side of the
bed...a white silk scarf is in her hand...her hips above his
face now, moving...slightly, oh-so slightly...his face
strains towards her.

The scarf in her hand...she ties his hands with it...gently...
to the brass bed...his eyes are closed...tighter...lowering
hips into his face...lower...over his chest...his navel.
The song plays.

He is inside her...his arms tied above him...on his back...
his eyes closed...she moves...grinding...he strains for her...
his head arches back...his throat white.

She arches her back...her hips grind...her breasts are
high...~~and they are high~~.

Her back arches back...back...her head tilts back...she
extends her arms...the right arm comes down suddenly...
the steel flashes...his throat is white...

He bucks, writhes, bucks, convulses...

It flashes up...it flashes down...and up...and down...and
up...and...

EXT. A BROWNSTONE IN PACIFIC HEIGHTS--MORNING

Winter ~~descends upon~~ (in) San Francisco: cold, foggy. Cop
cars everywhere. The lights play through the thick fog.
Two homicide detectives get out of the car, walk into the
house.

Nick Curran is 42. Trim, good-looking, a nice-suit: a face
urban, edged, shadowed. ~~His~~ Gus Moran is 64. Crew-cut,
silver beard, a suit rumpled and shiny, a hat out of the
50's: a face worn and ruined: the face of a backwoods
philosopher.

*"All I'm saying is, don't become a hooker;
respect yourself."*

Everything about Joe Eszterhas is larger than life: his warmth, graciousness, talent, income, style, and manner of being. At first glance you may think he is a giant, but he only *seems* that large. He has a great mane of well-trimmed red hair, beginning to tinge with gray, and a great red beard to match. On his finger he wears a huge brass ring fit for a giant, made by his son at school. He drives a huge van-like truck surely big enough to transport half the Marin County Fire Department, where he lives.

I first met Joe in front of the elegant Casa Madrona Hotel in Sausalito, California, across the Golden Gate Bridge from San Francisco. Joe had originally planned to fly down to Los Angeles for our interview as he had other business in L.A. However, something came up at the last minute that forced us to change our plans. "Take a plane up here for the weekend," Joe implored on the phone, "I've got you a hotel room in Sausalito, a car, and anything you need. It's on me," he cheerfully explained.

"But I can't let you do that," I replied, with enough sincerity to fill a thimble.

"But you've got to let me," insisted Joe, "besides, I've had a good year."

Knowing that part of the "good" year was the sale of a screenplay for a record-breaking three million dollars (not knowing about the other one he sold a few months later for "only" one point five million), my resistance collapsed.

Joe greeted me in front of the Casa Madrona and immediately suggested lunch "so we can get to know each other a little, first." It turned out, not to my surprise, that Joe knew most of the waiters in the large Chinese restaurant on the waterfront. Several, including the maitre d' and the manager, made a visit to our table to personally welcome Joe. I would not have been surprised if the mayor had shown up.

Joe and I enjoyed each other; we had Hollywood war stories to exchange, but our conversation instead focused on life stories. By the time the lunch was over I knew I liked this man enormously.

I suspect that when you read this transcript of our conversation, you will like him, too. And you will come to see why Hollywood screenwriters look to him as the bearer of the writers' standard. More than once during the dozen interviews in this book, screenwriters referred to Joe Eszterhas as their role model because he fights to protect his vision.

It seems that wherever Joe goes, the press follows. No screenwriter in memory has generated so much print and so many Hollywood hurricanes. While the winds of Hollywood sweep furiously around him, Joe lives quietly in Marin County, where the centerpiece of his life is clearly his family. He shields them from the fray by refusing to give his home address to anyone.

For me, it was certainly worth the trip to Sausalito to meet him. I think it will be worth it to you, too.

FROUG: What got you into *F.I.S.T.,* your first screenplay?

ESZTERHAS: Well, I had written a magazine piece for *Rolling Stone* called "Charlie Simpson's Apocalypse," which was about a boy in a small town, Harrisonville, Missouri, who flips out one day, shoots up some people in the town, and then kills himself. And the magazine piece turned into a book for Random House called *Charlie Simpson's Apocalypse,* which sold no copies and got what we can euphemistically call mixed reviews. But it was one of four books that were nominated for the National Book Award in, I think, '74. Marcia Nasatir at United Artists read the book and called me one day, and said, "I think that you write good dialogue and you write cinematically. Have you ever been interested in doing screenplays?" Well, I had really not been interested in doing screenplays, but *Rolling Stone* was about to move to New York. I didn't want to go to New York; I'd fallen in love with California. My wife was pregnant with our first child, and I was doing some bartending on the side at a little bar in Mill Valley. So I said to my wife, "This sounds like a pretty good idea. Let me go down and talk to her." I went down to Los Angeles and spoke to Marcia, and she said, "Why don't you go home and try to come up with like a half-dozen ideas that you'd like to do as a screenplay." So I came back and began to think about possible movie stories. I had grown up in Cleveland in a blue-collar neighborhood. I'd known a lot of kids whose dads had belonged to unions and heard all kinds of union stories. So, one of the ideas was to do a piece on the making of a union. Which, incidentally, from the very beginning, even in that story suggestion, was called *F.I.S.T.,* because I came up with the name of the union, and it simply worked out luckily as an acronym. The name was Federation of Interstate Truckers, and the acronym F.I.S.T. became the title.

FROUG: Did you have Sylvester Stallone involved at this point?

ESZTERHAS: Not at this point. So I sent this idea to Marcia, and she asked me to come down to see her again. She said that the producer Gene Corman had come in with a similar idea a few months ago, and she essentially said let's do it. It gets very funny from there on. But, let me back up. They said let's do it. So I went off into the Midwest and did three months of research, talking to old union guys in Detroit, Toledo, and Cleveland because I was going to set the whole piece in Cleveland. At the end of the three months, I wrote this bizarre bastard document, which they called the treatment. It was neither fiction nor nonfiction, neither novel nor short story, and it certainly wasn't a screenplay. But it was about seventy pages. I sent it to them, and they said, "Let's bring Bob Rafelson in to direct. We think he'd be interested in this." I was completely green, you have to understand. I didn't know anything at all about the movie business. Bob was literally the first director that I met. So they bring Bob in, and he was really sweet. I was very honest with Bob and said, "Look, I don't know anything about screenwriting." He said, "Don't worry about it. This is a terrific idea. We'll work together." So we made plans to hook up in Aspen, where Bob lived at the time. Let's say that the meeting was going to be Wednesday at noon in Aspen. Bob called me the day before and said he'd meet me at the airport and all that. About two hours after Bob called me to set up the meeting, I get a call from UA. They said, "Don't go to meet Bob." I said, "What do you mean?" And they said, "Well, Bob is no longer going to be the director." What had happened is that they had seen a cut of *Stay Hungry*. They didn't like it; they didn't think he'd do well.

FROUG: Disenchantment had set in?

ESZTERHAS: They said, "Bob's no longer going to be the director." Well, okay. The next day comes, when I'm supposed to get to Aspen, and Bob Rafelson calls me from the Aspen airport and says, "Where the fuck are you?" I said, "Well, what are you talking about?" He said, "We talked yesterday, and you were supposed to be here." I said, "Didn't anyone from UA talk to you?" He said, "What do you mean?" I said, "You mean you didn't hear from them yesterday?" And he said, "No. What's going on?" They had never informed Bob that he was off the project.

FROUG: That's very typical of Hollywood. Very typical.

ESZTERHAS: It goes on. So Bob's out, and they hook me up with Karel Reisz, who comes up to meet me in San Francisco. I like him very much, and I like some of his pictures. At that point, he had done *Morgan* and *Isadora*; he later did *The French Lieutenant's Woman*. He's a really sweet, gentle Englishman who liked the notion of doing a big picture about the making of an American labor union. We had a lot of fun talking in San Francisco. The next step was that I was to go to London to work with him further. So I'm about to go to London when UA calls me and says, "Don't go to London." I said, "What do you mean?" "Well, Karel Reisz is not going to direct the movie. He's no longer involved." And I said, "Well, have you talked to him and told him?" They said, "Yes we have." I said, "Are you sure?" They said, "Yes we have." Incidentally, as a postscript to that, they had indeed talked to him, but two years later I saw Karel in L.A. and he said, "Do you know what happened on *F.I.S.T.*? Why did they replace me?" He didn't understand it two years down the line. So they brought Norman Jewison in. He had seen the same bizarre bastard treatment document that I'd done. Norman literally took me under his wing for a year and a half. He taught me everything that he knew with an absolutely astounding generosity of spirit and a pure willingness to want to help. He worked with me in Malibu and at a place he has in Toronto and taught me about things that I simply didn't know anything about. Rhythms of screenwriting. And he taught me more important lessons than that, because Norman is a very feisty man who believes in fighting for the things he believes in. He taught me, for example, that you can get into fights with studios and win them, if you fight them well enough. There are two specific scenes with Norman I won't forget. One is when we were in the hot tub in Malibu, we had been talking a long time, and he said, "If you remember nothing else of all of this, remember that I've spent a good part of my life trying not to be cynical, and so far I've succeeded." And the other scene that I remember is when we got up one morning (we always worked very early, like at seven in the morning in Malibu, and we worked on his deck that looked out at the water), and he came down, I was out there earlier, and he said, "Do you know why I live down here, kid?" And I said, "No." He said, "So I can look out there at that water and I don't have to look back there at all that stuff." [*Laughter*] I owe Norman a great deal. I was so green and I had such chips on my shoulder that I didn't really understand the things that he was trying to teach me. I remember once he insisted that I go to a studio meeting with Mike Medavoy and Eric Pleskow. I said to him, "Norman, what do I want to go and see all these executives for?" And he said, "Because you're going to have a long career, kid, and I want you there." So he really exposed me and taught me a great many things, not only having to do with the notion that you can do screenplays that are at once commercial and that say something, but also more important things in terms of an entire attitude with fighting for your material and being able to win those things. That's how I got into movies.

FROUG: Taking a leap forward, for the moment, *Time* magazine reported that Carolco paid you three million dollars for *Basic Instinct.* Then the story went out that you were bounced off by the director, and then the story came out later that you were bounced back on again. Will you tell us the story of the *Basic Instinct* saga?

ESZTERHAS: Yeah, well . . .

FROUG: It's pretty crazy, isn't it?

ESZTERHAS: Well, I think it's a terrific story. I don't know if it's crazy, but I think it's a great story. I don't know what *Time* reported, but the reporting that the *L.A. Times* did was really accurate. I'm not sure that the story has an ending at this point, because *Basic Instinct* is not out. But the chain of circumstances was this: I wrote *Basic Instinct* as a spec script. Carolco paid three million dollars for it, and the deal was that Irwin Winkler would come in with me as producer. They paid Irwin one million dollars. Irwin and I had worked on four other things, and we continue to work on things. I wanted Irwin brought in to produce it.

FROUG: Do you have the clout to be able to say you want him to come in as the producer?

ESZTERHAS: Sure. In a spec situation like that, where the script is so hot that it gets three million dollars.

FROUG: Was that an auction situation?

ESZTERHAS: Yes, it was. It was so hot that we had every studio bidding. I mean, I have auctioned, all told, seven scripts through the years. This was the most successful one. This was the hot auction. When it escalates that way, and everyone in town is bidding, and you say, "I want Irwin Winkler to produce it," someone's going to go with that. And that's exactly what happened. Irwin got a million to produce it, and then I went off on vacation in Florida while Irwin stayed in town. Mario Kassar at Carolco picked Paul Verhoeven to direct it. Paul had just done *Total Recall* for Carolco, and he had done *Robocop* a couple of years previously. So he was coming off of two very big hit movies. Paul has done some terrific Dutch movies: *Soldier of Orange, Spetters, Turkish Delight.* The interesting thing about those movies is that they are movies with layers and depth. They have the same explosive quality that he has in *Robocop* and *Total Recall*, but they are very different types of movies. If we want to simplify and generalize, then they are more "intellectual" movies than his American pictures.

FROUG: That's interesting. So, anyway, now Irwin has decided to bring in Paul Verhoeven.

ESZTERHAS: No, Carolco has decided to bring Verhoeven in. So Irwin has a meeting in L.A. with Verhoeven and Mario Kassar. Then Irwin calls me in Florida and says, "Look, this is not one of the best meetings I've ever had. His only interest at this meeting was how we could put more tits and ass into this movie." To back up a second, *Basic Instinct* is a real erotic thriller. It's a psychological game between a man and a woman that extends into the bedroom. It is the most intense film and diabolical game imaginable, because it not only involves the psyche but also the senses, in every way. The woman involved is a kind of omnisexual who uses every part of her being to manipulate others. I backed up only to tell you that the point here is not to emphasize the erotic aspects, because it can cross the line and become so sensational that it tap dances into porn. The point is to emphasize the psychological aspects so that we have a balance on the piece. Anyway, Verhoeven's take was that he was going to emphasize the aspects that he shouldn't be emphasizing. He was interested solely in the erotic, the sensational, and the sexual aspects of the script. For example, Irwin said that he mentioned Meryl Streep, and Paul's response was, "When's the last time you've seen Meryl Streep's tits?" Okay? So I have this conversation with Irwin on the telephone, and I know that this possibly might not be a good situation. I finish my trip in Florida, and on the eighth of August we have a meeting at Irwin's house with Paul, Michael Douglas, and a Carolco representative.

FROUG: Michael Douglas is in what capacity?

ESZTERHAS: Michael Douglas is there as the star of the picture. I have just come back from Florida the night before, and the meeting blows up within five minutes. Verhoeven says that he thinks the beginning, middle, and ending of this should be changed; the script needs a great deal of rewriting in his mind. He wants to emphasize a lesbian relationship in the script (there is a lesbian backstory in the script), and he wants to show, actually show, a lesbian scene with two women making love. I say there's no reason for that. It's sensationalism. I say that you're wrong to want to make these changes in the script; all you're going to do is screw the whole thing up. I take great umbrage at the fact that we spend five minutes discussing which actress will or will not take her clothes off for the part, and I finally say to him, "Listen, we've spent all this time talking about who's going to do nudity. Why don't we talk about which actress can play this part? It's psychologically a very difficult part, and we need someone who is intelligent and manipulative, who can do all of these things, not a bimbo." He takes offense at me and, very loudly over this glass cocktail table, says, "I am the director, ja? I'm right and you are wrong, ja?" That bluntly, that simply. So the meeting ends, and Irwin and I look at each other. Irwin, who's made thirty-some pictures, says that this is the single worst meeting that he's ever had with a director since he's been working in films. I say to him, "He's going to clearly fuck this thing up." And he says, "Yes, he is." Irwin's take was, and I think it was valid, that Verhoeven simply didn't understand the material. Didn't get it.

FROUG: Why were you locked into this man? Since you picked the producer . . .

ESZTERHAS: Because Carolco picked him as the director.

FROUG: And you couldn't do anything about it?

ESZTERHAS: I couldn't do anything about it because we didn't have director approval. That we couldn't get.

FROUG: I see.

ESZTERHAS: But what's always happened in the past with me is that if you have somebody as strong as Irwin Winkler, even though by the contract he doesn't get director approval, they will be very careful and defer to what he wants. In this case, Mario Kassar simply overlooked what Irwin wanted and paid no attention to what he wanted.

FROUG: Did Irwin give him a list of directors he would accept?

ESZTERHAS: Sure. We wanted Milos Forman on the picture

and, through Robbie Lantz, we had gotten the script to Milos. Milos was on a bicycle trip through France and we had, through a great deal of trouble, actually gotten the script to the small town in France, where Milos picked it up and said yeah, he'd really be interested in doing it.

FROUG: Marvelous choice.

ESZTERHAS: Yeah, he would have been terrific. So anyway, we had no input into who the director would be. After this meeting, Irwin and I decided to pull out of the project together. First we tried to buy it back from Carolco, and the lawyers felt that it had gone to such a point with memorandums and everything else that it was impossible. Carolco refused to sell it back to us. We would have wound up in court for ten years.

FROUG: They couldn't understand this incredible difference between what they bought and what it was going to become on the screen?

ESZTERHAS: What they did was, essentially, defer to Verhoeven.

FROUG: What I'm kind of curious about is, if they can accept a director who comes in and turns the script totally around and inside out, aren't they concerned that they've bought something else? I mean, they've paid three million dollars for a picture, and now this guy's coming up with something else.

ESZTERHAS: If we're going to put an emphasis on the dollar signs in terms of how much they paid for the script, I think the way they viewed it was that they paid three million for the script, but Verhoeven had made *a hundred and sixty million* for them on *Total Recall.* Their position was that they'd totally defer to Paul. And he knew that. So Irwin and I pulled out. We said, "We want to be paid our full price, but we want to have nothing to do with this movie." I withdrew as executive producer and said that I would look at the rough cut to see whether I wanted my name on it as a writer. The settlement that Irwin made was that he was paid the full amount that he was owed, and he took his name off the movie. Well, this, of course, made terrific news.

FROUG: What was happening with Michael Douglas during all this? You've got the star sitting there watching all of this happening.

ESZTERHAS: Michael very much wants to work with Verhoeven. I wouldn't say Michael was very active in the meeting, but he certainly supported Paul. I think he was taken aback by the notion that we were going to have such a sharp and public disagreement here, but he certainly supported Paul. So Irwin and I, together, pulled out. It turned into a very celebrated pullout, with the headline across the top of *Daily Variety* and news stories going out all over the place. I wound up issuing a statement, because I felt that I wanted to clarify why I pulled out. I didn't pull out of it blithely at that point—I'd been paid a lot of money, and I felt simply that I was in a situation where, if I would have gone with Verhoeven's feelings and done the rewriting that he suggested, I would have sold out my own script. And I was not going to do that. That's simply what it came to in a nutshell. So we pulled out of the project. This is in August of 1990. We had nothing to do with the film from there on. In late February of 1991, Verhoeven sent me the rewrites of *Basic Instinct.*

FROUG: Done by whom?

ESZTERHAS: By Gary Goldman, who worked with Paul on *Total Recall.* And, first of all, the cover page is interesting. In big letters on top it says, "*Basic Instinct* by Joe Eszterhas," and in very small letters in the middle it says, "Revisions by Gary Goldman." And on the bottom it says, "Directed by Paul Verhoeven." I've been in this business for sixteen years, and I know that's usually not the way things go.

FROUG: No, it isn't.

ESZTERHAS: So I had come back from Cleveland—my father was sick—and late at night I opened this thing. I saw the cover page, and I thought, "I'm not going to read this thing tonight because I'll probably get so pissed off and have a stroke. I should rest up and read it tomorrow." But I couldn't hold myself back. I started reading it. To my bewilderment and shock, as I read more and more, there were no changes. There were like a half-dozen immaterial and irrelevant line changes. Absolutely no changes.

FROUG: Amazing.

ESZTERHAS: So the next day I called Irwin and I told him, and he was amazed. And I called Guy McElwaine and told him.

FROUG: He was your agent on this?

ESZTERHAS: Yeah. And right around that period of time—February of '91—I'd written a new original called *Original Sin*, which was also auctioned. Cinergi and Andy Vajna wound up buying it.

FROUG: What did they pay for that one?

ESZTERHAS: A million five fifty.

FROUG: That's all this year?

ESZTERHAS: I've had a good year. [*Laughing*]

FROUG: Four and a half million dollars for screenplays. That's a good year.

ESZTERHAS: The day after he buys *Original Sin*, Andy has a lunch previously scheduled with Verhoeven. In the course of that lunch, Andy says that he just bought this new Eszterhas original called *Original Sin*. And Verhoeven says to him, "I sent Joe the *Basic Instinct* script, and I don't know whether you know, but there are no changes." Andy says, "What do you mean?" And Verhoeven says, "Well, listen, I was wrong. I made a mistake, and I didn't understand his script. I worked with Gary Goldman for four drafts, and I realized that with each draft that what Joe wrote was better than what we were coming up with. We tried to change these things, and it simply didn't work."

FROUG: A breathtaking turn of events for a writer.

ESZTERHAS: Yes, breathtaking. And Verhoeven says to Andy, "Do you think there's any possibility of Joe and I getting together, because really we don't have any creative differences anymore." So Andy calls me and tells me his conversation with Verhoeven and tells me how up front

Paul was about the fact that he was simply wrong. So I call Paul and I say, "Look, I heard about your lunch with Vajna, and I've gotten the script, and we clearly don't have creative differences at this point. Why don't we get together?" He's overjoyed. He's thrilled. He says, "Terrific. Let's get together." The next week we have a dinner at Morton's with Paul, Michael Douglas, and McElwaine. And Verhoeven, once again, very openly said, "Look, I made a mistake. I'm not a perfect human being. I didn't understand the script. The script has a basement that I never saw—if you start messing with it, the whole thing falls apart. All I saw was what was above ground, and I've learned what it was through the four months of working with Gary Goldman." And he says, "If Joe would come back in as executive producer, I want to say this publicly: I made a mistake." So the blowup was so public in terms of big headlines in *Variety* that I said, "Terrific. Let's do it." So we did a series of interviews. Paul and I did an interview together with the *San Francisco Chronicle*, with the *L.A. Times*, and with *Variety*, in which he said the same things. The *Variety* headline was, "Eszterhas back. Verhoeven trusts instincts." He was very open, as the *L.A. Times* pointed out in their story. This had never happened, where a director had essentially said, "I was wrong. I made a mistake." I really admire the man. I think there are few directors who publicly would say, "Look, I simply made a mistake. I didn't get it, and I do get it now. I'm not going to change the script, because I think the script is wonderful."

FROUG: So then did you begin to talk casting for real?

ESZTERHAS: Well, by then it had been cast.

FROUG: Who was cast, by the way?

ESZTERHAS: Michael Douglas. Sharon Stone was cast as the woman. George Dzundza was cast as the policeman's friend Gus, and there were several people who had just done off-Broadway who were cast in the other parts.

FROUG: Was anybody concerned that Sharon Stone was kind

of an unknown.

ESZTERHAS: Yes. They went to a lot of people, wanting to cast that part. They had a great deal of difficulty.

FROUG: Because of the nudity?

ESZTERHAS: I'm not certain to this day, to be fair, whether the difficulty was because of Paul's emphasis on what he wanted to emphasize then, when he was doing the casting, or whether the script called for a certain amount of nudity that certain actresses weren't willing to do. There were other actresses who really wanted to do it. For example, Kelly McGillis really wanted to do it, and Mariel Hemingway really wanted to do it. They tested them, but both Michael and Paul felt that Sharon Stone's test was sensational. That's why they went with her. I think, the great challenge is, this is a very complex part. I think if Sharon Stone pulls this off, she's going to be a superstar, because of the complexity of the part. Paul has great confidence that she can do it, and so does Michael.

FROUG: The screenwriter as executive producer is a very rare thing indeed. Now you're executive producer of a project that has finally gotten back on track. They've already cast it and you've got a director who was imposed on you. What will your functions be now? What authority do you have?

ESZTERHAS: Well, you see, I think the screenwriter as executive producer is hypocrisy. All executive producer means is more points and more money. That doesn't give you any juice. That doesn't give you any more weight. Whatever weight you have as a screenwriter, you have individually in terms of your own persona and how much you're willing to fight. That title means dog shit.

FROUG: Actually, you were willing to fight and kissed it goodbye.

ESZTERHAS: Yeah. Well, I was willing to fight, and they said goodbye. Then they came around about six months later and said, "You were right." Had I not fought and had I done the changes that Paul wanted, that script would have been trashed. He wouldn't have discovered he was wrong with me sitting there saying, "Yes, Paul. I'll make these changes." What led him to that point was me saying, "No. Go fuck yourself. I'm not going to change this." He tried the changes, and he came back and said, "You were right." Now I think that really is a terrific selfless and egoless thing to do. I admire Verhoeven for that.

FROUG: Well, I agree with that. But let's talk about the screenwriter. So few screenwriters take that position, that they created a concept. I interviewed one screenwriter in this book who said that the function of the screenwriter, in effect, is to serve the vision of the director. What do you think of that?

ESZTERHAS: I don't think he's a screenwriter. I think he's a secretary. He takes dictation. I think he's in a different business than I am. I'm a screenwriter. The emphasis is on writer. I'm a writer. I tell stories. Maybe he makes a wonderful secretary and takes great dictation, but I wouldn't call him a storyteller.

FROUG: Suppose this writer says that the screenplay is the work of the screenwriter, but the film is the work of the director?

ESZTERHAS: No. You see, I think that's exactly the kind of thing that the auteur theorists fall into. If you're not just watching visual pyrotechnics and viewing it the same way that you would view a painting, if characters and story mean something, and if it's an original screenplay, who gives birth to those characters and that story? The writer gives birth to them. The director interprets it and puts it up on the screen. Now, in terms of this kind of thing, I make a great distinction between people who do original screenplays, who do adaptations, and who do rewrites. If it's taken from a novel, the original vision—where the story and characters came from—came from the novelist, certainly not the screenwriter.

FROUG: In your case, you have specialized in writing spec scripts, right?

ESZTERHAS: I think I've done something like sixteen, seventeen scripts over the years.

FROUG: How many have been made?

ESZTERHAS: Let's go through them: *F.I.S.T.*, *Flashdance*, *Jagged Edge*, *Big Shots*, *Checking Out*, *Hearts of Fire*, *Betrayed*, *Music Box*, and *Basic Instinct*. What is that, nine?

FROUG: Pretty good batting average.

ESZTERHAS: But there are some others that I haven't sold, of course.

FROUG: You've still got them in the trunk?

ESZTERHAS: Sure. A few of them. *Platinum, Magic Man.*

FROUG: Most of those filmed were originals?

ESZTERHAS: For the most part. *Flashdance* and *Hearts of Fire* were the only two rewrites. I did one adaptation in my life, very early, right after *F.I.S.T.* I did an adaptation of a Brian Moore war novel called *The Doctor's Wife*, which was the single worst experience that I've had in screenwriting. I didn't feel good working with someone else's characters, I had too much respect for the novel, and I felt claustrophobic all the way through.

FROUG: *Checking Out*, which I recently saw, is a fascinating satire on the fear of dying. It starts off as a delightful comedy, a comedy-satire, and then keeps going broader and broader and broader until it finally is spinning out of control. Did you have any control over *Checking Out*?

ESZTERHAS: Well, *Checking Out* is the only picture that I've done outside the studio system, and it was the worst experience I had, interestingly.

FROUG: You were executive producer originally, weren't you?

ESZTERHAS: Well, originally. Let me tell you the story. *Checking Out* was one of the scripts that I've auctioned through the years that didn't sell. I've done seven auctions; there were three that didn't sell: *Magic Man, Checking Out,* and *Platinum.* I did it as a spec script. I auctioned it; nobody came, and I was heartbroken with it, essentially. So about three years afterwards, a young producer here in Marin County asked me out to lunch. And he says, "Do you have anything in your trunk that you think would make an interesting movie?" I tell him about *Checking Out.* He says, "That's really great. I don't have much money, but I'll pay you a little money for an option. Let me see what I can do with it." I say, "Well, I'll tell you what: I'm making enough money. Don't pay me any money. I don't want your money, but take it and see what you can do." So he single-handedly, unrelentingly, for two years did nothing but try to push this project. Well, nobody knew who the fuck he was, but he kept badgering people and going after people. He somehow got it to a real small company who was interested and liked the script. They tried to put it together with directors, but it didn't work. David Leland, an English director, had just done a picture called *Wish You Were Here* and was sort of the hot, arty flavor of the moment. They got it to David, and he said he wanted to do it. Now I owned the material, because I'd written it, and the initial company decided at the last second that they didn't want to do it with David. But Handmade, George Harrison's company, wanted to do it with David. So David and I sit down at the Beverly Hilton with my friend Ben Myron, who's the producer. I say to David, "Look, I'm not out to make a lot of money on this, but what I am very interested in is to make sure that this is what ends up on screen." David looks me in the eye and says, "There's not a word of this I'd want to change."

FROUG: Famous last words.

ESZTERHAS: I say, "Terrific." And I sell the script to Handmade for three hundred grand. Ben Myron and I are co-producers. The deal is structured this way (you're gonna love this). The credits have to read: "A David Leland Film." And underneath it, in the same block, it has to say "A Joe Eszterhas Script," right? And it begins with "Ben Myron and Joe Eszterhas Present," right? Well, no one's ever gotten that kind of credit for a script, so I was very happy about it. What happens is that David changes his mind and, in the course of shooting, starts changing the script. Starts changing it to the point that when the foreign press comes around to the set, he puts his own name on the script when he shows it to them. Now it suddenly says, "*Checking Out*, by David Leland." Well, I hear about this, and I throw an absolute shit fit. I get my people involved in it and get my lawyers involved in it and we try to muscle Handmade. Handmade has a relationship with David, and they don't want to hear from me.

FROUG: I've heard again and again and again for years that when it becomes, as it did basically on *Basic Instinct*, a tussle between the writer and the director, the director's always right.

ESZTERHAS: During shooting.

FROUG: Or even before shooting, it appears.

ESZTERHAS: I'll get into it with what happened here. So the producer and I can't get anywhere with Handmade. I see the rough cut, and I loathe some of the things that happen in it. There's a crudeness in the rough cut; there is an anti-Semitism in the rough cut, with characters that David has created with Jewish names who are repellent and horrible. And now I'm really gone. I'm totally crazy. What I do now is write a letter to David, and I carbon Handmade and Warner Bros., who's going to release the picture. I detail these things—the characters with the anti-Semitic names he created in the middle of it, the fact that it's insulting to women. One of the things he did was a scene where a woman demands to be treated not on a sexual level but as a human being, and in the very next scene we see the woman fucking the guy that she made the speech to. So I send this letter out all over the place, and the next thing I know, Handmade has taken it away from David and is recutting the picture, partly because of pressure from Warner Brothers. The outcome was that we got rid of some of the things that really bugged me. Everything except a line of dialogue that couldn't be taken out. We got the anti-Semitism out of it, we got the scene where the woman fucks the guy after making the speech out of it—she closes the door now, and it ends there. A terrific amount of changes were made. David, of course, at that point, flipped out himself. He didn't want it to say "A David Leland Film." I didn't want it to say "A Joe Eszterhas Script." It says, "Directed by David Leland and Written by Joe Eszterhas." It was the single worst experience I've had with something getting changed and screwed over. Ironically, it happened not with a studio picture, but it happened with a little independent.

FROUG: Because of your strong stand for writers, I think, you are the leading spokesman for screenwriters today.

ESZTERHAS: I'm not a spokesman for anybody except myself, and I want to be very careful to say that I've never aspired to speak for all writers. I'm a spokesman for a forty-seven-year-old guy whose fingers ache when he types too hard, whose back goes out, who has the usual problems with his kids. That's the only person I speak for. [*Laughter*]

FROUG: Well, a lot of other screenwriters are delighted that you're saying what you're saying, because whether you mean to or not, you are a voice on behalf of the screen-writer. You believe in the screenwriter as the author of the film, and you believe in the right and the dignity of the screenwriter, which is not always stated so eloquently or forcefully.

ESZTERHAS: I believe in both of those things, but I shy from, in any way, being viewed as the voice of the screenwriter. I certainly believe in the things that you said, but I shy from that.

FROUG: Don't you think it's unavoidable when so few people, especially so few screenwriters, are willing to speak out the way you do?

ESZTERHAS: The things I say sound revolutionary and newsworthy, and they shouldn't. I think it says something about screenwriters and the lack of self-respect with which too many have worked through the years. See, I think that screenwriters through the years have not been viewed with a great deal of respect by the literary world and, to a great extent, by the news media. I think some of it, maybe a lot of it, is their own fault. You have screenwriters very publicly saying that they write what they are told to write, that in a situation where they are in a meeting with someone they know is speaking nonsense, what they will do is sit there, take notes, smile, and do what they're told. You have screenwriters who say that their function is to serve the vision of the director. There's a quote this month in *Premiere* from a screenwriter who says that he was so happy that someone bought his script that he was willing to make all the changes they asked him to do. I think it's hypocritical for these screenwriters to ask for a terrific amount of respect. All I'm saying is, don't become a hooker. Respect yourself. I'm not saying don't make changes if someone gives you lucid suggestions that you think are right, or someone says, "Look, this scene that you've written doesn't work as well as it could. This is why." If they can convince you of that, logically, rationally (and I've been convinced of that), then make the change, because ultimately the only thing you should be concerned about is the quality of the finished product. But if someone says to you, "Make these changes because I tell you to make them. I'm the director," and you feel that what they're saying is wrong and you still make them, then you are selling out what you've written, and you're selling out yourself as a writer, and, ultimately, it's going to destroy any self-respect that you have. I don't know how, if you do that, you can return to your typewriter and do something that's good, something that you believe in.

FROUG: Let me ask you some craft questions. When you sit down to begin one of your screenplays, do you generally start with a character? Do you work from the character out, or do you generally start with a plot idea?

ESZTERHAS: *Checking Out*, for example, came from very close personal experience. The day after I made my first real amount of money ever in life. I made it on the novelization of *F.I.S.T.*—Lynn Nesbitt sold it for four hundred thousand dollars. I grew up poor and I was broke all my life. Lynn Nesbitt sells it for four hundred grand, and suddenly I need accountants, because we have to do something with this money. I have a meeting in San Francisco with four accountants and my wife about what we're going to do with this money. I go home, and the next morning I get up, and I think I'm going to die. My heart feels like it's coming through my chest, I feel dizzy, I start thinking that my arm hurts. We called the paramedics. My children were babies, infants. The ambulances came and all that stuff. I called my doctor and said, "I think I'm having a heart attack." He said, "I don't think you're having a heart attack." The paramedics were there, but he said, "Get down here right away." I went down there and he said, "You had an anxiety attack. You had a classic panic attack." The damn money set it off—the four hundred grand. I'd been healthy all my life, and I'd never until that time paid a whole lot of attention to physical things, but the next year I thought I was going to die. I suddenly stopped swimming and doing the things that I like, paid attention to my pulse rate and all that. And finally, the way I got rid of the whole thing was that I wrote a comedy about it. I wrote *Checking Out*. It was about this guy . . .

FROUG: It was about you.

ESZTERHAS: It was about me.

FROUG: And if you don't quit smoking, schmuck, all that's going to come true. [*Eszterhas laughs*] Anyway, I think often the best stories come from within, from our own experiences. If we can learn to expose or dramatize the things that we're most afraid of, we often have good screenplays.

ESZTERHAS: Yes. Well, it helped me. I wrote that piece, and everything was okay. But that year was hellish. Some of the other movies, *Big Shots*, for example, came out of the notion of what would happen to my son. My boy at that age was very shy and very quiet and very attached to me. I wondered what would happen to him if I died, what would happen to him in life and all of that. It came out of that initial thing, combined with the notion, probably a fear, about how would my boy relate to the real world. I grew up in a working-class neighborhood, growing up with all kinds of kids—black kids, Puerto Rican kids, Jewish kids, German kids, hillbilly kids—and my boy grows up in a very nice, white suburb, an upscale suburb. That's sort of where *Big Shots* came from. *Betrayed*—I know exactly where that came from. My kids go to public schools in Marin County. Marin County is the most liberal area of California, liberal democrat. They come from school one day, and my boy tells me that he's gotten into a fight with a kid because he used the word "Jewboy" on the playground. Well, when the word "Jewboy" is being bandied about on a Marin County playground—at the same time they were having problems with racist things being scrawled into Little League bleacher seats—I thought, "Jesus, if this stuff is dribbling down in Marin County, what's going on?" And at the same time the whole neo-Nazi thing had happened with a series of robberies around the country, so I sort of combined it all into *Betrayed. Music Box* came from my own Hungarian experience. When I got to be about sixteen years old, I realized exactly what Hungary had done during the war. I realized, even with all of the heinous horrors that were done during the war, what Hungary did was really exceptional because the war was over, and the Hungarian people, not the German occupiers but the Hungarian people themselves, went on a rampage of mass murder of Jews. It frankly came out of my own guilt in terms of my Hungarian background. I felt that it was really important for somebody Hungarian to tell this story. I was born in Hungary; I grew up speaking the Hungarian language. I came to this country when I was six years old. I thought it was really important for somebody Hungarian to write this piece, because it was so awful.

FROUG: It's a good film. I was struck by something in *Music Box*. You're burdening a protagonist with a heavy load— I kind of think too heavy—throughout the film with her fighting for her father, who, the audience is increasingly convinced, happens to be a former Nazi who committed these heinous crimes. I just wonder, when you give the protagonist that kind of weight to carry, if we can ever really pull for her?

ESZTERHAS: Well, you see, one of the things that I've always thought was poppycock was the whole "rooting" notion. I think that's for football games and baseball games. I'm talking about drama and characters. I'm not interested in having to root for someone; I'm trying to get some sort of an understanding as to what makes people tick and what they're about. I've resisted the notion of creating people that you can root for. Don't forget the things that I do have a tendency to be so muddled sometimes that you don't know who the hell you can root for. In *Betrayed*, who are you really rooting for? In *Jagged Edge*, who are you rooting for? Well, you're rooting for Glenn Close, I guess, but you certainly don't like the fact that she's all wrapped up with Jeff Bridges. When you start viewing things in terms of who you're rooting for, you wind up writing formulaic things.

FROUG: That's a very good point. I think you're probably right. In *Jagged Edge*, which I just loved—I've seen it three or four times—you have a very thin thread holding that film together. The thin thread is whether Jeff Bridges is or isn't the guy who did that killing. Is he or isn't he a psychopath? That's a very thin line of dramatic tension. Did that concern you as you wrote, whether you could hold that or not?

ESZTERHAS: I felt that if we could perpetuate that game—if it worked to the point where you were never sure, right down to the ending—it was going to work and it was going to be fine. It worked in *Jagged Edge*. It didn't in *Music Box*, because in *Music Box* you weren't supposed to know that the father was guilty, and it didn't come off. I offer it as a contrasting example, because I agree with you that very many people, from an early point in that picture, simply thought he was guilty. We didn't have the shell game going that we had in *Jagged Edge*.

FROUG: It worked perfectly in *Jagged Edge.*

ESZTERHAS: Part of the reason it worked so perfectly is because Jeff, in playing the part, brought an entire all-American boy persona to it. It was ideal casting in my mind. He played it superbly, and all the baggage he brought with him in terms of the Jeff Bridges persona worked for us.

FROUG: I produced the first movie he ever starred in. It was a TV Movie-of-the-Week called *In Search of America.* He's a wonderful actor.

ESZTERHAS: I think he's a terrific human being, too. He's the most down-to-earth guy.

FROUG: In *Jagged Edge,* I think the creation of the detective singing the song of reality in her ear all the time is a wonderful device.

ESZTERHAS: Well, you know, what's interesting about that is that in my first draft—Sam Ransom is the detective's name—Sam is the same personality that you saw on screen, but he wasn't nearly as funny. And Richard Marquand, God bless him—he died a few years ago and I loved working with him—it was Richard's suggestion to make him funny. He originally had some humor, but he didn't have as much as he finally did. Richard's notion was make him funnier to relieve the tension that we have going, and the whole character's going to work more.

FROUG: So there's a case in which you say that when a director does have something positive to say that you think enhances the script, you willingly change it.

ESZTERHAS: Well, sure. With *Betrayed,* I think I did four drafts before the shooting was over. I've worked with Costa-Gavras twice, and we're going to work together again. Costa's not an easy man to work with. He's a world-renowned director. I think he does superb movies. I like him very much as an individual, but he has very strong ideas. I had to go up to the set in Canada because they discovered in the course of shooting that the goddamned thing was going to be two hours and fifty minutes if they shot it all. I have a tendency to write too long. That's one of my faults. Sometimes they discover it while they're filming and they freak. So I had to go up there and really revise. What made it very difficult was that I could only revise what hadn't been shot, so I had to trim those areas down.

FROUG: Don't they have a table reading with the script girl, as they used to call them, or the script supervisor?

ESZTERHAS: They had the old rule about one minute a page. It doesn't seem to work if you have a lot of dialogue. I happen to have a lot of dialogue in most of them, and it throws things out of whack.

FROUG: Yeah, one minute a page was the ballpark we always used. But in a heavily dialogued script, it depends on the pacing of the director.

ESZTERHAS: See, in my mind, what you have to be open to do is both things. Let me give you examples. Costa and I had a battle on *Betrayed* because he very strongly felt that at the end of the picture, when she comes back to face the townspeople, she is pregnant with Berenger's child, right? And I said, "You can't do that. It's going to open up an entire new can of worms. It's going to take away from the theme." We had a really nasty battle, and at the end of it Costa said, "You're right. I won't do it." Flipside with Costa: my final ten pages on *Music Box* were very different. He said, "If you do this, it's going to take away from your basic theme, which is the children. What this is about is successive generations, and we're going to lose sight of the fact that what holds this together is her child." I really fought him, but at the end of it I saw that he was right, and I said, "You're right." On *Flashdance*, Adrian Lyne and I had a fight because, at the last minute before shooting began, Adrian said that he thought a part of the girl's backstory should be that she was raped by her own father when she was eight years old. I said, "Adrian, this is a magical little fable about this girl who wants to dance. You inject those kinds of elements into it and it's going to ruin it." We had this battle in a final script session at Caesar's

Palace in Las Vegas. We disagreed for the whole day on this point and we weren't getting anywhere. I simply went upstairs to my suite, got my bags, and left. Checked out of the hotel, went to the airport and left. Don Simpson told me later that Adrian went racing up after me, found that I'd checked out, came back down to Don and said, "Don, he's left." And Simpson, who was sitting in a tub in the living room of this unbelievably grotesque suite, looked at him and said, "Well, Adrian, when the gorilla shits in your face, you gotta get out of the way." [*Laughter*]

FROUG: That's marvelous. I love that. *Flashdance* was, I think, a superb film. It was widely acclaimed, wasn't it?

ESZTERHAS: No. It got deadly reviews. The studio didn't support it, and actually wound up selling off a major part of their percentage. There was no advertising behind it, no stars.

FROUG: But it was a big hit.

ESZTERHAS: The first weekend it opened at something like two eight. Two million eight in eight hundred theaters on a weekend; it's nothing. The subsequent weekends, it held in and went up. They discovered it was solely word of mouth. People were talking about it. It was a total audience picture. It turned into a gigantic hit. It made something like two hundred and eighty million dollars.

FROUG: Do you have a piece?

ESZTERHAS: I did, and one of the things that was really interesting was that I had net points and made a lot of money off of them. During the Buchwald suit, Paramount asked me to testify on their behalf, saying that there were some writers who were indeed paid off with net points. I said, "Come on, guys. I'm not going to go testify against Art Buchwald." [*Laughter*] "What he's doing is wonderful." Just because I didn't happen to be cheated, and ninety-nine percent of the others are, I'm not going to testify on that side. Incidentally, the one thing that I want to say about *Flashdance* that I think is important is that it was not my original script. It was written by a guy named Tom Hedley.

Tom had the title, which was his, and he had the basic notion of a girl who does this kind of dancing that's between strip and a sort of high-fashion dancing. Without that, there wouldn't have been a movie. The story was considerably different, and I changed the story. His story was about a young girl who has a love affair with a man in his sixties who's married and who helps defend the neighborhood against Hells Angels, and so it's a totally different story. But what he did have, and there wouldn't be a movie without it, is the character—the basic notion of what she does.

FROUG: You were seized by the character.

ESZTERHAS: Yeah, I was seized. I'll tell you why I got involved in it. I've always loved rock and roll, and I wanted to do a musical kind of picture. When they wanted me to rewrite this, I went up to Toronto—Hedley lived in Toronto—and looked at the girls doing this kind of dancing. I found a really fascinating scene with all these girls who are blue collar doing this kind of thing, and I thought there was a richness there.

FROUG: Also you were going back to your own roots.

ESZTERHAS: Yes, I was. One of the things I blame screen-writers for is that screenwriters have a tendency to be awfully self-serving at times. We wind up fucking each other over. I would like to see more screenwriters give more credits to the guy who did the original screenplay instead of saying, "Well, this is mine." *Flashdance* is not mine; it is partly mine. To a great extent it is Tom Hedley's, because without that original spark, it wouldn't have been there.

FROUG: I'm glad you did say that, because it's true. I happen to like *Betrayed* very much. I saw some reviews that said that the chasing, the hunting sequence with the black boy, was sort of added in there. I didn't feel that way.

ESZTERHAS: I'll tell you the reason it was in there. The "mud hunt" comes from the verbiage that these people use. They advocate "mud hunts." I don't know how many black people they've killed through the years, but they have a thing called the "mud hunt." What I did was dramatize and show a mud hunt on screen.

FROUG: What were the roots of that story? It's a very unusual story of racism in America.

ESZTERHAS: Well, it began with what I told you about my boy and with seeing this neo-Nazi stuff. I don't know if you remember, at the time there were a whole series of robberies and criminal actions done by various neo-Nazi groups like the Posse Comitatus and several others. There were also a whole series of racial crimes: synagogue vandalism, black kids being beaten at colleges. I felt that what I was seeing was a rebirth of a kind of racism and anti-Semitism that was filtering into the popular culture. I have been dedicated to the proposition that no man has a right to hurt another man, and that the only thing that's going to make this the kind of society that my grandchildren will enjoy living in is the recognition that we are all of us equal. I wanted to write something about it. The actual way it happened is that I had had a three-picture deal that had just been set up with Jerry Weintraub when he was running UA, and they were blank. All the deal said was that they were original screenplays. I called Jerry one day and I said, "Listen, there's something that I really want to do here that I think is really important. I've got to talk to you about it." He said, "If it's that important, you'd better tell me about it on the phone." I did, and he said, "Well, you know, Irwin Winkler came in with the same idea three days ago." Now I had never met Irwin Winkler, and Jerry said, "I'm going to bring you together." So I went and met Irwin with Jerry. We were looking for a director, and I suggested Richard Marquand because he and I'd worked on *Jagged Edge* and *Hearts of Fire*. So Richard came in on the meeting and then decided he didn't want to do it. Irwin is a very strong producer, and, I think, frankly, Richard was sort of cowed by working with that kind of producer. So Richard pulled out, and then Irwin suggested Costa. That's how Costa came into the project.

FROUG: I always think of Costa-Gavras in terms of *Z* and in terms of the early political thrillers, and I was kind of surprised to see that he was the director on this.

ESZTERHAS: Costa would like to do different kinds of things. I'll tell you what's interesting, what Costa would really love to do is a musical. He loves dance and ballet and musicals and all that. But he has been pigeonholed to do a certain kind of political picture, and he finds it almost impossible to break out of that in this country. In France, he did a terrific little comedy called *Family Business*, which was the same theme as the *Family Business* picture in this country.

FROUG: Which was a dog here, wasn't it?

ESZTERHAS: Yeah, the one here was a dog. That's not the one Costa did. He did a little one in France with Johnny Halliday, the French rock-and-roll star, that's an absolutely brilliant little picture. It's just a goofy little comedy. So he can do that. He'd love to do it, but here, for the studio stuff, the only thing they want him to do is that kind of political film.

FROUG: Particularly left-wing political stories. Seems like they've pigeonholed him in two categories, both in genre and in politics.

ESZTERHAS: But you know what's interesting about the man is that he is very much a humanist. He did a picture in the late seventies called *The Confession*, which was a deadly attack on Eastern European communism. Costa is no knee-jerk leftie. Very few people have done that kind of picture, that goes after Eastern European communism and goes after it in terms of its Stalinism and narrowness and its fascistic tendencies. He's a great humanist, both personally and ideologically. I loved working with him. He's a very human person, and he loves the tug-of-war. Everything is up front with him. He's not passive-aggressive. And he said one of the nicest things any director ever said to me. It was the day before he began shooting *Music Box* in Chicago. We had dinner, and I walked him up to his room. He gave me a hug and he said, "Thank you for your help and your passion, Joe."

FROUG: Now you're working on another one with him. Is it another political thriller?

ESZTERHAS: Well, I want to do one more picture about extremism. *Betrayed* sort of does anti-Semitism and racism in this country today. And *Music Box* did it in terms of what happened in a country during the war, and I want to do a movie about what happened in this country during the war, with Father Coughlin, FDR.

FROUG: America First.

ESZTERHAS: America First stories, all of that stuff. And to get into the whole issue of American fascism. Father Coughlin, you know, was the dominant radio personality of his time. People don't know what an effect that man had on this country.

FROUG: Henry Ford was a big backer of his, I believe.

ESZTERHAS: Henry Ford was involved with him; there was a whole group of them. They worked together. There was a guy named Moseby, who was a military guy.

FROUG: Moseby's the guy who had the Brown Shirts in Canada, wasn't he?

ESZTERHAS: Yes. I want to do a picture that pulls all of that together, focusing on Coughlin. And I'd like Costa to do it.

FROUG: So you'll start from that germ and you'll build?

ESZTERHAS: Yes.

FROUG: You won't collaborate on the screenplay with Costa?

ESZTERHAS: I loathe talking about a story before I write. I think it's a waste of time in some ways. I don't know exactly what I'm going to write until I actually sit down and write.

FROUG: Do you step outline your screenplay before you start?

ESZTERHAS: I know my ending, and I do notes on my characters.

FROUG: Do you follow any kind of paradigm? Do you assume the first act should end around page twenty, twenty-five, for example?

ESZTERHAS: The only thing I do is draw up the names of my

characters and I describe them to myself. I know where I'm going to end. Usually.

FROUG: Do you work in a three-act structure? I don't think so, from what I've seen of your films.

ESZTERHAS: No, I just start writing. And sometimes I don't know where it's going to go. That's when it's really exciting to me, when I don't know where it's going to go, because it's not locked in, it's not set. We did that with *Betrayed*, but we had four or five meetings with Costa on *Betrayed*, in terms of talking about it. On *Music Box*, I just wrote the whole thing, and when it was done, we gave it to Costa, and Costa said, "Yes, terrific; I want to do it." It was that easy.

FROUG: It's a great working relationship. Do you think young filmwriters should go to film school?

ESZTERHAS: If all they want to be is screenwriters, I don't think they should. If they want to direct, then I think they should. Let me explain that. I think one of my strengths as a screenwriter is that I'm always talking to people. I spend extended time in different parts of the country. I've worked in journalism, which exposed me to all of the social class levels so that I can write a character like Teddy Barnes and I can write Johnny Kovak in *F.I.S.T.* What's given me strengths as a screenwriter is exposure to different people, different parts of the country, and different levels of society. I fear, sometimes, that the screenwriters who come out of the film schools wind up doing things that are so influenced by film characters as opposed to real-life ones that it all starts getting a bit incestuous. If they want to direct, I think they have to go to film school.

FROUG: To learn the mechanics of it?

ESZTERHAS: Yeah. Simply, so they won't be held hostage by their own ignorance.

FROUG: So the best way to learn to write is to write.

ESZTERHAS: Yes. Absolutely. There's a wonderful old German expression, "sitzfleisch," that I really believe in. It means the ability to sit on your ass.

Gregory Widen

1986   HIGHLANDER *(Sole Story and Shared Screenplay)*

1988   WEEKEND WAR [TV Movie] *(Shared Teleplay)*

1990   HIGHLANDER II *(Based on Characters Created by)*

1991   BACKDRAFT *(Written by)*

*IN THIS I WAS TRYING TO
DRAW TOGETHER THE IDEA OF
LOYALTY AND COMMITMENT TO AN
INSTITUTION,
AND HOW
THAT
CAN GO BAD
WHEN THE
REAL WORLD
PEEKS IN.*

INT. FIRE STATION 17 - STORAGE ROOM - 20 YRS. EARLIER

Darkness. Then the GLINT of a flashlight. Its beam rocks crazily to and fro across the inside of a small storage room as we hear two children arguing.

                    OLDER KID
          You're doing it wrong.

                    YOUNGER KID
          Shut up.

                    OLDER KID
          You're doing it wrong.

It's hard, but we get a sense of the room in the whipping beam of light. Huge, dark coats lined up like sides of beef on steel batons. Bent, stained helmets hung like African masks.

Beneath them BRIAN, 7, and STEPHEN, 12, are trying to struggle into a pair of the ludicrously massive coats over their pajamas.

                    STEPHEN
          It doesn't go like that.

                    BRIAN
          Who asked you?

                    STEPHEN
          If you do it like that it'll open in the
          fire. Then you'll get burned and DIE.

The door suddenly opens, morning sunlight roaring in. It's a fire station storage room full of fire gear. A fireman stands in the doorway, tall, athletic, their father; DENNIS McCAFFREY.

                    DENNIS
          Who's going to die?

                    STEPHEN
          Brian. He's not doing it right, dad. He
          never does it right.

                    DENNIS
          (gestures for them to come out) Well, let's
          have a look.

INT. FIRE STATION 17 - DAY   2

The two boys tromp out of the closet. The rubber turn-out boots are as high as their thighs. The ends of the coats drag on the floor. They salute, Brian's arm just an empty sleeve. Dennis kneels down and re-fastens Brian's coat.

"So it really helps to have a group of people you can lean on."

Greg Widen is a man of few words, but those few are often valuable. Like several other writers in this book, Greg was my student in a UCLA graduate screenwriting seminar. For me at least, Greg was not an easy man to know. We had little rapport. He spoke rarely in class but listened attentively. He was more serious than most of the students I came across. There was earnestness about him, and self-assurance without arrogance, that let you know that he was a man who kept his own council. If he didn't have that good quality early on in life, he surely must have acquired it during his three years as a fireman in the Los Angeles Fire Department; I'm certain he was as successful there as he has been as a writer.

Greg's early work showed this same self-confidence. As a teacher I knew he would come in with a solid, workable screenplay, and indeed he did. But I had learned many years earlier that there is no safe prediction in the wacky world of show biz. So, while I thought of him as a writer of substance and ability, I did not foresee that he would become the star screenwriter he has become since graduation.

Since our interview, *Backdraft*, filmed from the screenplay Greg wrote in my class, has become one of the big summer hits of 1991. It's a very exciting movie. As I watched it recently, I tried to visualize the screenplay I had read many years ago in early drafts, but I could not.

What came across loud and clear in the film, however, was that *Backdraft's* writer must know intimately the subject he was writing about. The writer would have to be a fireman with some considerable expertise to present this most difficult and complex work in such a clean, clear, and dramatic form. It's no easy job, and Greg deserves much of the credit for the film's smashing success.

Like many of the writers with whom I was privileged to work as a teacher, Gregory Widen has continued to grow in stature and talent as the years have passed. His admonition to his fellow writers—that the best way to learn to write is to keep doing it over and over again and to finish the screenplay you are working on at all costs before you move on to the next one—is solid gold. There's much here in this interview that is like Greg himself. Brief but valuable. Advice you can depend on.

FROUG: When you were in my class, you wrote two screen-plays. One was *Highlander*, which I found kind of con-fusing; I wasn't a big fan of that script.

WIDEN: Actually, I wrote that in Rich Walter's class.

FROUG: Okay. And the other one was *Backdraft*, which I happened to love. Then you left, and the next thing I know, you're a big success. Tell me, first, how you got an agent.

WIDEN: I did it the way you're not supposed to do it. I was so naive that I didn't know enough to know that you can't get an agent. I was always taught, as most people are taught, that you can only get an agent through a referral. But I didn't know any better, so I got a list from the Writers Guild and literally sent *Highlander* out with a cover letter. I said, "Hi, my name is Greg. Please represent me." And a handful of them wrote back.

FROUG: That's marvelous to hear. When the agents got the screenplay, how long did it take them to move it?

WIDEN: To sell it?

FROUG: Uh-huh.

WIDEN: I would say it was about four months. I walked away from *Highlander* with about two hundred and fifty thousand.

FROUG: Well, that's a nice walk.

WIDEN: Yeah, for a twenty-six-year-old college kid it wasn't bad.

FROUG: Tell me, when the film of *Highlander* came out, was

it what you expected?

WIDEN: No, not at all.

FROUG: In what way?

WIDEN: Well, it was a very personal script, and it was a lot more low-key than what was made. The producers wanted a lot more whiz-bang when they made it, and, in fact, I was replaced by other writers who worked on it.

FROUG: I couldn't make any sense of it. It was so confusing, with all the slam-bang and whiz-bang in the opening.

WIDEN: It lost all its heart. It had a lot of heart, from my perspective, when I wrote it. It was a much more personal story of these two guys and their struggle, and the film that was produced concentrated more on special effects and artistry of the camera and less on story.

FROUG: It did not make it at the box office, did it?

WIDEN: Well, yes and no. It did not make a lot of money in the United States, but it made over a hundred million dollars in Europe, and, in fact, at the time was the largest-grossing film in the history of France. So Jerry Lewis and me are geniuses in France. [*Laughter*] It was a huge financial success overseas.

FROUG: It that why they're doing *Highlander II*?

WIDEN: Yeah.

FROUG: Are you involved in *Highlander II*?

WIDEN: No, other than having to be paid a gob of money for them to do it. I chose not to be involved.

FROUG: Same production team?

WIDEN: Yeah. Same director.

FROUG: Then the next script you sold was *Backdraft*?

WIDEN: No. The next script I sold was a spec script I wrote in another class at UCLA. It was called *Clan of One*. I sold it to Warners for a six-figure option. That's when I really started my professional career, because even though I had sold *Highlander* a few years earlier and had written *Backdraft* (what would eventually become *Backdraft*), at that point in time, the option money for *Highlander* was very, very minuscule. It was a few thousand a year because it was with a very small company. Only when they linked up with a big funding source in Britain did the movie get made. And I didn't receive that money until the movie went into production in 1985, which was also the same year that I sold the spec script *Clan* to Warners. So 1985 was really the year I became a professional writer and started making a lot of money, even though I had some scripts in an option state for about three years before that.

FROUG: How many screenplays did you come out of UCLA with?

WIDEN: I came out with, I guess, four?

FROUG: Have you sold them all or optioned them?

WIDEN: Three of them. One of them I never showed to anybody. I'd like to show it someday.

FROUG: That's a terrific batting average. Do you recommend that young writers who might be reading this book go to film school?

WIDEN: Yeah.

FROUG: It was a good experience for you?

WIDEN: Yeah. Maybe not for the reasons you think. The best thing about film school, I think, is that you're forced to write.

FROUG: That's what we try to do with the UCLA program— make you write.

WIDEN: I think I wrote more in ten weeks at UCLA than I write now in ten weeks. [*Laughter*]

FROUG: Now that the wolf is not at your door.

WIDEN: I fear studio executives a lot less than I did instructors. I think that's probably the primary thing. The second thing is, you really form a very close bonding with a lot of friends in film school, which I think is really important later in life, because writing's a very lonely job. You spend a lot of time alone. People who don't do it, don't really understand it, understand what you go through. It really helps to have a group of people that you can lean on. I was very fortunate. I became very close friends with a lot of people I'm still close friends with today, and who are very successful. One of them, Randy Johnson, wrote the Doors movie that just came out.

FROUG: I remember Randy. He was in one of my UCLA classes. Did he write the Doors movie?

WIDEN: Yeah, with Oliver Stone.

FROUG: Good for him. Randy's really a good guy, and a good writer.

WIDEN: There was a group of us who were pretty successful. And we've stuck together. For me that was the greatest value, just having those people around to be able to hang out in coffee shops with and talk about writing. It's the atmosphere more than anything.

FROUG: Yeah, that's true. *Backdraft* is apparently set for major release, yes?

WIDEN: May 24 [1991].

FROUG: Who's in it?

WIDEN: Robert De Niro, Kurt Russell, Scott Glenn, William Baldwin, Jennifer Jason Leigh, Rebecca DeMornay, Jason Gedrick and Donald Sutherland.

FROUG: Big, important cast.

WIDEN: Yeah, it's a big movie.

FROUG: What do you think of it?

WIDEN: I love it. I'm really happy with it.

FROUG: Did they stick with your script?

WIDEN: Yeah. Very much so.

FROUG: That's rare, isn't it?

WIDEN: Yes, it is. [*Laughing*] I had a very unique experience on that film. Very often, as the writer, you're romanced heavily when they want to buy the script and fussed over when you're rewriting it, and then, if you're lucky, you don't have to be replaced. When it's actually made, very often as soon as the director comes into the picture, their attitude is "thank you very much, but please count your money outside the door." You're suddenly a threat, and they're very uncomfortable with you. *Backdraft* was very unique in the sense of the director Ron Howard. He's a very collaborative director, and he likes having his writers around. I was on the set every day by his desire. I helped pitch ideas and suggested performance ideas and suggested shots. All this for two reasons, I think: he is a very collaborative guy and I had the advantage of having been a fireman, and *Backdraft* is a movie about firemen.

FROUG: That was exclusively based on your experience in Los Angeles when you were a fireman?

WIDEN: Right.

FROUG: Do you recommend that students write out of their experiences?

WIDEN: Yes and no. I think one reason *Backdraft* was good enough to be made was that I reached a distance from it. If you write about your own experience, I think you need to take two steps back and look at it as someone who doesn't know the field would look at it. The great value is that you have a lot of anecdotal information that's particular only to people who have been there. That's what makes a film real. But, I think, for great thematic brushes, you really need to get back away from it. If you write it too close to your experience, it's a little dull or it can be a little too inside.

FROUG: In this case, you were a fireman to support yourself to go to UCLA and become a writer, yes?

WIDEN: Yeah. Oh, I also loved the job.

FROUG: How long were you a fireman?

WIDEN: Three years.

FROUG: That's a long stretch.

WIDEN: Yeah. Eighteen to twenty-one.

FROUG: I didn't know they hired them that young.

WIDEN: Some places they don't. Where I worked, they did.

FROUG: So that was a good experience, too.

WIDEN: I loved it, yeah.

FROUG: I read the script, and I could tell you loved it. It came through in the screenplay. What did you get paid for that one?

WIDEN: I walked away with in excess of five hundred

thousand.

FROUG: Is that a plateau that any of the scripts you write will reach automatically?

WIDEN: You mean in terms of price?

FROUG: Yeah.

WIDEN: My back end's actually bigger than that now. Not so much because I was paid that amount before, but because a big movie is coming out. *Backdraft's* perceived as a big movie. A normal writer, if he continues to work, crawls up in price, bit by bit by bit by bit. But I think once you get a big movie that comes out, it jumps sort of logarithmically.

FROUG: Then you become a big movie writer, so to speak.

WIDEN: At least for the moment.

FROUG: Do you get assignments to do rewriting?

WIDEN: I'm asked. I'm usually not interested in it.

FROUG: Because you want to write your own stuff?

WIDEN: I'm usually a writer who has my own ideas. Not exclusively, but I would say ninety percent of the time I do my own thing.

FROUG: You wrote *A Weekend War,* an ABC Movie-of-the-Week. How do you find the experience of working for television versus working for feature films?

WIDEN: It's a mix. On one hand, it's very rushed. The level of quality in terms of the directors is usually very low. The directors tend to be traffic cops. They're hired by the studio about the same way you hire a carpenter, at the very last minute. They're in there to get it in on time and under budget.

FROUG: Get the job done, right?

WIDEN: Right. They're not terribly creative people, I don't think. However, as a writer, ironically, despite the limited means, you are much more powerful, in a weird kind of way, in television than you are in film. In film, you serve purely at the discretion and whim of the director. I was deeply involved in *Backdraft.* And I had a wonderful experience, purely because the director wanted me to.

Otherwise, I wouldn't have been there. I had absolutely no rights. In television, however, the perception of the network, at least in my case, was that it was my movie, not the director's. Whenever a decision was made, everyone looked at me. I'd be in a room full of people—the director and the producer and network executives and studio executives—and every time a suggestion was proposed by the head of programming, everyone looked at me. When I'm in a room with Ron Howard, that doesn't happen. [*Laughter*]

FROUG: Jeff Boam told me that when he's in a conference now with these people (and he has a major number of hit movies out; he's up there in the big bucks) and they're talking about ideas for the movie, he presents an idea and they shoot it down easily and quickly. But when the director has an idea, it is immediately accepted. And if there's a question, they ask the director. They don't ask Jeff—the writer who has to make it work.

WIDEN: Yeah. In features, you shrink to about four inches when the director comes into the room. Television was nice because I was treated like I was the boss of the movie. I was a co-producer on the movie, too, which is very typical of writers in television. You just have that extra degree of power. I was involved in the whole process, much like with *Backdraft*. *Weekend War*, though, was the highest-rated TV movie that ABC had that year, and it got a lot of nice critical stuff written about it. It was not quite the piece of art that, say, *Backdraft* is. But, at the same time, I was very deeply involved in it, even though it was done over a very short period of time. We had twenty days to shoot it, and we were in Puerto Rico. What's also thrilling is that I wrote it in three weeks, shot it three weeks after that, and it was out three weeks after that. So the entire process—writing to on screen—was about two months.

FROUG: That's amazing.

WIDEN: In film, it can be years and years and years. So the

instant gratification was fun, too.

FROUG: Do you see yourself writing television as well as features?

WIDEN: It could interest me. Movies-of-the-Week I did more as a lark, a chance to produce, a chance to see how the system works. But Movies-of-the-Week are odd animals because there's extremely little money in them.

FROUG: Compared to features.

WIDEN: Compared to features, yeah. Compared to the real world, it's a lot of money. But relatively speaking, MOW writers are really underpaid.

FROUG: What, about fifty thousand?

WIDEN: Fifty, sixty thousand dollars. But series television is where most writers make tons of money. In fact, someone gave me a statistic that of the top twenty writers, in terms of pay, seventeen or eighteen of them were TV guys. Because if you invent a series . . .

FROUG: You're really up there.

WIDEN: Millions upon millions upon millions of dollars.

FROUG: Look at Norman Lear.

WIDEN: Speaking from a purely creative side, I'm very interested in doing series television, which is actually how I have this deal at the studio—through television.

FROUG: Because you are guaranteed to do a series?

WIDEN: Not guaranteed, but it's a first look. If I come up with an idea, I have to go to them first. In return I get this office space.

FROUG: Do you find yourself thinking in terms of TV ideas?

WIDEN: I try to. I'm not very good at it yet [*Laughing*], but I'm trying. The medium interests me. In television, you can develop characters in a way you really can't in movies because you don't have the time or the latitude.

FROUG: That's a very good point to make. If you do a series, the characters can grow over the span of the series.

WIDEN: I'm by no means arrogant or snobbish about television. I think there's a lot of really terrific television, and there are a lot of really rotten movies. I mean, I don't think I'd want to be just a writing jock on a TV show, because that's kind of numbing. But I'd love to create a television show and shepherd it if I believed in it.

FROUG: You would be the executive producer—the show-runner—that's the term. Bill Bryan introduced me to that nomenclature. Well, let me ask you this: when you're developing a screenplay, do you work from any kind of paradigm? You're looking for a first act curtain around page twenty, twenty-five or in between, a second act curtain around eighty, eighty-five, and then a short third act?

WIDEN: I don't really think in those terms, to be honest. I've never been a page-count guy. But I've always thought that you should understand the character—what he's doing, what his problems are—what the issues are going to be in the movie.

FROUG: In the first twenty pages?

WIDEN: In the first twenty pages, absolutely. In fact, I'm actually guest-teaching a course at UCLA this quarter. What I have to say, basically, is that I think a lot of screenplays are very well-written, with a lot of interesting dialogue and a lot of interesting stuff going on, but you have no idea what's at stake in the movie by page twenty. And the reality in life is a lot of people never get past page twenty.

FROUG: In reading.

WIDEN: In reading. And that's what I believe in. I think you have to really focus very early on what the character stake and story stake is. That's probably the only rule I have. That, and simply understanding the movie, which is not to be confused with the plot, in very simple terms.

FROUG: You say understand the movie versus the plot. Make the distinction for me.

WIDEN: When somebody says, "Tell me about your movie," a lot of people will sit there and give them the plot. Well, he does this, he does that, he goes through that door, he comes in this door, out that door, gets in his car, meets this person. And that's not really what the movie's about. That's what *happens* in the movie. What the movie is *about* is the emotional focus—why the movie's being made, what's at stake to the people involved.

FROUG: By that you mean the writer's emotional focus.

WIDEN: Exactly. And the focus of the people in it, too. For instance, one way to answer the question, "What's *Backdraft* about?" is to go on a lengthy discussion about an arson investigation and the relationship of two brothers and all that sort of thing. But if I really want to talk about what *Backdraft* is about, it's about people's loyalty to each other, to their institutions, how that gets all messed up and how in the midst of that—in the middle of that mix—against the background of an arson investigation, two brothers try to put their relationship back together again. That's really what the movie's about.

FROUG: I think that's a most interesting comment. Jeff Boam says that *Indiana Jones and the Last Crusade* is about Indy finding his own identity.

WIDEN: Exactly. That's exactly the kind of thing I'm talking about. And that should all be very clear right up front.

FROUG: Yeah. It's like Butch and Sundance. In the first scene, Bill Goldman says he sets the theme, which is, "Times are changing, buddy; you've got to change your ways, or you're doomed." And, of course, Butch won't. To avoid changing, he says, "Let's go to Bolivia." So "Let's go to Bolivia" is the spine of the movie. The theme of the movie is times change and you have to change with them or die. When you are about to launch a project, do you start with trying to figure out what it's about before you think about plots, or do you start with a character and see where the character takes you?

WIDEN: It depends. Sometimes I'm so interested in an environment and a story that I start with that, and then, along the way, try to find what the focus is. Occasionally you don't stumble across that focus until you've done a draft. You just simply have a plot structure, and only by writing it do you suddenly realize what it's really about. And you go back and you change it. Sometimes I know exactly what it's about before I begin, but, I think, sometimes you never find it. I've actually written scripts where I never found it, and the script was a failure. It had a very nice plot and everything clicked perfectly, but that focus never emerged, or hasn't emerged to this day. And the script was shelved, because it was hollow.

FROUG: I have a couple of those. I sold two screenplays that are shelved because I never figured out what they were about. I knew the plots, like you say, but I never knew what the themes of the stories were. Is teaching something that you think you might want to continue?

WIDEN: I enjoy it a lot. I was actually asked because they had an overflow and needed a guy.

FROUG: Do you find that the students are much different than you were when you were in school?

WIDEN: I don't know. I think I was particularly naive, even compared to my contemporaries at the time. They seem much hipper to me now than when I was there. But, I think, I was particularly unhip [*Laughing*] compared to my fellow students while I was there.

FROUG: You're still in your twenties, though, aren't you?

WIDEN: I'm thirty-one now.

FROUG: An old man. A student told me that their agent was going to set up a meeting for them with a network (this was a good ten years ago). The agent said, "By the way, how old are you?" And the student said, "Twenty-seven." The agent said, "Make it twenty-two." Was that you?

WIDEN: No, it wasn't my story. I never encounter that. I hear a lot of those stories, but I don't know anybody personally who can say that happened to them. I suspect that that may be more true in television. The whole ageism and discrimination aspect of movies, I hear a lot about it, but I've honestly never seen it.

FROUG: Well, you're young, that may be why.

WIDEN: Maybe that's part of it. In ten years, I'll be in a

protected class. [*Laughter*] But I think part of it may be more subtle. I think that maybe there's a cronyism. Guys you went to film school with start running the studios, so they're naturally hanging out with the people they went to film school with. Maybe as you get older, you get out of the loop. I don't know if it's anything direct, like "I don't want to work with you because you're over a certain age." I don't know how much that really exists.

FROUG: Well, there was the time, and this is not a rumor, when a network vice president (who shall be nameless for legal purposes) announced to his staff, "I don't want anybody over forty working at my network." According to the grapevine, he was a CBS executive in charge of programs. There was a time in Hollywood, a few years back, when those distinctions were made very strongly. The story of the agent is probably apocryphal, but some student did tell me the "Tell 'em you're twenty-two" story. But now I'm hearing more and more that that's disappearing. Let me ask you this: if you have a piece of advice for the young writers coming out of film school, what would be your best advice to them?

WIDEN: It's sort of dumb, but I think you've got to keep writing. Every day. Just do it. I know one guy who wrote twelve scripts before he had a movie produced. He simply went out there and wrote one script after another. That's what he had to do. Guys I knew who started in their early twenties as screenwriters, and this is one advantage of film school, wrote their projects in film school. It was okay to fail, because it was for class. You write, it sucks, you throw it away, you do another one. That was considered part of the process, the grind. You create, you chuck; you create, you chuck. What sometimes happens to people, I think, as they get older—not necessarily get older, but come into filmwriting not having gone to film school—is that when they sit down to write their first script, there's suddenly such a pressure on. This has to be the one that makes me a million dollars. This has to be the one that gets me my career. They don't give themselves the opportunity to write something and say, "This sucks," and write another, "This sucks," and write another one.

FROUG: Freedom to fail, right?

WIDEN: Freedom to fail and learn. And that can become paralytic. If a person has the attitude of, "this script has to be the one that makes it," then, suddenly, every idea they have isn't worthy. They begin it, they get about thirty pages into it and say, "This isn't worthy; this isn't the one." They don't follow it through. They don't understand that finishing that script, even if it's not worthy, is a worthy learning process in itself. I have friends who are that way, who have spent four years without finishing a script. They are so paralyzed by a desire that the next one they do has got to be *the* one that they only get halfway through scripts. They decide they're not worthy and they throw them away. They're not learning.

FROUG: And your advice is, once you start, to finish at all costs.

WIDEN: Absolutely.

FROUG: Couldn't agree more. Have you seen *Highlander II*? Is it finished?

WIDEN: It's finished, and I haven't seen it.

FROUG: Do you want to see it?

WIDEN: Not especially, no.

FROUG: Have you heard anything about it?

WIDEN: No. I know they're having trouble getting distribution in the United States. [*Laughing*]

FROUG: Because of *Highlander I*?

WIDEN: Well, I think it's because of *II*.

FROUG: Greg, what are you working on now?

WIDEN: I'm doing another project for Ron Howard's company. He bought an old script of mine. It has a working title of *OSS*, but it will be called something else when it comes out.

FROUG: That's back to World War II, long before your time.

WIDEN: Well, my uncle was in the OSS, and it's sort of a bit of his experiences.

FROUG: Is this an old-fashioned World War II story or a new-fashioned World War II story?

WIDEN: More new-fashioned. It's a lot about how all that stuff, that espionage stuff, got started for the first time, and there's a dark side to it, a kind of quirky side to it.

FROUG: Is this about Bill Donovan, who started it all for the United States?

WIDEN: Yeah.

FROUG: Did you have some background on Bill Donovan, or just researching?

WIDEN: Researching, and then also just my uncle.

FROUG: When you're starting a script, do you do much research?

WIDEN: Oh yeah; sure. Mainly because I enjoy it, the chance to get out of the writing room.

FROUG: Our friend Richard Walter, UCLA writing professor, encourages his students to write for an audience, and I believe that if the buyers don't read the script, or it never gets to production, there'll never be an audience. The key for me is to first write for myself. Otherwise, you're going to get no satisfaction and no money.

WIDEN: I think you don't have to be polar about it. I think that there's a truism in the middle. I think you have to write to please yourself, but at the same time you can take into account that ultimately your work has to be worth the consideration of others. You don't necessarily have to write for the masses as a possible audience, but I think you do have to write it so that someone else would want to care about this movie besides you. That's reality. That's, I think, what Richard meant. And I buy into that. As far as writing as a job, you should only write if you would write no matter what, even if you were never paid for it. That's the only reason you should write. If you're really doing it for the money, and if you're a person with any kind of talent at all, you should become a doctor or a lawyer or whatever, because you're more likely to make more money faster that way than you ever would in this business. The only reason that people stay in this business is because they really love to write. Otherwise, there would be very little reason to put up with all this baloney. I've been a very lucky person, but the ranks are few and far between. You know, it's a pain in the neck getting there, and it's also a pain in the neck staying there. It's a lot of effort and a lot of pain and a lot of hassle. So I think you've got to really love it to do it.

Daniel Pyne

1983   MATT HOUSTON [TV Series] *(four episodes)*

1984   MATT HOUSTON [TV Series] *(five episodes)*

1986   MIAMI VICE [TV Series] *(four episodes)*
THE EQUALIZER [TV Series] *(one episode)*
HARD COPY [TV Series] *(Shared Created by
plus four episodes)*

1987   DESPERADO [TV Series] *(one episode)*

1988   THE STREET [TV Series] *(Shared Created by
plus two episodes)*

1990   ANTAGONIST [TV Series] *(Written by)*
PACIFIC HEIGHTS *(Written)*
THE HARD WAY *(Shared Screenplay)*
DOC HOLLYWOOD *(Shared Screenplay)*

"White Sands"

— this is a Homeric odyssey,
the story of a small-town
deputy who gets seduced into
a twisted plot of con men
and arms dealers. It's a
modern western, about
a moral man
In an
amoral
world.
And,
ultimately,
it's a love
story about
a man
trying
to get back
home to
his wife.

FADE IN

A DESOLATE SWEEP OF LAND - DAY

greyblue sky bleeds into a dust-mottled horizon, and
disappears in the endless stretch of brown southwest
prairie. We hear the first few rusty bars of the Ry
Cooder/Steve Douglas duet of "Let It Be Me' underscoring
MAIN TITLES as they roll through what follows --

AN EMPTY DIRT ROAD

slashing diagonally across the screen, left to right, like
a surgical scar through the barren land.

A POND OF BRACKISH WATER

lifelessly filling a shallow, oblong dent in the ground.

THE BODY OF A WHITE ADULT MALE

face-down, legs splayed, arms outstretched, one hand
touching the water, as if testing the temperature with the
tips of his fingers. A black briefcase on the ground just
beyond its grasp. Cheap dark suit. White shirt. Black
dress shoes with leather-look soles. A thin shroud of
dust.

CLOSE - THE HAND IN THE POND

beneath it, barely embedded in the silt, there is a .45
magnum.

CLOSE - THE MAN'S HEAD

An **entrance** and exit wound in the tangle of jet-black hair.
Eyes **open**. Lips kissing the ground. What was once blood
is now just a dark splotch in the dirt.

CLOSE - THE OTHER HAND

fingernails neatly pared. A wristwatch with a dimestore
leather band, still ticking. Timex.

THE DIRT ROAD - DAY

a sheriff's department four-wheel drive station wagon tears
across the land-scar, siren silent, lights flashing, clouds
of dust billowing behind it.

"It's about writing. It's about becoming the best writer you can be."

About fifteen years ago, Dan Pyne, a tall, lanky, good-natured red-headed kid with a disarming smile, came into my UCLA office to apply for a spot in my graduate screenwriting seminar. He shyly handed me seven pages of a projected screenplay. "It's all I've got so far," he said, "I'd like to work on it in your class."

Any professional knows you can size up a screenwriter's talent in five or ten minutes by reading pages from a sample screenplay. If the characters leap off the page and define themselves, if they create their own dialog, you've got a talented writer on your hands.

Dan Pyne was clearly, from the git-go, such a writer. I welcomed him into our seminar.

Dan's biggest problem, I soon discovered, was that he did not believe in his work or in my enthusiasm for it.

When we met for this interview, it was the first time we'd seen each other in almost ten years. He is still the same tall, gangly kid with the haystack of red hair and the big, friendly grin. We talked for an hour and a half about the craft and conditions of life in the fast-track world of Hollywood. Still shy and self-effacing, Dan has at last begun to feel comfortable with his talent, yet is certainly not overly impressed with it.

I happily introduce Dan Pyne to you and know that you will find some helpful insights into the process of writing for film and television from an outstanding writer.

FROUG: I thought *Pacific Heights* was a wonderful movie, and *The Hard Way* was another hit. What led you into television?

PYNE: You did.

FROUG: [*Laughter*] Oh, no! How?

PYNE: When I was going back to rewrite my master's thesis for UCLA, which I never got done because I was in the middle of getting divorced and being broke and trying to earn money, I met a guy I'd gone to undergraduate school with at Stanford, Scott Shepherd. He is the exact opposite of me—very glib, very commercial—a good commercial writer. And the two of us kind of sat down and wrote some screenplays, not really together, but at the same time. We also came up with a TV pilot, because I knew that you had made a living in television, and I knew that there was the possibility to write good television. It seemed like screenplays were becoming a dead end for me. I kept writing them, and I wasn't getting anywhere. And that May you told me, "Sooner or later it's going to come together. Your sense of structure, your sense of tone; everything will come together, and you'll write something, and it'll be right. But you don't know when that will be." So I sat down with Scott, and we wrote a pilot for a TV series that never sold, but we managed to option it. Then, based on that, we got some interest in television. We got a job at Spelling on a show called "Matt Houston," where they quickly gobbled us up, hired us.

FROUG: A multiple deal?

PYNE: Yeah. We did one and then we did another one. Then they hired us on staff. And we just kept going. We stayed on staff, and it was more money than I'd ever made before, though it wasn't that much. It was half of a staff regular's salary. I said, "Well, I'll try this for a while. I'll do television for a while and see where I can go with it." I did that for a year. Then I left "Matt Houston" and went to "Miami Vice," where I met Tony Yerkovich and Michael Mann, and all these other very good writers who'd stayed in television and were doing good work. So I stayed there. On one hand, it was very frustrating because I feel like I'm a longer form writer. On the other hand, it taught me a lot of discipline: how to write quickly, how to write to the point, how to write on assignment. It taught me how writing is a business. It was a lesson that is important for me even now, because if I'm hired to do a job like *The Hard Way*, I will do what I'm hired to do or I won't take the job. A lot of producers have had the experience with screenwriters where they hire them to do a job, and the writers do something else. That's fine, you can justify it and say that you're an artist, but, I think, if you're paid up front to do a job, you're a gun for hire. So I did television for a while. I created a series called "Hard Copy" about journalists, and on that I met Richard Levinson and Bill Link.

FROUG: One of television's finest team of writers, ever. Dick Levinson was a good friend of mine. His death was a real loss to television. What did you do with Levinson and Link?

PYNE: I developed the series with them; then they didn't want to executive produce it, so they got me in touch with Bill Sackheim, who they said was the best producer in television, and who they promised would drive me crazy.

FROUG: So that's how you met Billy Sackheim. What a marvelous coincidence. You know, it's fascinating because he was *my* mentor. And now, another generation later, he's your mentor.

PYNE: He'll outlive us all.

FROUG: [*Laughing*] He's marvelous, a great teacher, isn't he?

PYNE: Yeah, he is. He was the one that brought me on to *The Hard Way*. It was a dying project at Universal. And because they had me under contract for television, they sort of had me work on the script under my TV deal, so they got a bargain. I fixed the script. It took about three years to get it made. In that time it went through a couple of directors. Finally Michael Fox committed to it, and they waited a year for him. But, based on my success with *The Hard Way*, I started getting offers. Everybody rediscovered me. I was doing okay in television, but nobody in film knew who I was. They thought I'd just crawled out of some hole and knew how to write. So I met with a bunch of people and I talked about a bunch of assignments and then decided that I'd write an original. I wrote a script called *White Sands*, which is a very complex, dark thriller set in the Southwest. Well-received, but not really—it was too challenging; it was too much. I got complaints from people that it was too hard to read. It took them two hours; they wanted to be able to read it in forty-five minutes by their pool. So, based on that reaction, I decided to write *Pacific Heights*, which was really my attempt to prove that I could write something very lean.

FROUG: It's a solid script.

PYNE: It was a challenge, and I didn't really think it would be a big movie. I thought maybe it would be a little thriller. I gave it to my agent and he thought it was too dark, but he put it on the market and it sold in a day. Morgan Creek bought it, and within a week and a half they'd set John Schlesinger. They started filming less than a year from when I finished it, so it was a very good first experience for an original.

FROUG: Did you get good money for it? What league did you get yourself into?

PYNE: I got into the half-million-dollar league, which was so much more money than I'd ever anticipated making. More importantly, I got to stay on the project and work with John Schlesinger, who's a director I've always admired. I got to do every draft. I got to come to the rehearsals. It was a great experience. I mean, it was so different from the experience of most screenwriters who complain that they're shut out.

FROUG: Most of them are.

PYNE: And I never really have been. It's been great so far.

FROUG: Was Schlesinger easy to work with?

PYNE: He was. He's very much a writer's director in that he wants you there all the time. He would have liked me to be on the set every day to talk about ideas. I couldn't, but he was very open, even to my comments over the phone. It turned out well, I think.

FROUG: It's a very good film.

PYNE: Thanks. The ending changed from what I had in mind. I learned my first commercial marketplace lesson, which was that I'd written *almost* a thriller. When Morgan Creek bought it, they decided they wanted it to be a thriller, through and through. So the ending became much more straightforward. But I still like it. I think it had a lot more depth than some of the critics saw in it. And it's done reasonably well. I think it will hold up over time.

FROUG: And *The Hard Way*'s a big hit, isn't it?

PYNE: Actually, *The Hard Way* is not doing as well as they expected. No one can quite figure out why. It got good reviews, good word-of-mouth, audiences seem to like it, Badham and Cohen think that maybe the buddy-film market dropped out. I don't know. They made some creative decisions after I left the project. They tried to make it a bigger, broader comedy. A stunt comedy. Originally, it was more of a relationship film. A lot like *Sullivan's Travels*—it had that feel to it. John wanted to make the stunts wilder and make the ending bigger.

FROUG: That was a Hitchcock ending.

PYNE: He was thinking of that. He likes to really take the audience on a roller coaster.

FROUG: How was he to work with? Did you find him taking

over, or did you find you were in the collaboration?

PYNE: He was fine to work with. Less of a collaborator than Schlesinger. More of a moviemaker. He had a sense of what he wanted to shoot, and all the elements of a script either fit that vision or they don't and he finds other ones. But I enjoyed working with him. He's a very nice man. Another Bill Sackheim protege. Bill gave him his first big break directing a back-door pilot for a TV show called "The Law." John's movie won just about every award.

FROUG: Yes. It was a superb series. When you got out of UCLA, you got to Aaron Spelling. How did you do that?

PYNE: More or less through a connection that Scott had. Scott's family is an industry family. His father is Richard Shepherd, agent-producer. His grandfather was William Goetz, who ran Universal for a while. And his great grandfather was Louis B. Mayer. However, Scott and I still lived in a little one-room apartment down on the beach, right down below where you lived, Bill, up on the cliff. We lived there for a year and wrote pretty hard before anything happened, so it wasn't as if we waltzed in and said, "Give us a shot." Scott was determined not to have to use his connections, but finally frustration wore us down, and a family friend got us through the door at Spelling, but we stayed in because we could write.

FROUG: I wrote some shows for Aaron Spelling, too. Very formula writing stuff, right?

PYNE: Very much. I spent a lot of time with my head on the desk, frustrated. [*Laughter*] But one of the things that I did learn, and that I try to pass on to writers who want to get in or writers who are frustrated by their inability to get in, was that at any level that you write, the people who are doing the show take it seriously.

FROUG: A very important point.

PYNE: They aren't really writing down to their audience. They're writing right across to them. A lot of good writers will come in to a place like Spelling and say, "Oh, these are light, very commercial, very simple shows." And they'll write down. Inevitably that sort of condescending attitude bleeds through the writing, and they get kicked out. Then they don't understand why they're not getting in other doors, why they're not getting more assignments. It's because they're not taking the job as seriously as the people they're working for. The people they're working for truly think that what they're doing is good, and for millions of people, it is. At Spelling, I worked for a man named Michael Fisher, who was the supervising producer on "Matt Houston." He's a good writer; his father was a screenwriter, Steve Fisher. I came to respect what Michael was doing, which was creating this kind of mainstream, very commercial sort of entertainment that was at that time the standard of the television industry. This is right around the time of "Hill Street," but "Hill Street" was the avant-garde.

FROUG: You're so right about that. It took me a long time to come to understand that those folks are never producing down. They believe in what they're doing.

PYNE: In a way, that's helped me in movies. I'm better able to ascertain at a first meeting whether the people that I'm working with are on the same wavelength or whether I'm on their wavelength. If I'm not, I bail out. I don't go any further. I'm not wasting anybody's time. It's one of the key lessons that I learned at Spelling. No matter what I do I'm always in this learning curve. I still feel like I'm at the very beginning. Kurosawa says (and he's what, eighty-five?), "I'm just beginning to understand what cinema can do." Which means I'm even further back on the learning curve, just barely beginning.

FROUG: Now, I've got to tell you this story. My wife and I are absolutely crazy about "Sunday Morning" with Charles Kuralt, and especially John Leonard, the critic. And the other morning John Leonard comes on and says something like, "I've seen a lot of lawyer shows. They come and go. However," he says, "there's one on tonight that's the best one that's ever been on. It's called 'The Antagonists.'" Then he went on to say the remarkable thing: "Writer and Executive Producer, Daniel Pyne." Whoever heard of such a thing, mentioning the writer? So tell me about that.

PYNE: It was remarkable. I got a call from somebody on the East Coast who'd been watching. They heard the show and they didn't know what the title was. And they heard my name and started running around the house screaming.

FROUG: Of course. We were screaming, too. I said, "God, did I pick a winner." [*Laughter*]

PYNE: It was odd, because the initial reviews on the show had been very lukewarm, and then John Leonard came out and gave this great review and cited me. Then the critic in the *Wall Street Journal* gave us a fantastic review, talked about the writing, and mentioned the writers.

FROUG: Are you doing this weekly now?

PYNE: Yeah.

FROUG: God, how do you do it?

PYNE: When I went to "Miami Vice," I signed a term deal with Universal with options. It was, like, five options. And then, in order to get released from motion pictures exclusivity, I gave them another couple of years. So, I'm still working all that time off.

FROUG: Are you paid living wages?

PYNE: Very much. Maybe this wasn't as true twenty years ago or even ten years ago, but these days it's feast or famine. You're either not making any money or you're making a lot of money. More than a living wage. I think that's the attraction to so many people about screenwriting.

FROUG: The big breakthrough and the sudden million-dollar script and all that?

PYNE: Yeah. I haven't experienced this, but they still say you can make more money in television than in motion pictures.

FROUG: If you read this book, you're going to read the interview with Bill Bryan, a man who went through the mill of writing screenplays on development deals—

screenplay after screenplay—and they all wound up on studio shelves. Yet he's a superb comedy writer, currently writing and producing "Anything But Love" and, before that, "Night Court." He made some convincing arguments that the real money is in television. When he told me the kind of bucks he's making, I just was astonished. Anyway, now you're on the weekly TV grind. It's a chore. It put me in the hospital. I produced thirty-five one-hour episodes one season for a short-lived NBC series called "Sam Benedict." I was working Saturday, Sunday, rewriting scripts, on stage, editing. I mean, everything. You were the only producer in those days. You didn't have a staff.

PYNE: And did you hire people from outside?

FROUG: Yes, it was totally freelance. Directors and writers.

PYNE: We did eight episodes of "The Antagonists." It was a mid-season pick-up series. We had a little bit of lead time. We were able to write scripts. I have two other writers. But I still wind up doing a lot of the rewriting. And I'm doing all the exec producing with Bill Sackheim. He's great.

FROUG: Does he still bang his head against the wall? Does he throw books?

PYNE: Yes, but I think he's calmed down. He still does throw scripts across the room if he doesn't like them. If he doesn't like them or if he really likes them he throws them across the room. I'm working with him on a lot of things.

FROUG: You mean you're developing other things along with "The Antagonists"?

PYNE: Yeah. Bill was one of the producers of *Pacific Heights*. Bill was also the producer on *The Hard Way*. Then I have another project at Pathe-MGM, if they stay together. Bill is one of the producers on that one with George Roy Hill. I've been pretty busy.

FROUG: I don't understand how you can produce a weekly series and be working over there on features? Where do you get the time? How did you get the time for this interview? [*Laughter*] You've got to be at the typewriter right now, no doubt.

PYNE: Fortunately, I wasn't doing any television when I wrote all these screenplays.

FROUG: These were all written on spec, right?

PYNE: *Pacific Heights* and *White Sands* were on spec. *The Hard Way* was a rewrite. The Pathe project was a development deal. It's not the only time I've done that. And now I've written a project for Universal and Brian DePalma that was a development deal.

FROUG: And that's a go project?

PYNE: Seems like it. I have to rewrite that one. The past six months have been a little bit crazy. Between trying to stay on top of the TV show and trying to juggle all these projects . . . there were a couple of times when I thought about bailing out of one of the movies, but I like them all too much.

FROUG: It's nice to have an embarrassment of riches, isn't it?

PYNE: It is. It's weird, too. A victim of my own success. I've stopped taking any more assignments and I'm just going to let all this stuff run its course. If "The Antagonists" gets picked up, and I hope it will . . .

FROUG: How are the ratings, by the way?

PYNE: They've been slowly climbing. Our ratings this week were better than the week before, and that show was better than the premiere, which hardly got any numbers at all.

FROUG: What was the premiere opposite?

PYNE: The premiere was opposite "Roseanne" and some ABC comedies. Now our time slot is opposite "Cheers," so we're never going to get great numbers. We share, I think, a lot of the same audience with "Cheers." Kind of sophisticated, more intelligent mystery-show fans. It's got a sense of humor, it's witty, and I think the people who watch "Cheers" for good writing would be the same people who watch our show.

FROUG: Are you writing most of them or are you farming them out?

PYNE: No, I farmed them all out. Plus, I have two writer-producers who have written one and rewritten a couple more. But I wound up rewriting about three of them on my own.

FROUG: Aren't all the producer credits on television actually writers who've negotiated for producer credit?

PYNE: Mostly, yes. Although there's a new trend that I'm particularly in favor of, where you find a great director and make him a staff producer.

FROUG: So he becomes the ongoing creative force?

PYNE: I have a friend who's a very good director, Aaron Lipstadt. We hired him as our line producer on "The Antagonists."

FROUG: As well as the director?

PYNE: He's directed a couple. It gives you more creative control of the project. It's what Steven Bochco did with Greg Hoblitt. Hoblitt does all his pilots, plus he stays around and produces the shows, helps to get the look of the show correct, helps to get the editing correct. It takes a lot of pressure off the writer-producer, because you're not worried about pulling in ten different directors and figuring out how to make their style work. You just don't have to think about it.

FROUG: You probably have four or five other producer credits, yes? Supervising producer, executive producer, which you share with Billy.

PYNE: Yeah. Bill and I are executive producers, Les Carter and Susan Sisko are the supervising producers, and then Aaron is the producer. We have a coproducer who's the UPM [Unit Production Manager], and an associate producer. Television has really expanded from the days when you and Sackheim were doing everything. Bill talks about that, the days when he was the *only* producer on a project. Even on "The Law," he was the producer, John Badham was the director, and that was it.

FROUG: When I produced "Twilight Zone," there was me, a casting director, and a production manager. Nobody else. No story editor, no staff, nothing. And Rod Serling had cut back on the number of scripts he was willing to write.

PYNE: No wonder you got a virus of the brain.

FROUG: Let me ask you a craft question. What do you think makes a screenplay great?

PYNE: What makes a screenplay great? A screenplay great or a screenplay that's filmed great? I think there's a difference.

FROUG: I'm talking about the screenplay.

PYNE: I think structure, obviously. Having a compelling story, well told in an interesting way, not by any formula. I completely eschew the formula of first, second and third act. I've run into too many writers who get lost in that old formula. They know where the first act ends, and they know where the second act ends, but their entire script is treading water because they're just writing from point to point

FROUG: They have no spine in the script?

PYNE: Right. I think a good script has a good spine. I also think that personality makes a great script. In terms of the characters and in terms of the writer. I think that you'll find that the better screenwriters and the great screenwriters put themselves into the script. When you read their screenplays, when you read a Bob Towne screenplay or a Joe Eszterhas screenplay, you're reading a piece of literature. You're reading the book of their movie. Of course, it's never going to be that way again. A director's going to remake it. But when you read the original script, you're reading something that's coming right out of their heart. I think that, as much as anything, is what differentiates a good, crafty screenplay from a great screenplay.

FROUG: You don't set any kind of pre-structure that you follow?

PYNE: I do a step outline, generally, a real broad one. I usually try to find about twenty-five to thirty-five kind of rough plot points. Then, as I start writing, I'll take it in sections and break down each section as I'm writing it. I'll try to find the flow of sequences. I was talking to somebody yesterday, a UCLA student, about how screenplays seem to break down into set pieces. If you'll look at *North By Northwest*, there's the end set piece, the piece at Mt. Rushmore. There's the UN sequence. There's the train sequence. The crop duster. The whole opening flows together from the opening phone page to the discovery that there's no one living at the house. I try to break down a script into those sections and find a rhythm in each one. The script that I'm doing for Brian DePalma is a remake of *The Seven Samurai*, which is one of my favorite films.

FROUG: What about *The Magnificent Seven*, which is Walter Newman's remake of *The Seven Samurai*?

PYNE: We're trying to make ours completely modern. Both the original *Seven Samurai* and *The Magnificent Seven* are period pieces. They're locked in history. We're updating the tale and setting it in Colombia, where Marxist guerrillas are in reality forcing villages to grow cocaine. And terrorizing them. Anyway, in analyzing Kurosawa's screenplay, I found that he broke things down into little tiny sections. There are introductions of characters, there's the set piece of protecting the town, and so on. So when I'm writing, I'll generally try to do that. I suppose I should also point out that I never write the same way twice.

FROUG: Is that consciously?

PYNE: Maybe. Just so that I'm always fresh.

FROUG: So you don't bore yourself to death?

PYNE: Right. So I try to come at ideas differently every time. But, generally, I start by finding the twenty-five or thirty beats of the story. Then I group those into sections. That way I can also manage my time better. I know I'm only writing to a certain point, and then I can step back and think about the next section. I don't have to be constantly worried about the entire script. Another thing that I've found that I do a lot is write the first fifteen or so pages in one sitting and then hold it for a year. I'll get an idea. I'll get a beginning. But I won't have it all worked out. Rather than sitting down and hammering it out, I'll write the first fifteen pages, which helps me figure out who the characters are. Then I'll just let it percolate for a while while I'm trying to figure out the best way to tell the story of these characters. Because ideas are all inherently different, I strive to find a technique that fits the idea rather than trying to find ideas that go with my technique. The Pathe project, *Winning Ugly*, is a simple story about an American coach who goes to Italy to turn around a losing football team. It had a kind of a built-in beginning and ending, but I had to figure out the middle. So it became a structural dilemma. I didn't want to do a *Rocky* story. I wanted to sort of subvert that form. I wrote *White Sands* without knowing where it was going. I had a character and I wrote the beginning. And then I just followed him through. It was a mystery. I actually used a technique that you had taught me about mystery stories, which was to surprise yourself and not necessarily know where you're going. You said that if you know you're writing to a certain ending, a lot of times you can get yourself in logic trouble. You can write yourself into a box. And you probably aren't exploring all the possibilities of the mystery. The characters aren't driving the story. I do like to let characters take over. That's another thing that I generally do, I guess—find the characters and let them run with the story, rather than forcing them to do things. They're revealed through action that way, which is the best way. The story begins to be driven by them, rather than by me. By what their needs are, by what their desires are. As I've said, I don't go by act one, two, and three. Sometimes I wonder if that's even relevant. Maybe only for studio story editors who are reading the scripts and breaking them down. Maybe that's who's taking all these screenwriting courses. Story editors or producers who want to write one. I met up with a guy yesterday, a very nice guy from Disney. He wants me to read something . . . if he writes it. For them, it's all about writing that one script and then cashing in on it. Whereas, I think, for the real writers it's about a career.

FROUG: Good point. The emphasis at UCLA is on getting the show script, and I'm not sure that necessarily builds a career.

PYNE: That was another thing that you worked on with me when I was there, and it was very helpful. I want you to put this in: you were instrumental in keeping me writing because, up to the point when I went to UCLA, I'd written a lot of fiction unsuccessfully and I'd studied in a creative-writing program as an undergraduate at Stanford, but I'd never been told to stay with it, that I would make it. You were the first person who said that.

FROUG: It was so obvious from reading your first script.

PYNE: Based on seven pages that I wrote for your class. And this was after I'd taken another class and gotten a B, which was crushing. The other thing that you kind of drummed into me was this notion that I tell everyone, that your best revenge is being a good writer. They can never take that away from you. Steven Bochco likes to say, when he's really hassled and they're beating on him to compromise one of his scripts and he won't do it, he says, "What are they gonna do? Take me out on the back lot and shoot me? What are they gonna do? They can't take my typewriter; it's mine. They can kick me off the lot, but I'll just write another one." That's kind of the way I began to approach writing, rather than worrying about getting a single script that was going to make or break me. It's about writing. It's about becoming the best writer that you can be. I think you also told me, or at least I learned in taking classes from you and working with you, the notion that you learn to write by writing. Keep writing. For writing as a career, writing is a thing that you perfect and you get good at and you take with you wherever you go. Do you remember Ann Hamilton?

FROUG: Sure, I remember her. A skinny, blond girl, right?

She's adorable.

PYNE: She struggled at UCLA. I met her toward the end of the program. I really liked her writing, but it was all over the place. It hadn't come together. It was the same problem I was having, but her own way. We became friends, and we would trade scripts back and forth. When I started working, she got really impatient and frustrated, because she didn't think she was ever going to make it. At the same time, what I was learning at "Matt Houston" was that the industry uses you in such a way that if you come in at a certain level, the temptation is to stay at that level. The money's great, your ego gets stroked. But I told Ann to aspire to the highest level she could reach and to continue to try to write well, because she might get stuck at whatever level she came in at. So it had better be as high as she wanted it to be. I kept telling that to Ann, and it finally worked out for her. She struggled and struggled, and she did a "Matt Houston" for us that didn't work out. Then she worked for me on "Hard Copy" and wrote a great script, a wonderful script. That got her a little bit more work and a good agent, and then she worked with me again on a show called "The Street" that I did with John Mankiewicz. Low budget, non-prime time, late-night series based in New Jersey. We'd shoot a show at night. Our total budget per show was fifty thousand dollars. We shot it hand-held, beta-cam. It was the precursor of the reality show "Cops." Only we were writing fiction; we were writing these little, fake-documentary, half-hour vignettes.

FROUG: Is this your concept?

PYNE: John and mine, yeah. We did about forty of those episodes. Ann wrote several of them, and, based on that, she got into "thirtysomething." They just grabbed her and yanked her in, and she's been writing great scripts ever since. It was that concept of continually trying to write better, rather than trying to learn how to just squeeze in and write a "Fantasy Island" or write a "Hunter" or something. She kept just trying to push herself and came in at a much higher level than she might have if she just stayed with this frustration about getting a job.

FROUG: What is the most difficult problem you've ever faced in a script, or, in general, what do you think is the most difficult problem for writers and how do they get over it?

PYNE: I know a difficult problem for many writers, if they write television and they write on a successful series, is coming off the series and writing anything else. Because television writing, I think, is both a blessing and a curse. You make a lot of money and you write a lot of material and you have a lot of power, but it's not like writing a screenplay. It's not the same feeling.

FROUG: Not at all. It's a formula. There's no freedom in it. You can make a good living, as you say, but you're locked into a formula.

PYNE: Right. Coming out of that formula and writing screenplays, I think, is extremely difficult for a lot of writers. It's something to definitely be aware of, I think, especially for a young writer going into television. To be aware that they'll try to use you, abuse you, and throw you away. But, let's see, the hardest thing for me is finding the simple core of the story, what it's really about. Sometimes I don't find it until I'm working with the director and we're going through and polishing, and the director figures it out. I think as a writer you have an idea, and then you complicate it. You layer it and layer it, and you make a screenplay out of it. It's a wonderful piece, but you're unconscious now of what the core was, what you were really inspired to write about. But when you go to make the movie, you've got to be able to explain to everybody on the movie, from the director on down, what that core idea was so that they can see where you started. You have to strip it all back away. That's an intellectual process that sometimes isn't that enjoyable for me, isn't that easy. I tend to write in a murky, complicated way, so finding the simple beat on the scene, so I can do it in five lines instead of five hundred, is always hard.

FROUG: So you write the draft, let's say, and then you come back and re-examine it to get the simplicity.

PYNE: Yeah. And as I'm going through I'm always trying to remind myself of what it's about. I do use certain pithy epigrams, like Paddy Chayefsky's "Who's your hero, what does he want, what stands in his way." Things like that sometimes help me to refocus in the middle of scenes so that I don't go do what Bill Sackheim calls tap dancing.

FROUG: Oh, I remember that when I was starting out. He'd say, "You're tap dancing with this scene."

PYNE: He says, "Any good writer can tap dance for sixty pages and make you think that they've written a great script." It reads well and everyone thinks it's great, and then you put it on the screen and it falls flat. You wonder why, and usually it's because they were tap dancing for sixty pages. They're not writing the important scenes; they're not writing what it's about. They're tap dancing around it. They're writing a lot of clever dialogue and cute characters and interesting situations.

FROUG: I remember once, so vividly, I'd rewritten a script for an episode of Alcoa/Goodyear Theater that I was producing (this is thirty years ago). I had a big rewrite to do. The script was short. I put in a scene with a cab driver. I vividly remember giving it to Sackheim, who was the executive producer of the series, and he says, "You're tap dancing!" He worked himself into a rage, threw some books across the room. "You're tap dancing!" He yelled at me, "What's that taxi scene doing in here?" It was a marvelous moment. He was certainly a demanding producer. Yet you couldn't help liking the son-of-a-bitch.

PYNE: I agree. A great producer is demanding. I think that's another thing that writers sometimes underestimate or we get carried away with, the concept of authorship. I know the Writers Guild is always into this. "In the beginning there was the word." But film is ultimately a collaborative medium. The only thing that isn't collaborative is your screenplay. So get it all out in your screenplay. Be the author of the screenplay. Put it on the page. Make it sing. But once it goes to the director, you've got to step back and realize that what you've done is the blueprint for a film. Now you've got to work with one hundred and whatever people to make the movie based on your screenplay. And it's never going to be what was in your mind. It'll be close, maybe, if you're lucky. It might be better; it might be worse. But, it'll always be different. I think the goal is to work with really good people who will help you find that other movie that's just as good, the collaborative movie based on your screenplay.

FROUG: Are you trepidant about finding good people? Working with DePalma?

PYNE: You know, I don't think I'm trepidant about anybody anymore. Anybody. What I admire about DePalma is the voice of his movies. I don't like all of them. Because I admire some of them, I'm able to look at the other ones and say, "Well, maybe I don't like this movie, but this is still his movie. His voice. He made the movie he wanted to make here." I admire that about him. I admire anybody who puts themselves on the line and puts themselves into their movies. What I'm most afraid of are the real commercial filmmakers who are more concerned with audience testing than with what their film's about. Who are more concerned with being universally liked, who are more concerned with finding some formula that will work, that will make them a million dollars, rather than finding a story they really care about. DePalma's very smart; he's very film literate; he admires a lot of the same films that I admire. I kind of prepared myself going in. I know that I'm doing an adaptation of something that I like.

FROUG: This is Kurosawa's *Seven Samurai.*

PYNE: I'm not as attached to it. I also know going in that I'm going to do two drafts and then he's going to make his movie from my drafts. So I'm going to kind of step back and see what he does. I might like it; I might not. But I do admire the independence of his attitude. I admire the personality he puts in his films. In that way he's like Scorsese and he's like Coppola and he's like all the great filmmakers that we have, the ones who really make films.

FROUG: Who commit themselves to it.

PYNE: Yeah, yeah. For better or worse. I mean, he's willing to take his lumps for his bad films or the films that don't do as well. I've been extremely fortunate with the film-makers that I've worked with so far: George Roy Hill, the same way, John Schlesinger . . .

FROUG: You've had some big-time guys.

PYNE: Yeah. Now, DePalma.

FROUG: It doesn't trouble either one of you guys that *The Magnificent Seven* was also a remake? You're remaking a remake of a remake, or what?

PYNE: It troubled me when he came to me with the project. I asked Brian about it. And his answer, I thought, was good. He looks at film differently, and I think it's evidenced in the way he shoots it. He talks about it in the way that a novelist talks about writing, where you take what's come before you and you speak in the language of the novel, or you speak in the language of film. What he wants to do is take this classic story, a tale that existed even before Kurosawa filmed it, and update it for a new generation of people who probably haven't seen *The Magnificent Seven* or *The Seven Samurai*. I mean, *The Magnificent Seven* was 1960 or something. Thirty years ago. There's a whole couple of generations of filmgoers who don't know these films. The other challenge to it is to make it a modern story and find the context for it. A film about modern war and modern warriors, in this world, this context.

FROUG: In other words, what you're doing, I gather, is keeping the theme and structuring a new story off the theme.

PYNE: Yeah, we're even keeping the structure, the basic structure of a film about groups of people, about a village of Indians, a group of mercenaries, a group of bad guys. The mercenaries and the bad guys are much closer to each other than they are to the villagers. But, for a turn of fate, these mercenaries could be bad guys or vice versa. All of those things from the original, I think, still work, particularly in light of Operation Desert Storm and all the discussion of military strategy and how America's redeemed itself now. All of that comes into play, because you can have seven characters representative of seven different agendas. What is the place of the warrior in the modern world? Does he exist? Kurosawa was writing about an age when samurai were being phased out. There wasn't a place for the samurai anymore. They were wandering around. The Walter Newman film was about how the gunfighter was being phased out. There was no work for these gunfighters. Now we're writing about a time where the mercenary's being phased out. Modern warfare isn't about hand-to-hand combat anymore. War is becoming about technology. It's about technology, politics, oil, big global perspective; and this is a battle that's about a village. It's about people. So, in a way, it becomes an old-fashioned war fought in modern times. That's where we're going with it. No doubt we'll get beaten up. I'm sure Brian will probably take the heat for taking a classic and destroying it.

FROUG: It'll be a new story when you get to it, right?

PYNE: Yeah, it is. And instead of going back to Walter's screenplay, we've, like Walter, gone back to the source. We've taken Kurosawa's screenplay, the original screenplay, and that's what we're working from.

FROUG: It doesn't sound like an easy job.

PYNE: It was a much harder project than I ever anticipated it would be. The economy with which Kurosawa tells his tale is remarkable. To try to duplicate that without just copying the images is very challenging. Yet, it's a fun project.

FROUG: How long do you think it will take you to do this?

PYNE: It took me four months to do the first draft.

FROUG: Is it going to involve a major polish?

PYNE: No. We've already been through it. My first drafts are like a lot of people's third or fourth drafts because I've been through them so many times.

FROUG: Before you turn them in?

PYNE: Yeah. By the time I've written it, I've really thought it through. I don't dash through to the end. It takes me three months to write one, and that's writing hard.

FROUG: This is a very good point for the student reader of this book. Work it through yourself, until what you present is the best possible script you can present.

PYNE: That goes back to what I was saying about putting your personality into it. Obviously you want compelling characters, you want a great struggle of some kind, you want tension, you want conflict. You want all these things. But more than anything, you want to put yourself into it. You want to write it from your heart, not your head.

FROUG: Lew Hunter tells me you have done a teaching stint at UCLA. How did that go?

PYNE: I had the opportunity to teach at UCLA this last winter quarter, and it was ten years to the day from when I had taken my first class from you, Bill. In the same classroom at the same time, I think. It was a Wednesday night class, seven to ten. It was a fascinating—it was kind of a journey back for me. In some respects, I didn't feel like I knew enough to teach. I sat in front of this class and thought, "What am I doing here?" Because you always had the notes, you had this whole thing about teaching, and you'd been writing for a long time. What struck me was the students that I have are so much better at structuring and the elements of storytelling than the students you had. But not at character and dialogue and scene construction. I don't know why that is.

FROUG: Well, maybe it's because being young, being immature, they're not yet able or ready to put themselves into the script. They're not able to get into that depth you get only when you explore yourself and what your feelings are.

PYNE: They seem like older students than we were. We were fighting with you because we all wanted to tell a non-linear, non-Western story. We all wanted to tell a story about a passive main character. [*Laughter*] We couldn't, but that was the goal, to tell this non-linear, wild experimental piece. And we were so frustrated by the structure. I remember going over to people's houses and trying to sort out what you were saying and what you were trying to teach us. My students seem much more capable of structuring the story, but it's disappointing that their struggle is to create compelling characters.

FROUG: Are they going for stories with depth or are they looking for the quick sale?

PYNE: They're looking for commercial scripts. I think the fact that people are selling screenplays for over a million dollars has changed the way a lot of writers come into the business. When I went in, I was going in just to make a living. I couldn't make a living writing fiction, so I tried this. Now, I think, people are going in because they want that quick kill, the quick catapulting into the mainstream of the industry, where suddenly you have ten development deals and you're offered a director's job. Like the guy who did *Radio Flyer*. He wrote the script, it sold for a million dollars, he was set up as the director, and ten days into shooting they fired him and they replaced him with Dick Donner. What happens to him? I don't know. I guess he's doing okay. He's got his million dollars.

FROUG: Do you find in these new students' eagerness to get commercial that they are shallower, that they have less depth?

PYNE: I find that they don't explore the depth. I don't know that the stories are inherently shallower. I find that many times the problem with the story will be that they have a biography for their main character, but they don't really *know* their main character. I'm not sure how much they care about their main character. I think when my generation writes, we're living that main character. Maybe it's because we were more idealistic, or because we came out of the latter half of the sixties. We're more idealistic, and we want to write deeper, we want to really get in there and figure out what the meaning of something is, or what the possibilities are. The gratifying thing for me so far in my career is that I haven't had to sell out. I haven't.

FROUG: You've been able to deal with Hollywood and still be true to yourself?

PYNE: I feel like that. I feel like, in a weird way, they've had to embrace me more or less on my terms. They aren't hard terms, because I'm flexible. I like working with people, but I haven't had to sell out and prostitute my art for the all-mighty dollar. And, in a way, as I travel further along in my career, I get more leeway. And that's gratifying. You run into people who might otherwise not care about what a film is about, and you tell them that's what *you* care about, and suddenly they care about it.

FROUG: Let's talk about this cautionary note. You were talking about young writers, that they often turn in a script looking for the quick buck, the commercial project, and then they're dumped and in comes a pro to save them. Tell me what the problem is here with these young writers who are writing this commercial stuff. I mean, are they looking for the fast buck?

PYNE: I think the problem is that they are not concentrating on being good writers. It's the problem of trying to find the quick commercial kill. The idea that will sell fast. You don't really care about how it's executed. You don't really care what it's about. It's a high-concept idea. You could sell it in a sentence, except that they won't buy it in a sentence. They want to see it packaged in a screenplay. They'll turn around and they'll go to a good writer; and they'll have him rewrite it. Ultimately, with a lot of those scripts, the idea's good, and it's a point of agreement for a studio, a director, and everybody, but you've got to get a good writer in there to create a good story. Because they're not going to make that film unless it works. A lot of films die on the shelf. A lot of big-selling films die on the shelf. And a lot of big-selling films from first-time writers get completely rewritten so they're completely unrecognizable.

FROUG: And the first-time writer doesn't recognize why it's happened to him?

PYNE: I wonder. I don't know that many, but I wonder if they recognize it. I also worry about what happens to them. You go to the effort and sell your first script, and then somebody trashes it and rewrites it—what do you really have left? You don't have a film that you can learn from. You didn't get the experience of working with anyone. You got thrown off the project. Everyone in town knows who rewrites these scripts. And those are the people who keep working, and you don't really benefit from having sold one. You just get a credit on a poster. That's all.

*This summer, my wife and I went to a local movie house where a new film called **Doc Hollywood**, the number-two hit of the summer, was playing. It was an absolute delight. I was surprised to read on the poster outside the theatre that Dan Pyne was one of the credited screenwriters, so I phoned him next day and asked him why he had not mentioned the film in our interview. I got the following response:*

PYNE: I was hired to rewrite *Doc Hollywood* because Michael Fox liked my work on *The Hard Way*. It was a dream re-write. It was a dry, badly structured doctor comedy, and I pushed it more toward the romantic side, with a touch of *Local Hero*. Michael committed to that draft, and I did another immediate polish. What wound up thirteen months later on the screen was as much mine as anyone's.

FROUG: What struck me is the many off-the-wall moments in an otherwise fairly routine story.

PYNE: What I'm most proud of is the way I took a pretty simple, familiar idea, and twisted it. It's probably the sweetest film I'll ever write. Left to my own devices, I travel to much darker, weirder worlds. But my mom and dad sure liked it.

Jeffrey Boam

INDIANA JONES AND THE LAST CRUSADE

FADE IN:

EXT. DESERT OF THE AMERICAN SOUTHWEST - DAY

A MOUNTAIN PEAK dominates the landscape.

TITLES BEGIN.

Riders on horseback cross the desert. From this distance
they appear to be a Company of Army Cavalry Soldiers.

CLOSER ANGLES ON THE RIDERS

reveal only details of saddles, hooves and uniforms.
The riders are silhouetted against the rising sun as
they ride into an ancient CLIFF PUEBLO.

THE OFFICER IN COMMAND raises his hand halting his troops.

                    OFFICER
          Dis-mount!

THE RIDERS climb down from their mounts . . . and only
now do we realize that this is a TROOP OF BOY SCOUTS,
all of them about thirteen years of age. The "Commanding
Officer" is only their SCOUTMASTER, Mr. Havelock.

One of the Scouts, a pudgy kid named HERMAN, steps away
from his horse, bends over and pukes. The other Scouts
rag on him.

                    FIRST SCOUT
          Herman's horsesick!

                    SECOND SCOUT
          Yeah, and he wet his saddle, too!

A BLOND SCOUT, however, befriends Herman. He has a
thatch of straw-colored hair and the no-nonsense expression
common to kids whose curiosity and appetite for knowledge
exceeds what they teach in school. Additionally, he
has adorned his uniform with an authentic HOPI INDIAN
WOVEN BELT.

                    SCOUTMASTER
          Don't anybody wander off. Some
          of the passageways in here
          run on for miles.

As the Scouts fall into step behind their leader WE
HEAR the following MUMBLED COMMENTS:

          "This better be good."

          "The circus arrives today.
          We could be watching them
          pitch the tents."

"There're hundreds and hundreds of jobs writing in Hollywood."

Every teacher has a student who stands out in his mind for a particular attribute. For me, Jeff Boam was the student who, more than any other, had the three qualities—along with talent, of course—a beginning screenwriter needs for success: Patience, Persistence, and Passion. Jeff was by no means the most talented screenwriting student who ever turned up in my classroom. But Jeff had the three "P"s plus talent in full measure.

When he applied for acceptance into my graduate screenwriting seminar, he presented me with two screenplays he had already written. One was about the Pilgrims and the Pequot Indians. It was, in a word, boring. The second was even less interesting. When I told Jeff how I felt about them, he was unfazed. "Well," he said, "I'll just have to write better." There was no arrogance in Jeffrey Boam, but there was absolute dedication and single-minded determination. As our school terms together continued, he got better and better, but he was still struggling.

One summer he asked me if I would read a treatment he'd written on the notorious bank robber of the thirties, John Dillinger. I was astonished by the research he'd done and the thoroughness of his understanding of this legendary character. Though his story was not well told, the material he gave me was very exciting.

Then he said, "Let's write the script together, if you're not working this summer." I had the summer off and we went to work on a daily schedule. I would write the scenes, based on his treatment, and he would come over to my place in the afternoon, read what I'd written, and make suggestions. We went like a cyclone. We worked superbly together. In three weeks we had a screenplay called *Johnnie*, the name and spelling Dillinger preferred to use for himself. The day we finished the screenplay, *The Hollywood Reporter* had a front-page story stating John Milius was about to direct his own screenplay for a film called *Dillinger.* Our hearts went down to our ankles. All was lost.

But all was not lost. NBC promptly optioned our screenplay and a producer named Ed Lewis, a man with considerable feature-film credits, met with me to tell me he was all set to go into production. We talked casting and I left our lunch on a Hollywood high. Which is one of the many false alarms that come your way when you work in the dizzy world of Hollywood film and/or television. Everybody, it seems, has a picture about to go, and they assure you it will take only one phone call and you're in business.

The only phone call I got was from the producer, weeks later, telling me NBC had a change of heart. New executives had come in. The project was dead.

This was by no means a new experience for me, but it had a major impact on Jeffrey. Boam took off on his typewriter like a rocket. Suddenly he was writing super scripts and, so it seemed to me, suddenly he was an "overnight" star. When I asked him how this happened, he said, "You jump-started me."

I had not seen Jeff since he was my student, many years ago. It was a great thrill to get together with him for this interview. We welcomed each other as the old friends we are and always will be. The following is a heavily edited transcript of our day-long discussion about the perils, the processes, and the experiences of being a Hollywood screen-writer. We talked almost all day, focusing on the profession that has lifted Jeffrey Boam to great heights. This is a long interview, but there's plenty of information here, information and wisdom in equal proportion.

Perhaps some of you may think I am envious of my former student, Jeffrey Boam. You can bet your boots on it.

FROUG: You're in an unusual position, my friend. In the last year, you've written two of the top box-office grossers of 1989, both supersmash hits, and now you're a star writer. You've even been written up in *People* magazine. That's rare for a screenwriter.

BOAM: It was remarkable. In fact, I think they told me that.

FROUG: What's your new deal at Warners?

BOAM: My deal with Warners is an exclusive deal. Since those movies came out, I said that I wanted it to be not an *ex*clusive deal, but an *in*clusive deal in that I wanted it to include anything I wanted to do. In other words, instead of just a writing deal, I want to be able to produce, write features, write television, direct if I have the opportunity, do cable (particularly HBO, which Warners owns). Anything that Warners is involved in I can be involved in. I can cut a record if I can talk them into it. I'm allowed to do anything, but it has to be under the Warner umbrella.

FROUG: And how long a deal is it?

BOAM: That deal was for three years. I've got about two years left on it.

FROUG: Do you get a percentage of the gross with your pictures?

BOAM: No. I get net points.

FROUG: Which is nothing.

BOAM: Which Eddie Murphy calls "monkey points." [*Laughter*] It's nothing. *Lethal Weapon*'s still in the red, as far as my deal is concerned. I'll never receive any money on it.

FROUG: Even though it's grossed probably eighty to a hundred million dollars?

BOAM: It did a hundred and fifty million domestically.

FROUG: A hundred and fifty million but still in the red?

BOAM: According to their bookkeeping. But every profit participant gets a different statement, a statement that reflects their definition of profits. I'm sure Mel Gibson's statement shows that there are profits, and he's getting a lot of money.

FROUG: My experience in the business was that nobody ever got any money off those net-profit deals. Isn't it still pretty standard today that the screenwriter gets five net points?

BOAM: I think so, on an original. I've been coming in on projects with other writers, so I get less, because there are points promised to the original writer.

FROUG: But you have something unique. Of all the writers I've known and all the films I've been seeing, you have the rare thing of often getting "Written by Jeffrey Boam" and there often is no other writer credit.

BOAM: I've shared screenplay credit on several of them, actually.

FROUG: Well, according to the Writers Guild, I think I have you down for most of them being sole screenplays.

BOAM: I have sole screenplay credit on *Indy III*, *Lethal Weapon II*, *Funny Farm*, and *The Dead Zone*.

FROUG: I was told you did a major salvage job on *The Lost Boys*.

BOAM: It was a pretty traditional rewrite. I didn't reinvent the concept, but I did rework the story, rework the characters, add a lot of things to it.

FROUG: Did you bring the humor to it?

BOAM: The script had some humor, but it was not my brand of humor. I brought my brand of humor.

FROUG: Your brand of humor was like that at the end, when the grandpa says, "I'm sick and tired of all those vampires around here." Right?

BOAM: Yeah, exactly.

FROUG: As he opens the fridge for a beer. That's pure Jeffrey Boam.

BOAM: I've rarely written a script where the director kept my last line. Endings are always being screwed around with. But when Joel Schumacher read *The Lost Boys* script, he said that was his favorite line, the last line.

FROUG: When you got out of UCLA, you went to work at Paramount, doing something in the shipping department, wasn't it?

BOAM: Film distribution.

FROUG: The thing that was singular about you in school was that you said, "I'm going to be a screenwriter. Nothing's going to stand in my way." When you went to work at Paramount, we talked on the phone a couple of times. Then you said, "I'm going to be a screenwriter, and I'm gonna marry Paula." [*Laughter*]

BOAM: And I did both.

FROUG: How'd you finally break in?

BOAM: Well, you helped me. I was working at Paramount in distribution. You called me up. You said you had a friend, a producer, who was looking for some cheap scripts from film students. He read my scripts and said, "These are good scripts, but they're not what I'm looking for." In fact, what he said was, "Do you have anything like *The Sting?*" [*Laughter*] This was about 1976. He said, "I can't use these scripts. Can I show them to my girlfriend? She's just become an agent and she has no clients." About a week later she called me and said, "I love these scripts. Do you need an agent?" And she became my agent. I became her first client.

FROUG: Having gotten an agent, how long did it take you to get into the business?

BOAM: Then things happened instantly. I was meeting with studio executives and producers. I had a couple of meetings every day for several weeks. Tony Bill at the time was a champion of young writers and read the scripts. He liked them a lot, and wanted to make a deal with me. He said, "Anything you want to write, I will subsidize." And what he was going to do was pay me what I was being paid at my current job. I now was working at Fox in film distribution. It was a clerical job. Booking the films into the theaters, making sure that the shipping room got them there. It was a very dreary job. Anyway, I was making maybe two hundred a week, so Tony Bill said, "I'll pay you two hundred a week to write this script. And when the script's done I've got a free option on it." Wouldn't even own it. He'd just have a free option.

FROUG: Have the right of first refusal.

BOAM: Yes. But before I could embark on that, Ulu Grosbard read one of my scripts, optioned it, and then took a directing job on a movie called *Straight Time*.

FROUG: Which already had a writer, didn't it?

BOAM: Several. Dustin Hoffman was going to direct it. He left and Ulu took over.

FROUG: It's a wonderful film. It still holds up.

BOAM: Ulu said, "Do you want to rewrite this for me?" And I said, "Sure, absolutely." I dropped everything to rewrite *Straight Time*. That was my first job.

FROUG: You didn't quit Fox to do it?

BOAM: I sure did. I've always had faith in myself, and I thought it was about time I had a shot. I assumed, naively, that one job would lead to another and I wouldn't have to worry anymore.

FROUG: Not naively, as it turned out.

BOAM: It turned out not to be naive. It turned out to be right.

FROUG: Were you still courting Paula at the time?

BOAM: No, we were married by then. I was married when I was between jobs. I was on unemployment when I got married, and Paula supported me. She supported me, and she supported my writing for about six to eight months. She was there for me at the lowest point.

FROUG: Her father was a big deal in the film business, wasn't he? He probably said to her, "I don't want you going with that bum out-of-work writer," right?

BOAM: He did. [*Laughter*] And now he likes me better than

his own children! We get along great. He's now a vice president at Paramount in post-production, so we really haven't had an opportunity to work on anything together. His name is Paul Haggar, and he's like a fixture at Paramount. They're even naming a building after him, I hear.

FROUG: I remember one thing vividly about *Straight Time*. I was living in a building called The Penthouse, 101 Ocean Avenue, Santa Monica. One day you came frantically up the elevator and said, "My God, you don't know what they're doing to my movie down there." I said, "What?" You said, "They're shooting *Straight Time* down there on the beach, and Dustin Hoffman and all those guys are changing all my lines. They're making it up as they go along." I remember that so vividly. You were frantic about it. We discussed it for a while.

BOAM: They ad-libbed many of the scenes. Actually they ad-libbed them when they rehearsed. We'd rehearse every scene the night before they shot it. While we were shooting it, we were making up the scenes. And so Dustin would improvise a scene with the actors. A scene that on screen would take two minutes took twenty minutes.

FROUG: In the rehearsal.

BOAM: In the rehearsal and in the improv. And then I would go away and find the scene.

FROUG: You'd distill the scene.

BOAM: And structure it and shape it and distill it to a page and a half.

FROUG: It's remarkable how well the film holds up. The tension is there, and it's a very thin line. It's like, is this guy going to make it back in the real world? That's really the only line.

BOAM: It is. It's the most realistic movie I've ever worked on.

FROUG: It didn't get the attention it deserved.

BOAM: It was dumped by Warner Brothers.

FROUG: I want to ask you about your next film.

BOAM: The next film I wrote, that I got credit for, was *The Dead Zone.*

FROUG: Nineteen eighty-three was *The Dead Zone.* It was based on a novel by Stephen King, screenplay by Jeffrey Boam, starring Christopher Walken. How does it become a David Cronenberg film?

BOAM: [*Laughing*] He directed it.

FROUG: Is it justice that, with a Stephen King novel, a Jeffrey Boam screenplay, and Christopher Walken starring in almost every scene, it should be called a David Cronenberg film?

BOAM: I actually don't have a problem with that.

FROUG: You don't? Why not?

BOAM: Because it's not David Cronenberg's *The Dead Zone.* It's a David Cronenberg film, which to me says a film directed by David Cronenberg. That's how I interpret it. I don't see it as meaning anything more than that. But I guess some people might interpret that as meaning David Cronenberg created the whole thing.

FROUG: But you don't see it that way?

BOAM: I see it more like a brand name than something that indicates possessiveness or creative origins.

FROUG: Do you think we'll ever get to the time where it will be a Jeffrey Boam film? I'm not talking about directing. If you write an original screenplay and it's a big release with big stars, do you think we'll ever reach a time in the industry where it will say "A Jeffrey Boam Film"?

BOAM: Not with me. But maybe with someone else. Neil Simon has that.

FROUG: Neil Simon has that, and the late Paddy Chayefsky; both writers richly deserved it.

BOAM: I think you have to acquire a nearly legendary status. Also you have to be a writer who is known for words, which I'm not known for.

FROUG: They're superb wordsmiths.

BOAM: They're known for their dialogue. I'm more interested in telling the story visually, through action and emotions, through things you create without dialogue.

FROUG: That's what you succeed so vividly with. In *The Lost Boys*, for example, so much of that are looks and attitudes, without dialogue. It's a very good film.

BOAM: Thank you. I like it, too. In fact, for some reason I was thinking about it as I was driving in today. There's a lot of good stuff in that movie.

FROUG: It was fun. It was kind of a Grand Guignol comedy. It was a horror comedy.

BOAM: Exactly. It's an audience pleaser and it did pretty well.

FROUG: In all your films, you is bring a wonderful overlay of, "Have a good time, folks. Though this is fraught with danger and suspense, don't take it too seriously. It's really only a movie." That's the imprint you give to a movie, and I love it.

BOAM: That's exactly my attitude. I want to entertain. I want audiences to come out happy. I don't want to be profound. I think, if I try to be profound, I'll just be pretentious. And to be pretentious, to me, is the worst disgrace of all. I'm quite happy to entertain. I've become addicted to audience reactions. When I write a movie, I hear the audience in my head either cheering or laughing or gasping, or something. And when I go to the theater, if I don't get those exact reactions at points where I intended them or heard them, it's crushing to me. I try to write scenes that are filled with these things, because I can't stand silence now. I want to hear a constant audience response.

FROUG: Nunnally Johnson said that as he was writing he was picturing a guy in the audience—this is an old-fashioned image—the guy is leaning forward in his seat in the theater reaching for his hat. In those days they had a hat rack under each seat. Nunnally said, "You know, I see this guy sitting there reaching for his hat, and I know that son-of-a-bitch is going to get out of the theater if I don't hold him with the script." He said he always wrote thinking about that guy reaching for his hat. So, in effect, you're doing kind of the same thing.

BOAM: I am. Although my image is the guy leaning back in his seat with the popcorn in his lap saying, "Entertain me." I don't feel like this guy's ready to leave, still I've got to show him something that will keep a smile on his face for two hours.

FROUG: That's not easy. What do you think makes a great screenplay?

BOAM: A great idea. I think that a great idea is gold. Without a great idea, it's hard to have a great screenplay. That's why I voted for *Ghost* for Best Screenplay. I was annoyed by a newspaper writer who was criticizing the Academy Awards the following day. He just scoffed at the notion that *Ghost* won the best writing award. "Best *writing*?" He put writing in italics, like *Ghost* is not writing because it's populist writing. To me it's writing. I know this is the type of critic or reviewer who thinks only Paddy Chayefsky is a writer because Paddy Chayefsky is a wordsmith. But *Ghost* had a great idea. And whether or not its author is a brilliant wordsmith is not important. He had a great idea and he executed it brilliantly. And that, to me, is what makes a great script.

FROUG: Certainly the Academy agrees with you, and certainly the audience agrees with you. It was a supersmash hit. Has it had an imprint on Hollywood? Here's a modestly budgeted—in the scheme of things—film which had no super-duper stars, no dazzling effects, no car crashes, no violence, no high-concept gimmick. There's some talk that films like *Ghost* and *Pretty Woman*, and recently a few others, are steering the studios away from films like *Lethal Weapon* or *Indiana Jones*, both of which you wrote, which are big, bombastic movies. Big, super-budget movies. What do you think?

BOAM: I don't think that's true. I think that all executives have been brought up short by the success of these movies. I think they feel that they are flukes. These "little pictures" probably have budgets of twenty-two million dollars. *Home Alone* was budgeted at eighteen million dollars. It seems like a lot of money for a movie about a kid in a house alone. *Ghost* was probably even more. So they're not really small-budget movies.

FROUG: But they are more intimate movies.

BOAM: They're a little more intimate because they're on a smaller scale in terms of their storytelling. But their production values and everything else are on the same scale as any *Lethal Weapon* or *Indiana Jones* movie. These are the kind of movies that you can't predict. Some will flop and some will be hits. You just don't know. So you can't count on those. But, I think generally you can count on sequels.

FROUG: Did *Lethal Weapon II* outperform *Lethal Weapon?*

BOAM: It grossed three times as much as *Lethal Weapon.*

FROUG: Are you going ahead with *Lethal Weapon III?*

BOAM: I'm working on it now.

FROUG: With Dick Donner?

BOAM: With Donner and Mel and Danny and Joel Silver, the whole gang. Everybody's back.

FROUG: You got Donner again? How are you doing with my old buddy Dicker?

BOAM: Dick is a handful. But I get through it. Dick is an intuitive filmmaker who operates out of his guts and his emotions. My job is to figure out how that translates into something I can put on the page.

FROUG: When you leave a meeting with these characters, are you able to sit down and clear your head and say, "I know what I want to do with this," or are you so churned up by all the schmooze?

BOAM: No, I try not to get churned up in meetings. I try to be very open-minded in meetings and not get defensive. If I have a point to make, I try to explain it in a calm and logical way. Only twice did I really lose my temper in a meeting. That's not many times after fourteen years of doing this. I try to keep control of the script as much as I can until the first draft is handed in. But after that, it's pretty much out of my hands and everybody starts messing with it.

FROUG: And they begin to pick at it and tear at it and want to change scenes. Do they rewrite it without consulting you?

BOAM: No. That's never happened. Occasionally, on the set, they come up with a line or something.

FROUG: Do they call you and ask you for a line?

BOAM: Usually they will, but on *Indy* they didn't have to. George is a writer, and, if they needed a line, he could provide it.

FROUG: There's a question I want to ask you before I move over to *Indy Jones*. With this enormous track record you've built up with these superhits, with all these films you've turned out that have been big moneymakers, and with as good a record as any writer in the industry, does all this give you big clout when you go into a meeting?

BOAM: No.

FROUG: No? They don't say, "Guys, we've got Jeffrey Boam here"?

BOAM: That's "NO," with capital letters, underlined, with an exclamation point. I get no more respect now than I did when I first started. Absolutely none. Which is a frustrating thing for me. This is why I actually had that argument with the producer we talked about. I feel that I've earned more respect than I'm getting. And that my ideas shouldn't be dismissed out of hand, which they often are. I'll throw out an idea in a meeting, and the director or the producer or the studio executive will say, "I hate it." They won't explain to me why; they feel like they don't even have to. They're not curious to know how I would actually execute this idea. They stop me and say, "That's terrible. We don't like it. Move on." You know, just like I'm the errand boy. And I feel that I have proven with these movies that I can execute the ideas I have; and the ideas I have are valid, they're good. They should be examined a little more closely and not just rejected. If I have an idea, I probably have a way of executing it and making it work. Many times, a studio executive (you'd be amazed at the low level of studio executives that I sometimes have to deal with) . . .

FROUG: No, I wouldn't be amazed.

BOAM: I get notes on a script from the lowest ranking junior executive's assistant reader, who suggests rewrites for dialogue. And I have to endure this.

FROUG: What do you do with them when you get them?

BOAM: I throw them away. I ignore them. I just pay no attention to them at all. You shouldn't fight it. You should just ignore it. But, it's very hard, because I think, basically, writers know more about how to create a movie than anybody. They see the movie in their head, and they create it. They can go from a complete stop to sixty miles an hour. No one else can do this. Everyone else has to hop on the moving train. Only a writer can go from a stop position. And I have to sit there and hear studio executives and producers and directors tell me why my ideas are flawed, or why they won't work. This is the thing I hate the most, when someone says, "That won't work." How can they say to me it won't work? I'm the one who knows if it will work or not, because I'm the one who has to make it work. But this is the most common phrase you hear as a writer: "That doesn't work." Without any explanation.

FROUG: Meaning, "I don't like it, therefore don't do it."

BOAM: It could mean a million things, but the catchall phrase is, "That doesn't work." Sometimes they say, "That doesn't work for me."

FROUG: Right, yeah. [*Laughter*] The caveat, right?

BOAM: Yes. But it doesn't make much difference. I know that if we film it, people will laugh or they'll cheer, or whatever they're supposed to do. I know they will. But they're telling me they won't. And I don't know how to argue against that. I felt that by achieving some success, I wouldn't have to. In my fantasies they'd say to me, "Do you think that will work?" I say, "You bet it will." And they say, "Go do it." [*Laughter*]

FROUG: That's only in the fantasies. Dick Donner, my life-long friend from our many television shows we did together and our many years of socializing together when we were both single, who now has these hit-movie credentials, do they say to him, "It won't work"?

BOAM: No. They don't treat directors this way. There's just a whole different set of standards for writers and directors. For example, before I get to write a script, like *Lethal III*, I have to explain to them what I'm going to do. And, okay, maybe there's some justification for that. I'm going to go off for three months, and they're going to pay me. They want to know what they're going to get. I can do that to a degree. But I can't do it in the detail they want. I can only get that detail by writing.

FROUG: By working through it.

BOAM: But once a director has a script and the studio says, "Well, we finally got a script out of Boam that we like; you go shoot it," they'll never say to the director, "Now, how are you gonna shoot this scene? Where are you gonna put the camera? What are the actors gonna wear? Are you gonna do this in a two-shot, or, if the camera is going to be moving, are you gonna have a dolly?" He doesn't have to explain his methods of operation or what he's going to do. He gets to go create.

FROUG: But he's actually interpreting what you created.

BOAM: He's interpreting, sure. He's doing his job. But he's doing his job without being probed in advance as to how he's going to do it. With me, they want to know exactly what I'm going to do and how I'm going to do it. And I can't answer those questions any more than a director can who feels he's got to get on the set to make these decisions.

FROUG: Right. He has to see what the location looks like in terms of his staging and camera moves.

BOAM: And I feel I've got to get into the scene, into the script, and then I'll know *where* it's going to go, *how* it's going to go.

FROUG: So, what you're basically saying is that the screenwriter is not much better off than he ever was?

BOAM: He's not better off at all, because screenwriting is kind of a no-win profession. Except that there's money in it.

FROUG: Enormous money.

BOAM: Which is not enormous compared to what the actors and directors are getting.

FROUG: It's just a ridiculous disparity there, isn't it?

BOAM: Absolutely. And I'm sure I can do what he does. I will do it. I won't say I can do it as well, and I guarantee you I'll do it differently. But, I'll do it.

FROUG: Are you going to direct your next one?

BOAM: I'd like to.

FROUG: You think you've got the clout now to say "I want to direct this one"?

BOAM: I think I can. If I can get *Lethal III* going, get that film made. If it comes out and it does well, then I feel like they can't stop me. They can't say no to me.

FROUG: Under your contract, have you a right to say "I want to direct"?

BOAM: Absolutely. But they have a right to say "No, you can't direct." But I also have a right to say, "I don't want to write any of your projects." I can say to them, "I'll rewrite this if I get to direct it." There's a possibility for many different kinds of negotiations.

FROUG: Is that the allure, basically, of directing—that the director has the power, has the control?

BOAM: The director has all the power and all the control, all the prestige, all the glamour, all the money. He has it all. It is the job to have.

FROUG: What do you look for to become deeply involved in a story, for you yourself to become deeply involved?

BOAM: Relationships, basically. Who is the main character

and what is the main relationship? This is what will hook me.

FROUG: Do you feel that your main character has to be likable?

BOAM: I prefer it if he's likable. I think this is just a change that I've undergone, myself, in my thinking. I used to be attracted to anti-heroes.

FROUG: Like *Lethal Weapon*?

BOAM: Like our screenplay about Dillinger.

FROUG: Dillinger, right. And like *Straight Time*.

BOAM: Like *Straight Time*. Now it could be that the times have changed or it could be that I've changed, or I've changed with the times, or the times have changed me. I don't think these characters are too appealing to audiences, and they're no longer appealing to me. I basically want to write movies that have heroes at the center. It may be a hero who's just a dad, or it may be a hero who conquers the Nazis and finds the Holy Grail. But he has to be a hero. I've turned down a lot of projects because the character at the center is not in charge of his own destiny. There are a lot of projects always being developed like that. They're kind of Hitchcock-type movies. The Everyman who gets swept up in something. I don't like stories about people who are swept up in anything. I want stories about people who take charge.

FROUG: What makes a great character, besides being likable?

BOAM: That's a hard one. His human qualities—his frailties and things that make him imperfect—are the things that I enjoy about him.

FROUG: When you're developing *Lethal Weapon III*, the Mel Gibson character is pretty cuckoo, but he is a hero.

BOAM: He's a hero, yeah.

FROUG: Do you feel a problem when you're working with that character, of him drifting off into absolute insanity?

BOAM: No, because I've actually steered him away from that. In the first *Lethal Weapon* . . .

FROUG: In the first one he almost went nuts.

BOAM: He was on the verge of a nervous breakdown and he was suicidal. He threw himself into situations that were life-threatening because he didn't care if he lived or died. That's what made him a good cop, and that was the whole premise. In *II*, we decided to pretty much abandon that dark aspect of the guy's nature and make him just a crazy cop who didn't know fear, who'd do anything to get the job done. But no longer motivated by this dark psychological need to self-destruct.

FROUG: A kind of underbelly of insanity.

BOAM: Yeah. And in *III* I think he's going to be even less that.

FROUG: He's going to be more normal, so to speak.

BOAM: More normal, and maybe more comic bookish. I think the logical evolution of sequels is toward being more comic bookish. Every sequel.

FROUG: James Bond did that.

BOAM: James Bond became a total comic strip. You cannot sustain that kind of seriousness over a series. You have to loosen up and lighten up. I think it's the only way to go. Eventually you run out of steam, and it's over. But everything ends. I think the last *Indiana Jones* movie had a lot more humor in it than the first two.

FROUG: What was it like working with Spielberg and Lucas?

BOAM: I spent most of my time working with George. We sat down in a room together for two solid weeks, about eight hours a day, and worked out an outline for the story. It was a great experience because I was working with a producer who was also a writer. A good writer, who has the mind of a writer. He knows how to structure things. He knows what the requirements are for a movie. He understands the number of characters you need. He understands the number of twists you need. He understands where the act breaks come. He understands what are the good ideas that elicit other ideas down the way, that have reverberations. He doesn't get hung up on minutiae like a lot of people do who really don't—or can't—see the whole picture. They see these little tiny pieces. They focus on the pieces and they don't have any sense of the whole.

FROUG: Directors tend to do that.

BOAM: Not Steven Spielberg, though.

FROUG: Tell me more about working with George Lucas.

BOAM: George lacks any sense of self-doubt. He's completely confident about everything he does. He said, "You and I will sit down and we'll create the story that will be the third *Indiana Jones* movie," and he blocked out the number of days we would need, cleared his schedule, and did not take any phone calls. And he was producing two movies at the time—*Willow* and *Tucker*, both big-budget movies that he was on the line for. His money was in those movies. But he shut all that out for two weeks, and we worked out the story. We worked it out beat for beat. We'd throw ideas back and forth and we'd go to lunch and we'd come back and we'd work till dinner time, and he'd go look at dailies of his movies and probably work until about three in the morning and then we'd start up again around nine or ten the next morning. He's driven, but he's not hyper. He's very laid-back, very calm, a man of few words. But he's constantly creating things. He's never at rest.

FROUG: Well, I had an interesting experience with him at USC. I was teaching a class in which I showed films and interviewed filmmakers, directors, writers, and producers. One day Gary Kurtz, Lucas' producer, called me and said, "George Lucas would like to show a film of his to your class." This was before anybody'd heard much of George Lucas. And Gary said, "Could we bring down a film?" I said, "Sure." He brought down *American Graffiti* and the class just loved it. Afterward Gary and George talked to the class. "We need your help," they said. "We can't get Universal to release our movie. They hate it. And the only thing that will help is if you students will call Universal and tell them you saw this in your USC film class and you think your friends would want to see the movie. Or write letters or do something and help us out." Everybody loved the film, and next week at class some of them told me they did phone. That was when George was finishing his first Hollywood film. It became the biggest hit Universal ever had. In spite of all this, George was a very calm and reasonable guy. That was when he was just out of USC film school himself.

BOAM: I'm sure he was always like that.

FROUG: He worked with you on the step outline. Was Steven Spielberg involved in the story structure at this point?

BOAM: No. Steven's attitude was "bring me a first draft," basically. We had a meeting with him after we did the story outline and went through it with him. Steven can be very preoccupied. Always thinking about something more important. [*Laughter*] No matter what it is, he's thinking about something more pressing. And at that point in his life, he probably had a movie he was editing, or a movie he was shooting, or a movie he was about to shoot. Hearing this story outline was not the most pressing thing in his career. We got through it very quickly and I went off to write the first draft. Actually there was a nice turning point, at least for me, in all this. Steven was going to do *Rain Man*, but still had some uncertainties about it. He felt that he had to make a choice between *Rain Man* and *Indy III*, because this was a commitment that he owed to George, to do the third *Indy* movie.

FROUG: Did you know as you worked this story out that this was to be the final *Indiana Jones* movie?

BOAM: No. The battlefield was littered with writers before I came onto the scene. There were four or five before me. Each writer had their script next to them covered with blood. [*Laughter*]

FROUG: Was it George who said, "I don't like it?"

BOAM: No, actually, Steven was ultimately the one who

turned everything down.

FROUG: So he was throwing out scripts by writer after writer?

BOAM: He knew he had to discharge this obligation sooner or later. Somehow he felt this would be a good time. But he had to choose either *Indy* or *Rain Man.* George called me up and said, "How are you doing with the script?" I said, "Well, I've got it about three-quarters of the way done." He said, "Well, how's it coming?" And I said, "It's real good." He said, "It better be, because Steven wants to read it, and he'll make a decision whether he's going to do *Rain Man* next or do *Indiana Jones.*" So I gave him the screenplay.

FROUG: While you were still writing it? That's rare, isn't it? To read a work in progress?

BOAM: It's rare *and* scary, because I'm always going back and making changes. George called me a couple of days later and said, "Congratulations. You did good. Steven's going to do our movie."

FROUG: Based on how many pages?

BOAM: Based on seventy-five pages. I was thrilled. Your life as a screenwriter is made up of little victories, all leading to the big victory. And this was just another little victory along the way. So then Steven was committed to it. And after that I finished the first draft.

FROUG: Do you remember how many pages your first draft ran?

BOAM: I don't think it was too long. This screenplay never was long. I never had a length problem.

FROUG: Because there was so much action?

BOAM: I really don't know why. I think it was because we plotted it out before I wrote it, which is something I've never done on any other movie—have a completely worked out outline. So it came in at about a hundred twenty-five, twenty-eight pages. Most of my first drafts hardly ever run longer than a hundred and thirty.

FROUG: *Lethal Weapon II* is about one hundred and thirty?

BOAM: The first draft. Ultimately, you never know. After you start rewriting it, and you start putting A and B pages in it, you really lose track.

FROUG: When you do the editing, do you assume you're going to cut about ten pages? The shooting script's going to run about what?

BOAM: They'd like to see it about a hundred and twenty or even less. The director always says, "I'd love to have a script that's about one hundred and fifteen pages." But if you write a hundred and fifteen page script, it always seems rushed and underdeveloped. So I think you have to write long, so the reader gets what you're trying to tell them. Many times I write very lengthy descriptions. I never write long descriptions of static things. I never describe the way a room looks, the way a person's dressed. I like to leave that to the imagination. But I write very detailed descriptions of actions—action pieces.

FROUG: Not to the extent of saying, "He hits him with a right, then a left, and then an uppercut"?

BOAM: Well, fights are a little different. I hate writing fights. I try to editorialize on a fight by saying, "These two professional killers are punishing each other beyond your imagination." And then let you imagine what that is. But if I have to write an action sequence . . . for example, in *Lethal II*, where the house comes crashing down . . .

FROUG: Where he hooks up the truck to the beams holding the house on its foundation and he pulls the house down.

BOAM: Right. I write that in great detail. Especially sounds. I love to write sounds. I feel I've got some of the noisiest scripts ever written. I capitalize all the sounds.

FROUG: Crash, crash?

BOAM: CRASH, CREAK, POP, SMACK. Whatever.

FROUG: Comic-strip stuff.

BOAM: It is comic-strip stuff.

FROUG: William Goldman said movies are comic strips.

BOAM: Well, they are. They're like comic books. And this forces the reader to think, "Snap, crack, and pop." There's no way to avoid evoking those sounds. I try to be very juicy about the descriptions of the way things break and come apart and crash, and especially how people are injured or maimed or killed. I try to be very visceral about that. Very graphic.

FROUG: Blood is spurting out of the arteries?

BOAM: Oh, I love that. And no one likes to read it. No one. The studio executives say, "I hate it. It's so gory. Do we actually have to see the blood squirting on the floor?" George Lucas, for example, has produced all these movies with gory effects, but at the end of *Indy III*, where one character drinks the wrong water, and he has this horrible transformation . . .

FROUG: I remember that.

BOAM: Well, I wrote that in great detail. Every grisly, ghoulish detail of his nails curling up and blackening and his skin flaking and the skull pressing through the flesh. And George said, "All you writers love this stuff, don't you? You just love to write this stuff. It's just—it's just so awful to read."

FROUG: It's there on the screen. George has been doing that for all his career.

BOAM: If you wrote that in a dry style, it would put the reader to sleep.

FROUG: "He's transformed, falls over dead." That puts you to sleep, right?

BOAM: Exactly. You have to, even though it may take a second for it to happen on screen and it may take you half a minute to read the description. You need that. That's the stuff that forces the reader to see the movie that you have in your head. And then, when you have to cut pages out of the script, after they've read it once or twice, then you can cut it back until it reads: "He pulls down the house."

FROUG: I stress to students that they are always writing a script to be read, no matter if they're being paid a million dollars or not. The first person they have to please is the reader, whether it's an agent or many agents, whether it's the director, the producer, the studio, the studio executives, star—it doesn't make any difference. What you put on paper is to be read, not to be shot. Read first, and then shot, hopefully.

BOAM: Absolutely.

FROUG: So you have that in mind, that you're writing for a reader?

BOAM: Oh, I'm always writing for the reader. And I think you have to keep it entertaining. Just like the movie. The movie has to be entertaining; the script has to be entertaining. The thing is, they entertain in two different ways, which is part of the difficulty of being a screenwriter. You have to describe things. You may have to take a page to describe something that happens on the screen in a second. But I hate reading scripts full of camera angles. I never wrote scripts that said "long shot" or "close-up."

FROUG: Nobody that I know of puts in camera angles anymore.

BOAM: People still do.

FROUG: Really?

BOAM: Yeah, but maybe not that diagrammatic, but they still use a lot of the typical things, like CU for close-up. I don't even like abbreviations, and sometimes I hate interior/exterior. If I'm writing a scene where there's a car chase, let's say we've got a police car, and it's part of the chase. Instead of writing "INT. POLICE CAR," I'll write "INSIDE THE POLICE CAR."

FROUG: You won't put a heading.

BOAM: I'll put a heading that'll say "INSIDE THE POLICE CAR."

FROUG: You won't use the official language.

BOAM: No. I want to make it more reader-friendly. I don't want it to be a heading. I want it to be part of the reading experience.

FROUG: So you want to encourage the reader to see the movie you're seeing as you write it?

BOAM: Exactly. I could say, "We cut to INSIDE THE POLICE CAR," as a heading, "where Riggs and Murtaugh are fighting over a hot dog." So it all reads like a sentence. It looks like screenplay, but it reads like a sentence, and there's no interruption. You don't have to constantly stop.

FROUG: Does the production manager go crazy trying to break down the script into camera setups?

BOAM: They don't. It's the people in the typing pool, or data processors, as we call them, who revert back to the formula they understand. I always have to say to them, "Just type it exactly the way it is. Don't try to make it standard screenplay form."

FROUG: Do you think that people who buy these screenplays and read them, as you did, realize the published screenplay is basically what the typing pool put in, in terms of headlines and sometimes even camera angles, that the writer basically is writing in master scenes, but they're rarely published in master scenes?

BOAM: I guess they're published in all different ways. I wasn't aware of that. In fact, my bible was the screenplay for *Tom Jones*. It was a great movie. I saw this movie when I was fourteen or fifteen, and it made the greatest impression on me in the world. It's the movie that ultimately made me want to be in movies. I saw that the script was published and I sent away for it. I must have read it twenty times. It was the most enlightening thing because I realized there was hardly any dialogue or speech that was more than two or three sentences. That was just a revelation for me.

FROUG: My wife and I just saw it on HBO or somewhere in the last few weeks. God, it's still marvelous.

BOAM: *Tom Jones* is a wonderful movie. It's so life-affirming, and that's the way I always felt when it was over, that life was worth living.

FROUG: I'm glad you brought that up, because that is the flavor you get in your movies, of exuberant, adventurous fun. They're full of affirmation and humor. In the darkest hour of your movies, somebody's going to crack some kind of joke and say, "Look, don't get too concerned here. We're having a good time, and you're supposed to have a good time."

BOAM: Exactly. It's that experience that I'm trying to recreate. *Tom Jones* gave me such a great experience that I thought, "That's what I'd like to do. I'd like to give that experience to someone else." I'd like someone to come out of a movie I wrote feeling the way I did coming out of that movie. I don't know if that's ever happened.

FROUG: Why'd they decide to end the *Indy* series? Do you know?

BOAM: I think everybody's just had enough. I think Harrison Ford is sick of it. Steven is, I think. His producing team, I think they're tired of globetrotting and eating weird meals in strange places. They've just had enough of it. But George hasn't, because he's now creating a series . . .

FROUG: A television series?

BOAM: He's creating a television series called "The Young Indiana Jones Chronicles."

FROUG: It takes place before the movies?

BOAM: A bit based on the opening of *Indy III*. It's Indiana Jones as a boy, age twelve to fourteen, and his early adventures.

FROUG: Does it give you concern when you're presented with an offer to carry on a series? "Oh my God, how do I top myself?" Does that worry you?

BOAM: Not until *Lethal III* it didn't.

FROUG: Tell me about that. That worries you?

BOAM: *Lethal III* worries me because I don't think that we're all heading in the same direction. I think we all have different ideas of how this third movie should evolve.

FROUG: Do you have a time limit on how long you can worry about *Lethal III*?

BOAM: They keep changing this. About a month ago, we decided it was time for me to start writing this, that they wanted to shoot the movie in March or February of 1992.

I said to the studio, "That sounds like a long time away, about a year, but I'm going to need every day of that time because it's going to be hard to get it right; it's going to be hard for me to please myself; it's going to be even harder for me to please you; it's going to be harder yet to please Dick Donner, let alone Mel Gibson and Joel Silver. I'll need the whole year." Then, about a month after that, they say, "We want to move it up. We'd like to do it sooner. We'd like to do it, maybe, in December." I said, "Well, that's okay. We can still do it." Then a couple of days ago Dick called me and said, "I've got to shoot this movie no later than September." Because of another commitment he has. We'll just have to do it faster.

FROUG: That puts a lot of pressure on you.

BOAM: It's not over. And then the next day, which was yesterday, Joel Silver called me and said, "I just spoke to Mel. He wants to go in August." August! Gee! That's five months away. And I said, "You know, we can do this. This is possible. It's doable. But we all have to agree on the movie and we can't experiment." Which is what we did last time. I did one script, then I did another script. Then I did a combination of the two scripts.

FROUG: What is the hardest problem you've ever faced in writing a screenplay?

BOAM: Every project brings with it its own nut that's hard to crack. What was the hardest thing I ever had to deal with? Well, actually, there were hard problems on *Funny Farm*, believe it or not. The Chevy Chase movie. It was adapted from a book that had absolutely no structure to it. No spine to it at all. There were a lot of funny incidents, but they weren't adding up to anything. There was just no conflict, no drama, no problem to be worked out. And that was probably the hardest thing to solve.

FROUG: What did you finally come up with to solve it?

BOAM: We worked in that his wife was actually doing the writing while he was merely trying to write without success. We tried to make that the central issue, that this journalist had a dream to be a novelist. He had a romanticized vision of what that is. He goes out to the country and he turns his life upside down to achieve this dream and finds out that he's not capable of achieving it. But his wife, behind his back, has succeeded. That's the most conflict, the most drama, the most throughline we were able to come up with. And it's spread very thin. It's not quite enough to hold the movie together. It was just a very difficult thing to make work successfully.

FROUG: I liked the script better than I liked the movie, frankly.

BOAM: The first version of the script was much raunchier, and it had a lot of more sophomoric humor in it, more Chevy Chase kind of humor.

FROUG: Like the eel? Where he's fishing and he pulls up the eel?

BOAM: Yeah. A lot more physical humor, low humor.

FROUG: I notice you're very good with toilets. A lot of your movies have toilet jokes. Exploding toilets in *Lethal Weapon II* and in *Lost Boys*. How much, if any, censorship do you face? When you're writing, do you think, "Oh, I'll never get this past the rating board"? Or, "Do I write to an R rating or do I write to a PG?" or what?

BOAM: I don't usually write anything that would be too offensive.

FROUG: In your own mind.

BOAM: Yeah, to the point where we'd get an X. Certainly I do a lot of R movies because of the action. Or the language. But even the language I try and tone down a little bit. I find the studios actually are very prissy about certain things.

FROUG: Language?

BOAM: Language and violence. They're a little uptight.

FROUG: That's a new attitude, isn't it?

BOAM: Maybe it's just a personal attitude of some of the executives at Warner Brothers, but they don't like to see a lot of blood, they don't like to hear a lot of foul language.

I think it's just a personal thing.

FROUG: I think it's a healthy trend.

BOAM: I think it is, too. I find that it's easy to write vulgar dialogue, and, because it's easy, I'm suspicious of it. I wonder if it's ultimately debasing and demeaning to movies. But with *Lethal Weapon*, it's hard not to put in a few "fucks."

FROUG: The two cops in *Lethal Weapon* are in a patrol car, they're being chased, and they're saying, "All right, fuck you, man." You know, "Fuck you, man," which seems to be key lingo in most contemporary movies. Are those guys kind of improvising that as they're shooting?

BOAM: Sometimes they do. I know Mel threw in a couple of additional "fucks" that I did not write. But I try to avoid that. If you do a movie like *Goodfellas*, in which every other word is "fuck," "fuck," "fuck," that's the language of the characters. The idea is to overuse it to the point where it becomes meaningless. You don't even notice it. It's just like saying, "uh," or "you know." They say "fuck," and that's what they fill in the gaps with. It's a hard word to know when to use. It's so easy to just sprinkle it in arbitrarily.

FROUG: We were talking about censorship. What about self-censorship when you are writing? Are you afraid, for example, of offending folks if you get into issues like politics? For example, the villains in *Lethal Weapon II* are the South Africans and apartheid. You don't worry that, if you slant this politically, it's going to turn off an audience?

BOAM: No, I don't. I worry about, "Can we get away with this? Are we somehow breaking the law? Is some judge going to come in and confiscate all the film because we've slandered somebody?" That kind of thing does concern me. In fact, on *Lethal III* I had flirted with the idea of one of the villains owning a car dealership. Then I realized that no car maker will allow their name to be used if a villain is running it. So I just abandoned that idea. I guess that's a kind of censorship. I'm not going to waste my time writing that idea only to have it rejected well before it's shot. I never worry about being controversial. The stuff I do isn't usually controversial. But, I think there was something controversial about *The Dead Zone.*

FROUG: Because you had a neo-Fascist running for office?

BOAM: That's right. And the hero tries to assassinate him. I was worried that the movie in some way was an endorsement of these nuts who assassinate politicians. Because, from the point of view of everybody else in the movie, the lead character was one of these crazy characters with a gun. They weren't privy to the information that the audience was.

FROUG: Was *Dead Zone* based on any scientific research or was it Stephen King's imagination?

BOAM: I think just Stephen King's imagination.

FROUG: It was a very interesting concept. I liked the film. Do you recommend film school for young filmwriters?

BOAM: I don't know. It worked out well for me because I met you.

FROUG: Well, thank you.

BOAM: In fact, it's about the only thing . . . no, there's two things I feel I got out of film school. I met you and we worked together. That was worth two years of tuition [*Laughter*] for the one summer we worked together. And I got to see a lot of movies. That was it for me.

FROUG: Say a guy's picking up this book and he's got aspirations to be a filmwriter, and he's got some screenplays he's been writing like you did. He's a guy like you were in your twenties, and he's thinking, "I want to make a career of screenwriting. I want to be Jeffrey Boam. Let's face it, I want to make four million dollars." What would you advise that guy or gal, whichever the case may be?

BOAM: To write and write and write and write. That sounds like advice you once gave me. You have to just write and write, and eventually you'll see if you have some talent. The problem is, there are too many people around who don't have talent. They wonder why they're not succeeding, but they never question their own talent. But writing's still the easiest job in Hollywood to go from a nothing to a success.

FROUG: Because you're creating the property, as they call it here, out of your own head in your own room anytime you want to.

BOAM: Exactly.

FROUG: And all you have to have is blank paper and a pencil.

BOAM: You can come to the studio with a finished product. A product as finished as any professional writer, whereas an actor or director or producer, whoever, really doesn't have that capability. They have to find other ways to prove what they can do. A writer can prove what he can do by doing it.

FROUG: Right. On his own.

BOAM: And the thing to do is just keep writing. Show it to your girlfriend, boyfriend, or your wife, or whomever, and see if they like it. Then show it to your friends and see if they like it. You keep accumulating these little victories along the way. Pretty soon you're showing it to an agent, and your agent's showing it to a producer, and your producer's showing to a director; the director's showing it to an audience, and it's just an escalation of these little victories that you have to go through to get to where you're a successful writer. It's not a fun process. It's like homework. I don't think you can really leapfrog from writing a screenplay to the big premiere with the klieg lights, which I think is the image that every writer has.

FROUG: Are there writing jobs?

BOAM: Oh, there're hundreds and hundreds of jobs writing in Hollywood. There are always open assignments at all studios. In fact, young writers are highly prized because they're easy to work with. They're enthusiastic. They're cheap. A young writer who demonstrates talent will have no trouble getting a job in Hollywood.

FROUG: And to get a job, you have to show scripts, right?

BOAM: Right. Your calling-card script. This is the script that every writer should have. You should have two of these scripts that are quite different. This is what writers should be working on, these scripts that everybody enjoys reading. They shouldn't worry about, "Am I going to sell this script for two million dollars? Am I going to get De Niro to be in this script? Is Spielberg going to direct this script?" I think all of that is just wishful thinking and a waste of energy. Write the script that's going to impress somebody enough to say, "Boy, this guy can write." And then you'll get a job writing.

FROUG: My experience as a teacher is exactly that, Jeff. I've very rarely heard of a writer selling the show script. But the show script, if it's good enough, has gotten them job after job after job, even though that script never gets made. It's not important. It's important to show, as you said, that you can write.

BOAM: That's what I did, and that's why I'm still working. A lot of writers have an idea, a brilliant idea, and they execute it and it gets sold and that's it. You never hear from them again. That's all they had, that one idea, and they got lucky enough to sell it, but they're not truly writers.

FROUG: I've known a lot of those folks. Do you find that there are a lot of young, or new, writers who think they have an idea out there and somebody's going to steal it? Do you find much actual plagiarism going on, or do you think that's mostly a kind of paranoia?

BOAM: I think it's paranoia. I really don't think people steal from each other.

FROUG: What do you hope is your future in film or whatever? What is your goal? You've got all the money in the world . . .

BOAM: Oh, hardly. [*Laughter*] I need to make more, much more money . . .

FROUG: Well, okay. You've reached the peak of your profession as a screenwriter, so what's the next step?

BOAM: I'm realizing that I'm getting tired of pleasing other people. I've wondered why I haven't decided to be a director before now. I've always imagined what it would be like to be a director, but I've always been quite content to write scripts. I can understand why. It was a nice, comfortable way to live, to be left alone and make your own hours. But my life isn't like that anymore. I have a schedule, I have a secretary and a producing partner and a development person, and I feel like I'm no longer living this quiet, contemplative life of a writer. I'm not getting that benefit anymore, and I've gotten to the point where I'm losing my patience with directors and producers. I feel, "Why do I have to please these people? Why do I have to knock myself out to please them? Come back to them with idea after idea after idea. They're all good but they reject them so often. I'm just sick of it." I can do what they do just as well. So, I'm thinking I should do that. I should produce, I should write, I should direct, I should somehow not have to please anybody but myself.

FROUG: So you formed a production entity?

BOAM: It's a partnership with a fellow named Carlton Cuse. He was an assistant to a producer at one point. I met him at a meeting with this producer and we hit it off. He's very smart and we are in sync creatively. He has an ability that I do not have, which is the ability to be involved in the "business" end of the business. He just has a natural grasp for how all these things fit together. Much more sociable than I am, likes to take people to lunch. He can talk to agents on the phone. He likes to do all the things I hate to do, but I know that I've got to do. He's a tremendous asset to me.

FROUG: What is your goal for this production company?

BOAM: Our most immediate goal is to produce a movie. Produce a movie under our own banner that I would write and direct and that Carlton would produce.

FROUG: During lunch, we got into talking about the youth craze of the previous few years, where anybody over twenty was suspect. Do you find that still true?

BOAM: Definitely not. No. As I said, that trend has come to an end.

FROUG: That's great. There was a time when nobody could get a job if they were much over twenty-two.

BOAM: I can't imagine the executives I deal with, who are all about my age, early forties, some in their late thirties, advocating that point of view, because I think it would make them feel like they're getting older, like they have already outlived their usefulness.

FROUG: Good point. But it's the baby-boomers who've come in—the baby-boomers themselves who've all grown older. All of you now are in your late thirties or early forties, and you're all aware, I guess, that the audiences you're appealing to have also gotten older.

BOAM: But I still think the audience who came to see *Easy Rider* back then, which was the movie that kicked off this youth trend, is still the same age. I think the key audience the studio is looking for are the eighteen-to-twenty-something crowd.

FROUG: Because they come back and see a movie again?

BOAM: Because they come back and see it again and again. And this is the age that goes out on dates a lot.

FROUG: I'd like to go back and talk about *Lethal Weapon II*. You raised a good point about theme. I've always believed the writer ought to have a theme in mind, have something that's behind the plot. Regarding *Lethal Weapon II*, you mentioned something at lunch that's very important.

BOAM: What I was saying was that anybody you ask will probably say *Lethal Weapon II* is about two cops who break up a ring of diplomatic criminals. I think the director would say that. I think the star would say that. But I know better. I wrote it. I know what the movie's about. The movie is about Mel Gibson's character discovering the truth about his wife's death. For me, that was the big scene in the movie. It was the scene I was writing toward. I think that anytime I'm writing a script, I need one scene that I'm writing toward, and I just keep moving forward until I get there. It was the most crucial scene in the movie. It doesn't really register on people that that's what the movie is about. I don't know why. For me it was what kept me going through the script.

FROUG: I think that's really fascinating and important, because I think writers have to remember theme when they're writing. Theme is a proposition leading to a conclusion, and it's not always revealed. You don't have to come out at the end of the movie and say, "Folks, this was a movie about the death of my wife." It never has to be stated, but it has to carry you along as a writer.

BOAM: I think a theme could be very slight, actually, and it doesn't have to be about a big idea, it doesn't have to be about racial injustice. It can be about a very small thing. And it has nothing to do with how entertaining it is. I'm just talking of structural things. I think one of the first lessons and best lessons I actually learned from you is when to reveal information. Information and exposition are the hobgoblins of dramatic writing. A lot of writers feel that they need to get all the exposition out up front. That, for some reason, you need to know all this useless information to understand the characters or to understand the story. And it's the worst way to deliver information. The best way to deliver information is when it's absolutely essential because a point is being made. You'll find this throughout William Goldman's excellent screenplay for *Butch Cassidy and The Sundance Kid*. There are a couple of moments that I think illustrate this perfectly. There's one where Butch Cassidy reveals that he never shot a man. Goldman has withheld this information, allowed us to ride along on an obvious assumption, and then he surprises us by giving this piece of information just at the moment when it's meaningful. If, at the beginning of the movie, Butch said, "I never shot a man," it would destroy the whole joy of discovering it at the right moment, which is when he has to engage in a gunfight. And there's another moment where Redford's character, Sundance, says he's from New Jersey, which is a small thing. But, again, we assume this guy was born in the West, but he's from New Jersey. I think an inexperienced writer would put that up front because they think, "Oh, this is such good information, that this outlaw is from New Jersey. Let's just tell it right away." And then it only becomes exposition. But when you save it for the right moment, it becomes drama.

FROUG: It's like Hitchcock said, "The person who tells you everything right away is a bore." You reveal as little of the character as possible, and as little at a time as necessary, on a need-to-know basis.

BOAM: This is actually a battle I have with studios a lot. Literal-thinking and linear-thinking executives are always saying to me, "Well, gee, we have to know about the character. We have to know that he's an orphan in the first act. Why do you delay that knowledge for so long?" I would have delayed it for a reason, because I want you to know it at the best moment to know it, but they just want to drop it in up front. For no reason other than in their simplistic thinking, they feel that this is valuable information. It's backstory (which is a terrible phrase and an expression you hear all the time). As if we need to know something that happened before the thing started. I'm always fighting to just show what you need to see and that's all.

FROUG: Sometimes it is the difference between a really good writer and a writer who never grows. The really good writer keeps you from knowing, keeps you wanting to know more. The really weak writer spills his guts right away, and it's boring. Naked exposition. I hate it.

BOAM: It's a hard lesson to learn. It's so easy to fall into the trap of revealing information. There's nothing more boring than information.

FROUG: True. If you can reveal it almost without the audience being aware that it's being revealed, that's wonderful. That's basically, to me, the difference between film and theater writing. In writing theatrical pieces, it seems to me that the characters stand up there right away and say, "Mother's coming to visit. She's been in the hospital for six weeks with chemotherapy," and the husband says, "Good God, we have to put up with her again. Remember the last time she was here? She did so-and-so." It seems to me in plays the actors stand up front and tell the audience the story, because they can't cut to close-up, they can't cut to the hospital, they can't cut to the car arriving.

BOAM: That's true, although I think a lot of playwrights become better screenwriters than novelists do. Because playwrights are writing drama. Novelists are writing narratives. And narratives are filled with exposition. I've enjoyed many movies that have been written by playwrights. They're usually small in scope, but I like the way playwrights tell stories.

FROUG: How do you lay out your story before you write the screenplay, in three acts, with a beginning, middle, and end?

BOAM: I think I instinctively envision three acts, but I try not to overanalyze it. I just sense that they're there.

FROUG: Do you follow a paradigm? Do you say, "Somewhere between page twenty and twenty-five I've gotta have a first-act curtain"?

BOAM: No, not at all. I've got no rules, no rules of thumb, no guidelines to use. It's all pretty instinctive.

FROUG: They apparently work.

BOAM: I'll tell you, the biggest and most helpful rule I have is, when I'm bored, the screenplay is boring. And it's going to be boring for an audience.

FROUG: Absolutely.

BOAM: In fact, I had a screening of *Lethal Weapon II* and somebody came up to me and said, "How do they do it? How do they make it happen so fast? It's just bam, bam. One thing after another. How do you do that?" I said to this guy, "It's real simple. You cut out all the boring stuff and just do all the rest." So many movies have boring things in them that I think the makers feel are obligatory—"I know it's boring, but we've got to have this." For whatever reason. But that's about the only gauge I use: Am I bored, or am I not bored?

FROUG: That's the most important gauge. You don't sit down and lay out scene cards up on the bulletin board and say, "Well, I need to get my climax on page eighty-five or ninety, or my first-act curtain on page twenty-five," what some call a turning point? You don't say, "Here it is page twenty. I wonder if I've got a turning point?"

BOAM: No, I don't use any of those techniques, tricks, whatever they are. I think you should just tell the story, and if you have a sense of drama and character, and if you know what you're writing about, it'll all work out, I'm convinced.

FROUG: How much do you need to know about your characters before you can write them?

BOAM: Not a lot. I don't think you need to know their life story.

FROUG: You don't write a biography of them?

BOAM: Never. No. And the last few movies I've worked on have been sequels, so the characters came pretty much developed.

FROUG: Well, those are the protagonists. What about the rest of the characters?

BOAM: I only need to know what I see.

FROUG: What you see in your mind's eye?

BOAM: What you see on the screen. I personally don't need to know more about the character than I reveal.

FROUG: So they can talk to you, yes? In that movie you've created in your head, you need to know how they're going to behave and how they're going to talk, right?

BOAM: You need to find a voice for them and you need to find a behavioral attitude for them. Attitude is very important. What is the attitude that the character carries around with him? What is his attitude in any given scene? Once I know that, then I know how he'll behave.

FROUG: But that's all you need to know.

BOAM: I need to know what's my take on the character.

FROUG: On secondary characters, do you need to know much about them?

BOAM: Secondary characters are hard to write because you want to make them distinctive, you want to make them interesting. We'll never get to learn too much about them, so what you need to do is find some kind of quirky mannerism for the character, something that distinguishes him from the rest of the group.

FROUG: Joe Pesci's character, for example, in *Lethal Weapon II*, was singled out by every critic as being special. What was your take in your mind on him?

BOAM: Well, the character is kind of self-evident. Now you're asking me to analyze him.

FROUG: All I'm saying is, going in, as you're sitting down, you see this character in your mind's eye, the money launderer. You see this character, and he speaks to you, obviously. When you're writing, do you experience that he's doing the lines, and you are kind of unconsciously putting them down?

BOAM: Yeah, in a way. I think the character starts to speak for himself. But I did have a take on the character, which was that he would be kind of a nuisance, a pest, extremely friendly, extremely likable, very positive, very upbeat, rascally, sneaky. Maybe that covers the character.

FROUG: In other words, you enjoyed him.

BOAM: I enjoyed him.

FROUG: You enjoyed writing him, and you enjoyed seeing him in the movie in your mind.

BOAM: Absolutely. And I'm going to enjoy writing him in *Lethal III.*

FROUG: Are you thinking in terms of, for *Lethal III*, some kind of political theme like you had in *Lethal II*?

BOAM: It's not a political theme. I think there's an important social theme, which is the proliferation of guns in our society. It's going to be an anti-gun movie.

FROUG: Long overdue.

BOAM: Talk about concern and self-censorship. I do have a concern: Can I write an action movie where the heroes are solving their problems with guns and also make an anti-gun statement?

FROUG: Can you make it so the studio won't bow to The National Rifle Association and say, "The NRA won't stand for this"?

BOAM: I don't think the NRA will ever enter into it.

FROUG: That will be a real achievement, Jeff, if you can make a film in which everybody uses guns, which is fundamentally a violent type of movie, and still at the same time talk about how we're overarmed. We're all armed and dangerous. There are too many guns around.

BOAM: I know. It's as bad a situation as drugs.

FROUG: It is.

BOAM: If not worse. My final image for this movie has always been Mel tossing his gun in the ocean. I'll probably never use that, but just as an emotional signpost, I like it. But I'm hoping that the audience won't feel betrayed if I let them feast on two hours of gunplay and then, at the end, throw the gun in the ocean as if to say, "This doesn't solve anything." Will they feel, "We've been betrayed. We've just invested two hours in enjoying gunplay, and now you're telling us it's a bad thing?" I don't know exactly how that's going to work out.

FROUG: The critics loved and quoted often in many of the reviews your line in *Indy, The Last Crusade*, when Sean Connery says to Harrison Ford, "But I was the first man."

BOAM: The line was, "I'm as human as the next man." And Indy says, "I *was* the next man." They having slept with the same girl.

FROUG: That was singled out as a special thing.

BOAM: We debated that point a lot. There were several things we debated in that movie a lot and, in my mind, we filmed them all. When I write something, I imagine it filmed. There were so many different variations on that and on the girl dying at the end. Does she die? Does she not die? Do they rescue her? Does she ride off in the sunset with Indy? Without Indy? Does she stay behind? Does she wind up in the pit? It's just amazing how difficult it was trying to figure out the best way to dispose of, or dispense with, this character.

FROUG: That was you and George in these hours-long meetings.

BOAM: George, and Steven, too, because, once he came along, I did many drafts with his involvement. And that was constantly changing. The thing about the father having slept with the girl was an on-again-off-again thing. It was in, it was out, it was in, it was out, depending on who read the script, actually. Steven would give the script to a woman, just to get her opinion, and she would hate it and we'd take it out. We'd give it to somebody else, they'd love it, and we'd put it back in.

FROUG: So in terms of this, the struggles were always how do we find the best audience reaction.

BOAM: Exactly. What else are you shooting for? I don't necessarily believe in some kind of internal integrity that a piece has, that it has to go in a certain direction, even though the audience won't enjoy it. I think it is just foolhardy to say, "The audience won't want to see this, but we have to be true to the piece, and this is where it goes." I think that's just self-defeating. That's suicide.

FROUG: I understand that very well, but the only question I have is, even with Spielberg's record, your record, and George Lucas and his incredible record, do you always know what the audience is going to feel?

BOAM: Oh, of course not. At best it's an educated guess. They fool us. I've never been fooled on a large scale, but I've been fooled many times on a small scale. Certain bits I thought would work didn't. Certain bits I thought didn't have a chance of working did. But I never felt like I, or the people I was involved with, made a grave and serious error that just killed us.

FROUG: So you thrash these points out in terms of what you think this response would be, and, I gather, most of the time you're right.

BOAM: I think so. Again, like saying, I don't write stuff that bores me, because it will bore someone else—the opposite is true as well. If something excites me and entertains me and amuses me, it usually does the same thing to an audience. I think I have a nice middlebrow sensibility.

FROUG: Have you ever been broadly or wildly thrown by the audience response. Is there any time that you said, "My God, I was amazed at their response."

BOAM: Yes. In *Lethal Weapon II*, when they're all sitting around to watch the commercial that the girl's in and the camera pans down in the commercial itself to this box of condoms. It's the biggest laugh I've ever had in a theater.

FROUG: You didn't know it was going to be that big a laugh.

BOAM: No. I never thought it'd be that big of a laugh.

FROUG: You figured what? It would be just a chuckle?

BOAM: Yeah. I figured it'd be a laugh. But it's a roar. It's a roar that goes on, and you can't hear the next two or three lines. It's unbelievable. It's a bigger laugh than I've ever gotten in anything that's just a comedy.

FROUG: Well, in view of that, if you had it to do over, would you in the editing have allowed more space for the laugh?

BOAM: Maybe you'd want to leave a little pause there.

FROUG: Do they do previews where they screen the thing and then recut them to the audience reaction?

BOAM: Every movie I've been involved in has been previewed. But I think mostly it's the response that the director has at the moment that determines what's going to be cut and not cut. Not necessarily the cards. I've never seen a movie changed because the cards say, "We hate this scene" or "We hate this character."

FROUG: They don't change for that reason.

BOAM: I don't think so. I think it's because . . .

FROUG: If Donner came out of the preview screening saying, "God, I hate that scene," out it goes, huh?

BOAM: I think so.

FROUG: But if you come out of the preview screening saying, "God, I hate that scene," what happens?

BOAM: No one cares. Unless they already agree with me. But even if Dick said it, I think that if there was resistance on the part of the studio, it would be left in.

FROUG: Fascinating.

BOAM: Certain directors have more power than others, but ultimately, even the most powerful director, even someone like Steven, listens to people. He believes that other people's opinions have merit.

FROUG: In the working group.

BOAM: Yes, that's right. He doesn't reject the opinions of studio executives; he doesn't dismiss them. He listens to them and thinks about them. And I think he feels compelled to make some concessions to the people who are putting up the money.

FROUG: Somebody puts up forty or fifty million dollars, you gotta give him a little credence.

BOAM: You have to.

FROUG: Right. Jeff, you are to me, without question the most singular of the writers I knew at UCLA because you had the perseverance and the determination to press on at all costs. You said, "I am going to make it. I'm going to be a screenwriter no matter what."

BOAM: I did. Still, you learn as you go. You do improve; you don't have to be a full-blown screenwriter the minute you sit down to write a script.

FROUG: Hang in there, if you believe in it, right?

BOAM: Hang in there.

Bill Bryan

In TV, you know who you're writing for, and you try to go to their strengths. Jamie Lee Curtis as a temptress always works and Richard Lewis is at his best when he's suffering.

(BB)

ANYTHING BUT LOVE

INT. DINER - MORNING

(HANNAH AND MARTY AT COUNTER, READING THE PAPER.)

                    MARTY
          How about that. The sex act
          lasts an average of two minutes.

                    HANNAH
          Says who, Roger Rabbit?

                    MARTY
          No, Masters and Johnson.

(HE TRIES TO SHOW HER THE ARTICLE HE'S READING.)

                    HANNAH
          Forget it, I don't need any
          study to tell me what I like.
          It's better to start slooow.

(THEY EACH BEGIN TO DRIFT INTO FANTASIES.)

                    MARTY
          I admit, slow has its merits.

                    HANNAH
          That way you get to gradually
          builllld.

                    MARTY
          Who could forget the building?

                    HANNAH
          Pretty soon you're going faster,
          and faster, until you feel
          yourself break free of time and
          space and blast off into a state
          of uncontrollable ecstasy.
(BEAT)
          I don't think I could ever
          finish in two minutes. What
          about you?

                    MARTY
          I think I'm already finished.

"We're going to shoot this tomorrow."

Bill Bryan and I became friends the moment he walked into my UCLA graduate writing seminar. It was a happy chemistry and is a friendship that has lasted over the years through heavy-duty trials and tribulations for each of us in our own different ways. Maybe I remind him of his father or maybe he reminds me of my son, for whom I have similar feelings.

For whatever reason, I have followed Bill's career with both concern and interest. He has not had it easy since he graduated from UCLA and entered the shark-infested waters of Hollywood. Some of his troubles, I'm sure he would agree, are of his own making. Others come with the territory.

During our first seminar together, Bill gave me a copy of his screenplay-in-progress. I forget the original title but it has since been named *Sex and Violence*, no doubt because it contains none of either.

Parts of the script sent me into uncontrollable laughter, tears rolling down my cheeks, and me almost rolling out of my chair. In twenty years of teaching, I had never come across a talent such as this. Finding a comedy writer who can write hard comedy (defined as creating out-and-out laughter) is as rare as discovering another Hope diamond, and just as valuable. Writers of soft comedy (chuckles, smiles, etc.) are not so rare and not nearly as in demand. In my years of teaching, I discovered quite a few soft-comedy writers but Bill Bryan was the only hard-comedy writer I ever came across, with but one exception.*

We screenwriting teachers readily teach the fundamentals of writing drama, but nobody can teach a writer how to write funny. The writer of hard comedy can write his own ticket anywhere in Hollywood for incredibly huge sums of money.

Alas, this is not true of us drama writers. Think of Neil Simon, who has made more money off his extraordinary comedy-writing talent than Shakespeare, Eugene O'Neill, Tennessee Williams, and Arthur Miller all combined. It is not a slur on the human race to note that people would rather laugh than cry.

Bill Bryan has walked through the valley of career death and survived relatively unscathed, but a whole lot wiser. Bill's early troubles make an excellent cautionary tale for all of you would-be screenwriters. Listen up. There's wisdom here.

---

*The one exception is Sheldon Bull, who leaped from my UCLA class a decade earlier into big-time TV sitcoms as a writer-producer with "Newhart."

FROUG: During your time at UCLA, you wrote far and away the funniest student screenplay I have read.

BRYAN: I think that's enough of an interview right there.

FROUG: It was called *Sex and Violence* and was your show script, or calling-card script. New screenwriters will want to know about your experience in the world of Hollywood. Going out there with your show script. How did you come up with the idea for that script?

BRYAN: It's based on a true story. Through college, I'd worked in TV news, and I knew a guy who had suddenly, out of nowhere, become a big-market TV anchor. So I originally wrote a pretty bad melodrama based on that notion, and then set it aside. And when I was taking your class at UCLA, I wrote another screenplay, and your reaction to it was—if you recall—"Well, I think you're a good writer, but the parts that seem to be the most inspired here are the funny parts, when you're really trying to get laughs. Comedy writers are always in the shortest supply in the business. Why don't you try writing a flat-out comedy?" So I thought about what I might attempt in that direction. I thought, "What if I take this idea of a guy springing up out of the sticks to become a big-time TV anchor? What if I do that as a comedy?" So I introduced the female character and constructed a battle-of-the-sexes plot. In its bare bones, the story is similar to *Broadcast News*, but this was years before *Broadcast News* was out. I think I wrote it in 1981.

FROUG: You've got this wonderful script, and now you're out there.

BRYAN: Again, you deserve a prominent place in the story. It was quite remarkable. You asked me, essentially, "What would you like to be when you grow up?" I said, "Well, I guess, in an ideal world I'd like to be a writer and perhaps a director of films and television." "Well, do you want to get this script to an agent?" "Yes." And within a week I had an agent. Within a month I had three development deals at major studios and one hundred thousand dollars, which, of course, I had to write the three scripts to collect. I was to write a screenplay and a set of revisions of three different stories. In the first case, it was a one-sentence idea from a major producer at a major studio who said, "Can you come up with something out of this?" In the next case, it was more or less the same, a little complicated by the fact there was an existing script, but, again, the same kind of job-for-hire. In the third case it was a matter of my having a slightly more fleshed-out idea that I pitched to a studio and was paid to develop and write.

FROUG: What was the pitch like for a comedy writer?

BRYAN: Terrible. Hard.

FROUG: You can't exactly sit in a room with these executives or these producers or functionaries and be funny, really, can you?

BRYAN: You try. But many comedy writers are not terribly outgoing. If we were, we'd be at the Comedy Store doing stand-up instead of sitting in our offices. I think any pitching is murderously difficult. There's the obvious problem of self-consciousness. There's also the difficulty in comedy of trying to give a sense of something being funny when, in fact, you could take any story—a basic story—and depending on how you write it, have it come out as a comedy or a drama. In other words, the bare bones of a story are not inherently funny.

FROUG: It could go either way. Comedy must also have a dramatic spine or line of dramatic tension.

BRYAN: Right. So you're put in a position of having to give some kind of a hybrid. You're mostly pitching the basic idea and then throwing in a few jokes along the way. You're trying to say, "And these characters are all really hilarious." What you're really riding on is your previous script—the script that got you in in the first place—and the fact that they perceive you as funny.

FROUG: Now, with that show script and these meetings, this was one hundred thousand dollars if you came up with a script for these people?

BRYAN: No. These were guaranteed deals—for very small dollars in today's terms. This was a total for these three projects, all three from different studios, for a first draft and a set of changes for each one. It was not, *if* I came up with an idea. The deals were made based on given ideas.

FROUG: So, you had three firm commitments for three screenplays.

BRYAN: Right. I simply had to write the scripts and turn them in. Usually it's twelve weeks to write a first-draft screenplay. Then there's a reading period when various people—producers and studio executives—read it and make their notes and give it back to you, and that's typically four weeks. Then you have another four weeks to do revisions. That's a total of twenty weeks, or less than half a year, in which you're supposed to do this.

FROUG: Three complete comedy screenplays.

BRYAN: . . . in the space of slightly over a year. And, of course, it doesn't happen that way.

FROUG: Which one did you tackle first?

BRYAN: Well, the first deal was with MGM (at that time it was MGM-UA; I've lost track of what it is now). It was a teenage sex-comedy, a genre then in vogue. This was either shortly before or right after *Porkys*, which followed a few years after *Animal House* and a whole spate of films. I had actually gone to prep school . . .

FROUG: So you were going to do a kind of *Animal House* in a prep school?

BRYAN: It doesn't sound very valorous, but yes. I did that first.

FROUG: You turned in the screenplay, and then what?

BRYAN: I went through a cycle that was to become quite

familiar. The first few people that you hear from are the lowest in power, and they tend to be wildly enthusiastic. In this case it was the development person working for this producer who was saying things like, "We're going to shoot this next month." A writer who doesn't know any better takes it at face value. Evidently, the producer himself was also quite pleased. Then it gets to the studio level. You hear that they're very positive, but they want to have a meeting and talk about it. So you have this meeting, and at the end of it you want to say, "Now, exactly, what was the part you liked?" I don't know how much of that is excess defensiveness on the part of a first-time writer with countless character defects or how much of it is just a really strange process. That meeting was after the so-called reading period, and it was time to do another draft.

FROUG: The next draft incorporates all of this feedback they gave you?

BRYAN: Right. Much of which is self-contradictory and is coming from different sources. The writer is the only person who really has to try to make sense out of all these things at once. Everybody else has the luxury of tossing out whatever they want, and then it's left in your lap. This is where, again, inexperience is a problem because you tend to want to please them. These people have important jobs, credentials, and are all intelligent—I've never known anybody in the business who was obviously stupid. So you have a tendency to want to fulfill all these things. You're also intimidated and afraid to say no. And then you go home and try to make sense of it all. In many cases, as I said, it's impossible to execute all the notes because they're so fundamentally contradictory to each other and to your understanding of what you were doing in the first place. If you were to follow all the notes, you would essentially be throwing out everything and starting over. I couldn't actually tell you, after all these years, what happened with that project except that it got turned in and then it didn't get made. And from time to time somebody or other will call up and say, "Hey, we're really going to try to get this going." You say, as a writer, "Oh, great."

FROUG: And that's the last you hear of it?

BRYAN: Yeah, then a year later somebody else calls.

FROUG: Periodically you get somebody calling and saying, "That's a wonderful script. I'm going to go to work getting it filmed," yes?

BRYAN: Yeah. It was particularly true with the script I wrote at UCLA, *Sex and Violence*. Ten years later, the calls still come at least two or three times a year.

FROUG: Occasionally these people would phone and say we're really working on this—your MGM script—but, as the weeks turned to months, it just vanished?

BRYAN: Yeah. This town is terrible at delivering bad news.

FROUG: You read it in the trade papers?

BRYAN: Nothing as direct as that—just silence.

FROUG: Let's talk about the next one.

BRYAN: The next one was at Paramount. The then-head of production, Jeff Katzenberg, who was then a powerhouse and has since become a mega-powerhouse at Disney, responded very well to *Sex and Violence* and told the people who worked under him to find something in their slate of projects that I could do. They had a script about a bum and a little girl who befriends him and brings him home for Christmas. They were looking at everything in their script inventory that Eddie Murphy could do. He was the coming star. *48 Hours* had just come out, and it was the perfect time because everyone was saying he's going to be great, but he was still attainable. So, somebody said, "What about this bum-for-Christmas project?" And then somebody else said, "Well, what if he's an angel?" It was sort of a scatter-shot affair. Anyway, I was called in and had this meeting with Paramount.

FROUG: Where'd the angel come from?

BRYAN: From an executive, I believe. I'm a little unclear

about this. It may have been in the existing story that they owned, that this bum turned out to be an angel, or it may have been a development made by one of the executives on the project. All I know is, when I got hold of it, it was about Eddie Murphy as an angel. It involved a little girl and it was a Christmas story. So I took that much and they made a deal with me based on that idea. I came up with a story and I called it *Hell of an Angel*. The title's probably the best thing I contributed to the project—it's very important to any motion picture.

FROUG: The title?

BRYAN: Yeah. It instantly elevated the project. I came up with it while I was driving to the dry cleaners. That moved the project from the lower rung to the upper rung of the projects in work. Now it was something that could actually happen.

FROUG: And *Hell of an Angel* right away tells you it's a comedy, yes?

BRYAN: Right. And tells you a lot about it, right there. When you see him on the poster with that title, you've got a pretty good sense of the movie. I wrote it in short order, and I again got this tremendous response, even bigger than the one to the first draft of my first script. It got to the top level of the studio, to Jeff Katzenberg. There the response was also positive, but somewhat more muted in the sense of, you know, this needs work. We need to fix this and get rid of that. So I was told this *could* be Eddie's next movie. By this time "the next Eddie Murphy movie" had become kind of a script derby.

FROUG: You were just one of many?

BRYAN: One of many, many.

FROUG: Whoever got this movie would presumably be a star writer, right?

BRYAN: Absolutely. This was really going to make some money. So I did another draft that didn't come as easily. I should also back up a little and say that before I wrote the first draft, I'd had numerous meetings with the producer on the project, the development executives, everybody connected with this project. All of them have gone on to nothing but fame and fortune. Actually, everybody on the project was at sort of the same level in their career as I was. The two executives on it were, at that time, really lower-rung people. They each now run their own major studio. The producer, who was not a well-known guy at the time, has since produced some major films and has eight hundred development deals everywhere. Anyway, the point I was really going to make was that we had a bunch of meetings and developed the story in a particular direction, and I was struggling with it and not making progress. Ultimately, I went off to a very remote location—a mountain cabin, literally—for a ten-day period and threw out virtually all of what we had discussed and worked on. I wrote a new script from scratch without an outline, without anything. It was really just a pure form of turning the pages over and doing it. I came back, and the initial response that I got was surprise.

FROUG: Because it wasn't what they bargained for?

BRYAN: Right. But the two people who really knew what they'd bargained for, the studio people who were in on the story meetings, were entranced enough with it that they didn't complain. They were happy about it. Anyway, on the second draft I realized that this throwing everything out and starting over was not in the cards, would not be appreciated. But I couldn't do everything they wanted. I had a more difficult time making the changes, and essentially the script went through the usual process. It died in a similar fashion as the thing at MGM. Then there were various things I heard: that Eddie's manager got ahold of the script and sneaked it to Eddie, who liked it. I heard things like that, but nothing happened with it. Something like a year later, most of those top people who were running Paramount—Michael Eisner and Jeff Katzenberg and those people—left and went to Disney. And the one person who was left out of the original group that was involved—now promoted to an upper-level executive—got ahold of me and he said, "I recommended this as Eddie's next picture." And Eddie had made another movie in the meantime—*Beverly Hills Cop*.

FROUG: Now Eddie Murphy is a big star.

BRYAN: The biggest. It's no longer, "We still want it to be a Christmas movie." Now it's, "We don't want this little girl. We want the second part to be something another comic leading man can play, a Dan Aykroyd or Chevy Chase or Bill Murray." I was living in New York at the time, but I was brought back to L.A. by the studio in kind of a spare-no-expense fashion. Again, a major script race was on. There were other projects I knew about that were competing to be Eddie Murphy's next movie, but at this point it seemed like we had a really good track on it. I did a script in a pretty short period of time. As I was getting ready to finish it there was an article on the cover of the *L.A. Times* Sunday *Calendar* magazine that was about who would win the Eddie Murphy script derby. It listed the contenders, handicapping the top thirty projects at Paramount. I think *Hell of an Angel* was in position three. But, alas, it turned out to be another also-ran.

FROUG: Okay, so that just quietly vanished beneath the waves. Then what did you do? Now you've gone through this grind of development, which is a very good way to tell new writers that this is what lies in store for most of them.

BRYAN: I don't know, by the way, how true that is. I've taken myself out of the feature development business, but I hear from some people that it's not done as much anymore as it was then, that there is some trend away from it. I hear from others that it's only gotten worse. I don't know.

FROUG: Okay, so now what? Now you've had this wall of silence.

BRYAN: Yeah, the way you find out is by the phone not ringing. While I was finishing that draft, that revised *Hell of an Angel* with the male co-lead, I was getting daily and hourly phone calls, you know, "What page are you on? When are we gonna get it? We're going to pre-production in two weeks with this movie." And I responded to that. I believed it, you know, and I was working hard on it. Anyway, I turned it in and caught the next plane back to New York and expected that the phone would be ringing by the time I arrived. The producer was actually very good about it. I heard his very enthusiastic reaction within a day or so, but I don't think I heard for about two weeks from the studio executive who I'd been talking to every day. I went through the range of emotions—all the way from excitement and irritation to fury and disappointment to the point where I was actually surprised when the call did not come. It's not just pure indifference to writers' feelings that causes this to happen. Generally, when calls aren't coming, it's because people don't like to deliver bad news or they don't have any news. They don't like to acknowledge that they alone are not capable of making decisions, so they tend not to call. In the meantime, between those two incarnations of *Hell of an Angel*, I had written the third project that I had originally sold in that spate of development.

FROUG: You've gone through Metro and Paramount. Where are you now?

BRYAN: I'd done a picture at CBS Theatrical, which I always like to put on my résumé with the footnote "Bankrupted the company." I believe one of the last checks they wrote was to me. That was a theatrical film division of CBS that never made it. It went down the tubes, and that project went with it. Then, another producer, who was at the time of modest stature and now runs yet another major studio, said, "I'm going to make *Sex and Violence*." So I worked on it. It needed some rewrites, and I worked with a script consultant he hired who, as a director, had come up with some ideas that had become movies made by this producer. I hit it off really well with this director. So we worked together on trying to refashion *Sex and Violence*.

We also were dealing with a number of actors who were hot at the time and were considered appropriate for the male lead.

FROUG: What's the average life span, do you think, of these actors being hot?

BRYAN: There was something interesting about that in the William Goldman book, *Adventures in the Screen Trade*. I don't know that there is any average, but it's clear that if you look at a period of ten years, no one remains on the list. Maybe one name, but the ten most popular actors will not be the same. And, probably, now it's down to even less. I mean, last year the big names all took a pretty bad pounding at the box office.

FROUG: So now where are you?

BRYAN: I was having this terrible experience in development deals, so I did the natural thing: I made another one. I decided that by lowering my sights in terms of a picture's budget and trying to make a smaller picture on which I'd have greater control, I'd have a better chance. I made a deal in partnership with this director I met on *Sex and Violence*. We packaged ourselves on a studio project that could be made for a low budget. We took almost none of our fees up front—just the Writers Guild minimum.

FROUG: Get yours at the back end?

BRYAN: Yeah. And, again, you know, it was a can't-miss proposition. It was a case where we and the studio were trying to capitalize on the existence of another film. It was thought that it would be a good companion to the original. We finished the script the day the first film opened, and it died.

FROUG: It was planned to be a big box-office hit? Can you mention what the title of that film was?

BRYAN: It's silly, but the film I was doing was based on the board game Monopoly, and the other movie was *Clue*. The thought was that *Clue* was going to be a sure-fire winner. It was a universally recognized name—the game—and it's a mystery, a form that works in drama. But it flopped, and that was the end of *Monopoly.*

FROUG: Well, let's just say that we're at a point, maybe a bit of a shortcut, where you've got yet another development deal which is not going to go through. So, now, at what point did you decide that development deals are not a good thing?

BRYAN: Well, for financial reasons, I took several more deals, and, ultimately, I had a more and more difficult time finishing them.

FROUG: You kind of know at this point that nothing's likely to happen with them.

BRYAN: Yeah. All of us think, to one degree or another, that willpower is what makes you do things. If you want to do anything badly enough, you can. But, I don't think we actually work that way. Things like the belief that things will actually happen, rewards, all those things, play a much bigger role than our piddling willpower. When you start to get the message that you can do these development deals till the end of time and you don't have much to show for it, it takes a toll and it makes it more difficult to work. So I was having a hard time finishing the projects. Ultimately, my relationships became strained with the people I was working with, and I decided that it was time to pack up and leave for Northern California, where I grew up. (It coincided with the time my wife and I learned we were going to have my first child. I got very neurotic about the idea of him breathing Los Angeles air in his early life.) In Northern California I would work on spec, which is something that all the big writers were then doing. That would solve all my problems. But, by then, I had become hooked on development writing.

FROUG: On money.

BRYAN: Exactly.

FROUG: You were well-paid during all your frustrating years?

BRYAN: Very well. And, you know, I had a nice life. I never had to put on anything but shorts and sandals, except to go to an occasional meeting. But, except for the screenplay I wrote that got me into UCLA in the first place, I'd never written anything without a gun to my head, and I found that I was incapable of doing it. So, nine months later, when my first son was born and financial reality set in, I essentially went out and got a bigger gun, which was called television.

FROUG: That's the biggest gun of all.

BRYAN: Yeah. There it's always at your head.

FROUG: Now that you're in it, what are the benefits? A lot of students I've had have turned in scripts that they have been well-paid for, but they are still sitting on the shelf. They're looking for some kind of credit out there, to establish some sort of name. Suppose they make this move and say, "Okay, we'll try television." What are the benefits of television?

BRYAN: There are a lot. If you're lucky enough to work on staff of a TV series or if you do freelance scripts for one, what you write will get made. It may not get made in exactly the way you first wrote it. If you're on staff, you have a greater ability to influence that than if you're not. But it will get made, quickly, and you will get a credit. That's the first good thing. The second is that the writer is much, much stronger in television than in the movie business. In fact, with few exceptions, writers run every TV show, especially comedies.

FROUG: Every producer credit we see on a TV show is basically a writer, isn't it?

BRYAN: Let's say eighty or ninety percent. One of those names is the line producer, who deals with the nuts and bolts of production, and another may be someone with an ownership position in the show. But the rest are writers.

FROUG: There's an executive producer, a supervising producer, co-producer, ad nauseam, yes?

BRYAN: Yeah. And then all the titles below producer—story editor, executive story editor, script consultant, executive script consultant—are all staff writers.

FROUG: How did you make the move from the development field of movies into television?

BRYAN: Well, I asked my agent how to do it, and he told me to write a spec episode of an existing series. He was able to give me a good leg up by sending me tapes of three pilots that he guaranteed would be hits in the coming television season.

FROUG: He knew because of the time slot or because of the people in them?

BRYAN: Because of the overall heat from the project. They were the ones everybody was talking about. There are a lot of shows that get put on the air about which people say, "Well, maybe." And then there are the few—in this particular year, it was extraordinary, there were three that everybody was certain were going to get on the air and stay on. They were "Roseanne," "Dear John," and "Murphy Brown." They also happened to all be packaged or represented in some way by my agency, William Morris.

FROUG: Okay, so . . .

BRYAN: I thought that the one that I could best write a spec script for was "Murphy Brown," because of my TV news background and a similarity in style to my own work. Based on the characters that I saw on this pilot, I sat down to write an outline first, which was difficult.

FROUG: The format, right?

BRYAN: Yeah. The important thing about format, by the way, is not how you type it on the page. It's story structure. How many acts? How quickly do they set things up? How many stories do they tell in a half hour? Typically, they tell one main story and one lesser story, and then have one sort of running gag that doesn't really qualify as a story, but that they will hit a couple of times. By the time I sat down to write, I was able to get my hands on a couple of scripts from the show. It wasn't on the air, but they were already shooting episodes, so I was able to take a couple of them apart and really see how they ticked. This is not a process I was entirely comfortable with. One could stand accused of writing "to a formula," because it's obviously what you're doing. You're attempting to mimic the structure of something while finding a different story to tell. But I think it's absolutely necessary. As you go on, you can find new ways to build the tale. But you can't get around beginning, middle and end; you can't get around the fact that before the commercial you have to do something interesting that will make the audience come back from the kitchen. So my advice is to start out copying structure and sort of plug in your own story and jokes and things. That's what I did. I sent the script down to my agent, and I got multiple job offers to be on staff in the following television season . . .

FROUG: Based on that one spec "Murphy Brown," you got multiple offers?

BRYAN: Yeah. Which I hear is not a universal experience. Many people write spec script after spec script in an attempt just to get a freelance assignment. So, it was a piece of good fortune.

FROUG: I'm told that "Cheers" receives truckloads of scripts, year in and year out, and that they have a skiploader that comes up to the back of the production offices and picks up the scripts that have been submitted and dumps them out somewhere.

BRYAN: Yes, I believe there's a subdivision somewhere in the valley that's built entirely on bad "Cheers" scripts.

FROUG: Based on this one script for "Murphy Brown," now you've got offers. Tell me what that did for you.

BRYAN: Well, I got to pick from a number of good shows, to be on the writing staff. And I chose "Night Court" because I liked the show, I liked the people, and I *really* liked the money. The show was in the unique position of having a two-season pickup. They were able to guarantee me two years at a generous per-episode fee (for a beginner) because the show was already such an enormous moneymaker for the studio. It was into its sixth and a half or seventh year at that point, well into syndication, making a fortune. They could afford to spread it around a little.

FROUG: Of the ones you named, though, that's one that we would call low comedy as opposed to "Murphy Brown," which is sophisticated comedy. Which is really what you've been writing.

BRYAN: I don't agree with that. To some people, "Night Court" has a reputation for low comedy because of certain broad situations and characters, particularly Bull. But it also has the reputation among writers as always having been a very well-written show. Basically, it's like vaudeville—a place where different actors play different kinds of comedy. I think that has something to do with its appeal. In any case, I never felt, on anything that I did there, like I was writing down.

FROUG: Do you have a better standing in the community as a comedy writer if the show is considered sophisticated?

BRYAN: Yes, you do. Although, again, "Night Court" is not a bad credit. It has one of the best track records for where its writers wind up. We had a staff of seven, and everybody on that staff is now doing incredibly well. Beyond that, the answer to your question is "yes." If you are perceived as working on a better show, you're thought of as a better writer. There are shows (which I would not name at gunpoint) from which a credit is worth very little. One of the guys who was executive producer of "Night Court" when I was there (and who is now very well-regarded) suffered from this. Half a dozen years before "Night Court," he had been a story editor on one of these more kid-oriented shows. He went through several years of unemployment and hard times because that was not a good credit. He and a partner then wrote a spec "Cheers" and essentially reentered the business from the bottom.

FROUG: "Cheers" immediately elevated him to another status?

BRYAN: Yes, it was one of the scripts to write to show you could do good stuff.

FROUG: He had to prove that he could write more sophisticated comedy. When you say it was a very good deal as one of these seven staff writers, what kind of money can you expect if you're a new guy coming in, and this is your first job in television? What kind of money were you paid?

BRYAN: Okay, here we go with the really tacky indiscretions. I made about two hundred and fifty thousand the first year. I stayed one year, and the staff changed. The two guys who were running it left, and I had an offer to go to a show that was more universally respected by people who thought that "Night Court" was low comedy. It was called "Anything But Love." I really, really liked the show.

FROUG: Understanding television on the comedy level is not too easy sometimes. They came to you with a better offer and you were free to move away from "Night Court"?

BRYAN: It's complicated. I was not contractually free to move. But, generally, if somebody strongly expresses a desire to leave, it will be respected. In other words, they don't want people around who aren't happy. You don't want to cut and run too often, however, because you get a reputation as somebody who is a malcontent or who doesn't honor their commitments.

FROUG: This is really a small town, isn't it?

BRYAN: Very. Very. Very. I mean, I've been in television for a grand total of two years. I went to a taping of a new show the other night, and I must have seen fifty people that I knew there, just from these two shows. And this was for a different studio, different network.

FROUG: That's important to pass along. If you have a bad reputation on one show, the word quickly spreads. Right away the word is, you can't rely on this guy, he'll quit on you.

BRYAN: Television's all about being able to rely on people.

FROUG: Right. It's so hard to get material for that tube, isn't it?

BRYAN: Yeah, it sucks it up at a furious clip, and erratic brilliance doesn't have a place, at least in writing.

FROUG: Actors get away with it all the time.

BRYAN: When they do, it's because it's tough to fire them. Their face is what people think they're tuning in to see. It's all you can promote. When you're going to sell a new show, you're mostly selling it with names, recognizable names of actors who are in it. Now, occasionally, a network or studio will try to send actors a message by showing they can dump somebody. But the mandate is almost always to accommodate the star.

FROUG: I've been in that producer's spot where I knew I meant nothing but the actor meant everything.

BRYAN: The only power you have, really, is to walk out yourself. The better actors recognize who are the better writers and try to avoid that from happening. On one of the two shows I've worked on, there were a number of standoffs between the actors and the writers. But even in that atmosphere, it was understood by everybody that there were good people on both sides and that you didn't necessarily want to lose them. You had to find a way to get along.

FROUG: Is "Anything But Love" a hit?

BRYAN: No, regrettably. I would have to categorize it as a sort of a middle-ground ratings performer. It's a critical sensation. Virtually every major critic has written these love poems to the show, saying it's the smartest comedy on television. It deserves better treatment.

FROUG: Does that do anything for you in television?

BRYAN: Yes. But not as much as if it were accompanied by big ratings. Basically, the moral of the story is, in company with the answer to your earlier question about what happens if you work on a not-well-respected show, what you really need is both. You need to be loved and respected, you need to get critical response at some level, and you need ratings success. If not, you keep searching for whichever of those two things you're missing.

FROUG: Now you've earned yourself that producer-writer status, correct?

BRYAN: Right.

FROUG: Now you have more and more responsibility to meet that awesome deadline every week, right?

BRYAN: Yeah, but only to the extent that I have more money and more reputation. In terms of real responsibility, that doesn't change on a staff until you're the executive producer. He or she is called the show runner, the head writer. He makes all the critical casting and production decisions and usually writes scripts, too.

FROUG: That's a very awesome responsibility, isn't it?

BRYAN: Yeah.

FROUG: Do you want to be a show runner?

BRYAN: Yeah. But I'm not necessarily anxious to do it this year or next. The last few years have been chaotic: doing movies and television, having two children. I'm reaching sort of a level of comfort and competence in the business, being on staff, where it's not such a bad thing to be called a producer but not really have to produce.

FROUG: What you have to produce is a script. You're doing fresh comedy every week.

BRYAN: Yeah. And you're critiquing and revising all the scripts that are done on the show, not just writing your own. The way the money breaks down is that you get a per-episode fee for whatever your title is. In my case now it's producer. In theory, for that money you are in meetings at the beginning of the year to determine the overall sweep of the series. Then you are coming up with individual story ideas, pitching out the stories.

FROUG: Which somebody else, your staff, writes, yes?

BRYAN: Well, no. The producers *are* the staff.

FROUG: On "Anything But Love"? You're it?

BRYAN: On "Anything But Love" this last year, there were three of us who had various kinds of producer titles and one story editor. No staff writers. There really aren't any staff writers to speak of around town. The lowest rung now is usually story editor. The point is, it's four of us in a room, and we're pitching these stories out. One of us is then going to take that story and go and write it.

FROUG: You just rotate this?

BRYAN: Yeah. The show runner—the executive producer—is making the decisions. Everybody is throwing ideas out, and then he's the one that says let's do it this way, let's do it that way. So the individual writer of that episode will go out and write an outline, and then everybody reads it and makes their notes on it.

FROUG: How long have they got to write the outline? Overnight, or what?

BRYAN: Typically, people take about a week.

FROUG: To write an outline?

BRYAN: Yeah. It really should be done faster. It basically should be transcribing and editing the notes from the story-pitch meeting, but people—myself included—tend to want to make it a complete thing. So you put a lot into making that outline as good as possible, and then people give you their notes and response.

FROUG: When the outline's delivered, who's going to write the script? You or somebody else?

BRYAN: The person who writes the outline writes the first draft and the second draft. First, notes (comments and suggestions) are given on the outline. A first draft is written, and the same process is repeated. Your colleagues say, "We had the wrong idea here. Go back and do a second draft incorporating those notes." And then it gets to what's called the table, which is where another draft is done, where the revisions are made out loud.

FROUG: This is a rehearsal?

BRYAN: No. This is again just among the writers. Another draft, called the table draft, is made. It's based on the second draft, and improvements and deletions and things are made out loud. All the writers on the show are present, including the writer who wrote the episode, and the executive is making the decisions about what to do.

FROUG: The show runner?

BRYAN: Yeah. On some shows that rewriting is done behind closed doors. The executive producer and any other person that they designate, whether it be a script doctor who's a friend of theirs or another member of the staff, is off rewriting in private. I prefer not to work on a show where it's done this way.

FROUG: That undermines the staff, doesn't it?

BRYAN: Yeah, it does. It's a tough blow, I think, for the person who wrote the original draft. That's how it always is, by the way, in the motion-picture business. I don't want to have much to do with it anymore. Even if you write a picture that's a big success and your name is on it as a writer, you will have been rewritten when you're not there.

FROUG: That doesn't happen in TV comedy? It certainly happened in TV drama when I was doing it.

BRYAN: It can also happen in comedy. For instance, you asked if I was free to leave "Night Court," how that all went about. One of the reasons that I kind of insisted upon it was because the new system that came into place in between seasons did involve some of that style of work, and I didn't care for it.

FROUG: I don't blame you. Now to the new writer who's considering writing a spec script for movies, and is hearing the trepidation and indeed the pounding you took, is television a better route to go in your opinion?

BRYAN: Absolutely. Without question. If you have what it takes, and one of the things that it takes is a really strong constitution, I think TV is a wonderful place to learn. Even if I were going to go back into the motion-picture business tomorrow and never work in television again, I'd really value what I've absorbed, structure-wise and especially performance-wise. Because, like it or not, it's all about actors up there in front of the camera.

FROUG: When you're there taping, you get to observe, I guess?

BRYAN: Well, not just taping. Sitcoms are revised continuously for a week. Your typical production begins Monday morning with what's called a table reading, not to be confused with the table draft. The table reading is the actors sitting around a table with the writers, on stage, reading the script out loud. You get some feel for what works and what doesn't work, just based on that, and you spend the rest of the day rewriting. The following day you see the first of what are called run-throughs. Rehearsals. Generally the actors are not what's called off-book, in other words they haven't memorized the script at that point. They're walking around with the script in their hands. Again you're getting the feeling of what's going to work and not going to work. Typically that's on Tuesday afternoon. Tuesday night is the big rewrite. You go back to the writers' room and everything that didn't work, or didn't work as well as you'd hoped, you're fixing, and you're also cutting for time.

FROUG: Do you have a lot of input from the actors?

BRYAN: It varies. Some offer more than others, and some have their input responded to more than others, according to how useful it is and to the principles first articulated by Mr. Darwin. Responding takes two forms: saying "Okay, I'll try to fix it," and saying "No."

FROUG: If you say "I got your idea, but no thanks, it doesn't work," is that a problem with the actors?

BRYAN: Depends on the actor and on how you say it.

FROUG: If the star says no, it doesn't work—that carries more weight than the second banana, yes?

BRYAN: Absolutely. And oftentimes actors say things that are correct. So you have to be a big enough person to recognize that. But if they're not correct, or if they may be technically correct but are not seeing the big picture, or there's some other reason why you can't make the change, you have to be able to sell it to them. And if you can't sell it to them or scare them you have to persuade them to do it your way, anyway.

FROUG: Many of the interviews for this book are unearthing these astronomical fees that screenwriters are making. Anywhere from new writers who are getting from three hundred thousand to five hundred thousand a screenplay and up. Joe Eszterhas just got three million for a screenplay. What kind of a financial lure does television have to offer?

BRYAN: More. Joe Eszterhas is a small player in the television scheme of things. He's the biggest guy in the movies, right? But his counterparts in television, the Jim Brookses of the world, could buy and sell him.

FROUG: Really? What kind of money is that?

BRYAN: Tens of millions of dollars.

FROUG: Tens of millions. I know Gary Goldberg sold "Family Ties" for something astronomical.

BRYAN: Right. That's the big payoff, when you've created a show.

FROUG: And it lasts for years.

BRYAN: It only comes when you've had the wisdom and the guts and the financial position to take a large part of your money on the back end. The guy who created "Night Court" did the same thing, and he's made in excess of fifty million, as I understand.

FROUG: Where do you stand now on your climb?

BRYAN: Where do I stand? Somehow it was easier to say what I made than what I'm making. Rather than say where I stand, I'll give you a typical profile of what someone might expect to make.

FROUG: Okay, give me a profile of Mr. or Ms. X.

BRYAN: If you're very fortunate and you get into an established show right off the bat, a quarter of a million a year is not too much to expect by any means for a staff position. You will be stuck at or around that figure, with modest increases, for the term of your original deal, generally two years. If you have done well off of that, you can expect to approximately double it.

FROUG: Half a million a year, if you reach the producer-writer status?

BRYAN: Yeah. On a good show, and again, you'll be at that basic level for the term of that deal, two or three years, at which point you can again expect to double.

FROUG: You go to a million dollars a year? Writing television?

BRYAN: Yeah. Because if you are moving up the line, the presumption is that at some point you're going to get the opportunity to run a show. Whether you have actually run one or you've gotten close enough to the top—the supervising-producer level—you are perceived as somebody who's likely to be able to run that show or another show. That's when the million-dollar-and-up money becomes available. And then, beyond that, for the people who have created shows or, in extraordinary cases, people who are associated on a high level with a really big show like "Murphy Brown," you can be getting some really high figures, getting up into the two, three, four, five million dollars.

FROUG: Incredible.

BRYAN: I keep hearing this year that's all going to tighten up.

FROUG: That's what CAA says, that the numbers are going to come down. Do you think that's true?

BRYAN: God, I hope not.

FROUG: What is your next move?

BRYAN: Well, I don't know. We're speaking in the middle of April 1991, when I think more television people are saying, "I don't know," than at any other time of the year.

FROUG: Do you know whether your show's been picked up?

BRYAN: No. Only the people who are returning to major hit shows know for sure. I could end up staying with "Anything But Love." It would be tremendously gratifying to me if it were renewed because I think we did great work last year. But I don't really know if it will be. It could go either way. I could go to a show that's been on for a number of years, but the ones that appeal to me have very few staff positions open. The other possibility is to run my own show.

FROUG: Do you have something in the fire for that?

BRYAN: Yeah. I'm developing a pilot.

FROUG: You'd have a piece of the action? So here's your chance to become Gary Goldberg or Norman Lear, yes?

BRYAN: Well, not exactly. I was not in a position to demand a big piece this time around, and I didn't because I didn't figure this was going to be the deal where I made the next "Night Court" or the next "Family Ties" or something. It happens, I guess, that people unwittingly create hit shows. So I'm creating a show now that, if it does take off, while I certainly won't be poor, I won't make Gary Goldberg or Norman Lear kind of money.

FROUG: You won't make a hundred million dollars? This is a long-shot business. You're getting a new show going, and it depends on whether the actor clicks with an audience, which you don't really know, and whether the time slot is good, and whether the network stands behind it. You just don't know those things, do you?

BRYAN: It's the ultimate long-shot business. I couldn't tolerate it as a guy with a young family, except that the studio guarantees and protects you to a certain, quite comfortable point. Fundamentally, everybody who has any demonstrated ability to do television comedy has a deal somewhere, which is called an overall deal.

FROUG: I know you've suffered long and hard at different times from writer's block. Tell me about it.

BRYAN: Well, first of all, the definition of writer's block is fear, basically. Fear of failure, fear that what you're doing is worthless, that you shouldn't be doing it. I have dealt with my fear by confronting it with a bigger fear, the fear of not finishing the job I was assigned to do and not getting paid.

FROUG: Going broke.

BRYAN: Yeah. I think an awful lot of people do that. Even some people who write on spec are operating with that drive. If I could offer a word of advice, I think it's a mode of operation to be avoided at all costs. It takes a high personal toll. It's a perfectly tidy and even amusing thing to say, "Well, I confronted my fear with a bigger fear and it went away." It keeps the money coming in, to be sure, but, I don't know.

FROUG: What do you mean, "It keeps the money coming in," the bigger fear?

BRYAN: Whatever gets you to keep working keeps the money coming in. If you're not producing, fear of not having a script ready to shoot next week, you know. That's why I thought television would be a better place for me. Because of the weekly deadline. But I don't know, maybe there are people somewhere who happily function under deadlines. I tend to think not. It seems to me that if you have yourself organized to be able to function only under a deadline, that means you are only able to function with fear. And fear just is not a good thing to carry around with you all the time. In television, I feel like I essentially get things done out of fear of not getting them done. This hasn't hurt anybody but me. I wrote four and a half "Night Court" episodes in a short period of time. I wrote three "Anything But Love" episodes on schedule. My reputation in television is as a guy who delivers. But . . .

FROUG: You beat yourself up in the process?

BRYAN: Yeah. It's not a lot of fun.

FROUG: Jack Epps said something that I felt was succinctly put and quite accurate. He said, "It's a very punishing business."

BRYAN: There are all kinds of punishments. I know people who don't have the writing problems that I do, who, nevertheless, are equally beaten up by other aspects of the business. By the inability to control the end results of our work.

FROUG: But in television you feel you have more control?

BRYAN: Much more. And in the case of the kind of stuff that I do, I just plain prefer television. There's by far more good TV comedy done in a year than good film comedy. The best films in both drama and comedy—the Oscar stuff and some of the great foreign films—will transcend what's done in television. But in terms of having what I would call consistent, reliable entertainment, give me any episode of "Cheers" over the latest Chevy Chase movie. It's just flat-out better.

Laurence Dworet

BLACK SCREEN. FADE UP CHATTER:

YOUNG MAN (V.O.)
Thirty-eight million from Midland Bank to Chase...

FADE INTO the harried YOUNG MAN speaking on the phone as he checks his
COMPUTER SCREEN, filled with numbers and bank names.

YOUNG MAN (CONT'D)
... key code 6523786.

TRACK PAST HIM AND DOZENS OF OTHER WORKERS busily working phones and
computers. The chatter's the same: dollars - by the tens and hundreds of millions - moving
electronically from one bank to another.

HOLD ON LEWIN, a short, hot-tempered, emaciated man in his late 50's, talking into the
phone as he angrily punches the keys:

LEWIN
Sure I got it! Sixteen point eight from B of A to Citi.
You don't need my name, just the number: 6523801.
Three point five from Security Pacific to First
Interstate?
(the computer screen scrambles)
Nope, too late. The computer's down til morning.
That's right, buddy, the first Thursday of every month.

He hangs up, exhausted, and lights a cigarette. His eyes are pale, faded, the look of someone
with a terminal disease.

OPEN WIDE TO REVEAL THE ENORMOUS MAIN COMMUNICATIONS ROOM OF
THE BANK, the HUNDRED OR SO WORKERS straightening out their cubicles, getting
ready to leave.

ON LEWIN - crossing toward the SECURITY GUARD sitting in front of the glassed-in
MAIN COMPUTER ROOM. Lewin drags his left leg, his face set, not about to admit the
pain.

LEWIN
I wanna check some numbers on a Chase Transfer.

FED GUARD #1
I hear you got cancer, Lew. I'm sorry.

LEWIN
(signing the logbook)
I'm not dyin'! What the hell do doctors know?

The Guard, ill at ease, quickly buzzes him into the

COMPUTER ROOM

"Gratification in Hollywood takes a long, long time."

One of the exciting aspects of teaching graduate film and TV writing at the University of California at Los Angeles was working with students who came from all walks of life. None was more unique, however, than Laury Dworet, an emergency-room physician determined to build a parallel career as a screenwriter in Hollywood. I've encountered several lawyers, many professionals in various fields, and one fireman, but Laury was my first doctor.

The immediate thing one recognizes in Laury is his high level of intelligence, intensity, and his deep concentration. During our several quarters together I learned nothing what-soever about his life as a doctor. I don't recall it ever being mentioned. Though once he confided to me that he financed his way through film school with one night a week in the emergency room.

When our second quarter together was over, he handed me a complete and thoroughly polished screenplay titled *Code Blue*. It was all there. The drama, the intensity, the high stakes, the dedication, and, yes, the stamina of the men and women who devote their lives to saving the lives of strangers. It takes a very special kind of dedication to endure and even succeed in that constant life-and-death environment. It surely isn't for the faint of heart.

One reading of *Code Blue* told me this doctor was one hell of a screenwriter. And it was all his—he neither asked for nor did I give him much input. This screenplay could only have been written by a person who lived the experience.

Code Blue went on to win the much-prized Samuel Goldwyn Award, given each year at UCLA to the student writer of the best screenplay.

In spite of all I know about Hollywood after living and working in the "Business," I nonetheless foolishly assumed Laury Dworet was off and running toward a dazzling career as a screenwriter. I had forgotten how really tough it is to get into our industry, no matter how much talent you have. The only "overnight" successes I know about firsthand are years in the making. Dr. Dworet is no exception to this harsh truth. First you take your lumps, and just when you think you can't take another, you get some more. If you can still hold on to your dreams after years of obstacles and punishment, you have a real chance of achieving your goal. Laury is another example of a screenwriter who possesses the three key ingredients screenwriters must have if they are to take on the challenge of making it in the big leagues: passion, patience, and persistence. If you are determined enough, you won't settle for less, and you won't get less. As a screenwriter (in both your screenplays and your life), nothing makes for success better than an obsessed character for a protagonist. Laury Dworet is a splendid example of the man who already has a lifetime of achievements to attest to the power of will and determination (and he is only forty years of age). Show me a "nothing will stand in my way" protagonist in your screenplay and I will assure you that half the battle is already won. Read the saga of Dr. Laurence Dworet and you will meet a man who knows this lesson well.

FROUG: First, I want to ask you the obvious question: Why does an emergency room physician become a screenwriter? What is the drive that pulls you away from surgery and your medical career into screenwriting?

DWORET: Well, medicine is a good career, but when I was about sixteen years old, I decided, for some reason that I'm not one-hundred percent sure of, that I was going to be a film director. I used to play hookey from school and watch movies. I would fake my illness. I used to take the thermometer, put it to the light bulb, and my mother thought I had a 104-degree fever. [*Laughter*] I'd stay home all day and watch movies. I was always fascinated by movies. Even then I was interested in how pictures were set up. I mean, how a shot was composed. I always was interested in that. I come from a family of artists—my mother, my uncle, my aunt.

FROUG: Where was this?

DWORET: In Newton, Massachusetts. Somehow I was never an artist, yet I was always interested in the visual aspects of things. I grew up quite independent. My parents divorced when I was young, and I was basically on my own since I was nine or ten. I was living in the back of our small house, and I used to sneak out to play cards all night long. Poker, for big stakes. I was a pretty good gambler. I would have to hire older kids as my protection so I could take my winnings home with me. Actually, I'm going to make a movie about some of this.

FROUG: It's a good story.

DWORET: It is a good movie. I was very involved in school. And I played in a band. I was a musician.

FROUG: What did you play?

DWORET: Drums. I played in orchestras, in jazz and rock bands. I started playing professionally when I was about nine or ten. With a couple of other friends, we'd play bar mitzvahs. And we'd play all these clubs. We were doing it very actively. I thought about becoming a professional musician at one time. In high school I became addicted to playing bridge. So, instead of going to high school, I'd play tournament bridge all the time. I'd play high stakes bridge for money. I remember one game, I was playing in Boston right before I went to college, and I literally almost lost my scholarship in one hand. This guy, one of the biggest landowners in Boston, was assigned to me as a partner. Here I am, an impoverished about-to-be college student with my scholarship on the line, playing with one of the wealthiest guys in Boston, and he blew the hand. I just saw my life fading away. [*Laughter*] Anyway, somehow between the bridge and the music, I decided to become a film director. I was going to the University of Chicago and didn't really have a major. It was my first year, and as soon as I got there I applied to transfer to film school. I was going to get a scholarship at UCLA, but they said, "We won't give you money to make movies. You have to come up with it yourself." And my parents were dirt poor. My father went bankrupt a number of times, and my mother didn't have an income. I was on a full scholarship at Chicago.

FROUG: You must have been very bright to get a scholarship.

DWORET: Well, I think a lot of it's need, to be honest. They're a wealthy school. I did okay academically. I loved it at Chicago. I was able (since I wasn't planning on staying) to take any courses I wanted. I took a lot of courses in art—art history, things like that. Then I found out that I didn't really have the money to go to film school. Or maybe it was a lack of nerve. So here I was going to undertake not just a career that I didn't know much about—film—I only knew that I wanted to do it, and I'd never been further west than Chicago. I was now going to go to Los Angeles without any money. I decided I better think about this. I had to figure out a better way to make movies, which was still my ambition.

FROUG: Becoming a doctor was a way to a career in film?

DWORET: Exactly. I decided to stay at Chicago and find another way to make a living so that I could become a film director. I decided I would become a doctor. My father always told me, "Be a doctor, be a doctor." It was like this endless Jewish litany. [*Laughter*] "Be a doctor." My father was a salesman, a very bright guy—he'd been to Harvard and a number of other schools. He went off on his own to start all these businesses that eventually went bankrupt. Anyway, to make a long story short, I decided I would go to medical school and then go to film school. This was a rash decision, based on not so much my father's advice but just, "Gee, that will give me the money to make movies." And I wasn't sure how it was going to give me the money to make movies, but I felt I'd figure this out as I went along. I hadn't had any science courses at all in high school. This was a major impediment. [*Laughter*] So I decided to take all the science courses and still be an art-history major. I did well in college. Loved it. Took all the science courses, the physics, organic chemistry. And then got into a lot of really top medical schools. And I chose the University of California at San Francisco.

FROUG: One of the best medical schools in the country. You must have had an incredible record.

DWORET: Yeah, I did have a really good record. Chicago was very intellectually challenging. I mean, it was so cold that you always studied. And there was a lot of competition and I'm very competitive, whether it's playing bridge, music, anything in my life. College was actually easier than high school in some sense. My high school was unusual. Every one of my teachers was trained at Harvard. When I was in the fourth grade, Pete Seeger was my music teacher one day. In retrospect it was great. At the time it was like, "Who's this weird guy? [*Laughter*] Why do I have to listen to this when I could be out running around?" I didn't appreciate it.

FROUG: How old were you when you entered medical school?

DWORET: I must have been twenty-one. I was still fascinated by film. And I would still read film books. I remember, in the sixties I couldn't buy enough film books or see enough movies. This was before medical school, but even in medical school it was the same thing. I'd be reading books on film, studying film, going to movies, thinking about film a lot. I remember my first day in anatomy—I told them that at Chicago we never really had to memorize things, it was all based on principles, even chemistry. Organic chemistry's the killer course, because you have to memorize a lot. But in Chicago it was always the theoretical aspect of things, so you didn't have to just memorize. And when we came to anatomy, I said to the dean (I was really naive or arrogant or whatever), "I'm not memorizing all this stuff. [*Laughter*] I just don't believe in it, you know." He said, "Well, you've got your ticket out of here fast." I was also on scholarship to medical school, and I said, "I'm going to film school as soon as I get out of here." [*Laughter*] He wasn't pleased about that. But I knew I was gonna get out. And I'd never liked the sight of blood. Couldn't stand the sight of blood.

FROUG: Kind of an impediment to being a medical student.

DWORET: It was. I remember when we were playing bridge when I was eleven or twelve and the brother of one of my friends came in with a cut head. All the men just about fainted, but my sister just handled it immediately. She was born to be a doctor. She's a pediatrician. And my brother's a doctor, too, an anesthesiologist.

FROUG: So, at this point you've gone off to medical school in San Francisco.

DWORET: I went to San Francisco, and I took a screenwriting course when I was there. It was taught by a documentary filmmaker who said, "Put in every shot." It was the craziest and worst experience of my life. He turned out to be completely nuts. He did teach us a little bit about film, but he said you have to describe every shot—extreme closeup, cut to, moderate closeup, whatever. And so I wrote this script that must have had three hundred pages, mostly shot directions. The script was about a woman doctor, and there was a pretty good story in there. I decided I would get a Hollywood agent to sell it while I was in San Francisco. But I couldn't get an agent. Nobody would take my calls. So I used a friend's office and said, "I'm doctor . . ." (I wasn't a doctor at the time, I was a medical student.) I got the whole list of agents from the Writers Guild. I started calling these agents and I told them I was this doctor. I would call one after another after another. Many of them thought I was their own doctor calling. [*Laughter*] One of them I remember said, "Doctor, doctor, thank God you called. I'm about to kill myself. I've been calling you for hours and hours. What should I do?" This really happened; here I was in medical school in San Francisco, and he thought I was his psychiatrist. [*Laughter*]

FROUG: Funny story. You gotta write this. This is a movie.

DWORET: Yeah, I know. And eventually it reached the point where, to get to some of the real top agents, I basically had to say I'm coming down to deliver a lecture in Los Angeles, you know, I'm a prize-winning doctor about to get the Nobel Prize. [*Laughter*]

FROUG: Were you saying that?

DWORET: That's what I was saying to these agents. You had to impress them. It was like you had to be the president of the United States to get to Mike Ovitz. The story grew and grew: I was coming down, and I had literally a few hours in Los Angeles to meet with them, but no more than that, and I would send them the script. So they all read the script. Most of them didn't like it. Most of them couldn't find the story in the shot directions. But I did meet a number of the agents. It was quite an experience. At that point—it must have been around '73, '74—buckskin was in. [*Laughter*] The agents were all wearing buckskin. And they're looking at me like I'm some freak because I'm not wearing buckskin. [*Laughter*] That was my first experience in Hollywood. I didn't have buckskin, and wearing buckskin was more important than what was on the page.

FROUG: That's a funny experience.

DWORET: Anyway, that was it. I finished school. And then, when I moved down here, I decided that I actually enjoyed medicine. But I knew I was going to write. I was getting ideas for screenplays in medical school, yet I was more interested in directing. I never was really interested in writing. I'd written well when I was a kid. I remember being in the fifth and sixth grades and writing stories that were always read aloud by the teacher. Maybe writing was an extension of being a lonely kid. I was younger than my classmates because I'd skipped a grade, which was a major mistake. And so, emotionally and physically, I wasn't the peer of these kids.

FROUG: Let's go back to when you graduated from medical school in San Francisco.

DWORET: Graduated medical school, did an internship.

FROUG: Where'd you do the internship?

DWORET: In Oakland, a county hospital. Blood and guts and excitement every minute.

FROUG: That's what steered you toward emergency room medicine?

DWORET: Emergency-room medicine because emergency medicine then was coming into its birth. There never had been emergency-room doctors, really, who were special- ists. Here was this opportune moment where I could work a couple of days a week and write, or do whatever else I wanted. After a year of that, I joined a partnership that would take me all over the state or, if I wanted, anywhere in the country to do emergency medicine for a day at a time. This is an idea I've been trying to sell as a TV series. It would be a great TV series, traveling around the country, each week in a different town.

FROUG: I once did a presentation many years ago on an emergency-room surgeon, strangely enough, who was operating out of southern France. Jim Moser and I did it. We never could sell it.

DWORET: Yeah. It's one of the things that's just expensive for them. It was like "Route 66" and "The Fugitive." Changing locations is expensive. They're worried about it. And I can understand that. Still, it's a wonderful idea.

FROUG: At what point did you apply to UCLA?

DWORET: In 1977 I applied to film school at UCLA and USC and got into UCLA. That's when I came here. My partnership had hospitals in Los Angeles; I could practice medicine. I was all set up. I could work at night and go to film school during the day.

FROUG: It sounds like a tough schedule.

DWORET: It was. It was really pretty brutal, working all those nights and going to film school and trying to make movies. I still bump into ex-film students at UCLA who remember me because I was the only one who could pick up the tab for lunch. [*Laughter*] When I made a student film, I paid my actors because I just felt too guilty not to. And also I wanted them to show up, and I knew that they'd be there if I paid them. So I was at film school, and I took a number of writing courses. I became more interested in writing because I felt that you have to understand writing to really understand storytelling in film. It wasn't just what to do with the camera. I'd always been good with the camera. When I was in medical school, I developed a tremendous interest in still photography. Did all my own work. I would stay up nights when I wasn't working, just doing still photography. And I thought about being a still photographer. Commercially, you know, doing that as a career, along with medicine. But I still wanted to be a filmmaker. I'm obsessive in a certain way. Good emergency doctors are obsessive-compulsive. You have to be. You can't forget little things. You have to be complete. Forget one little thing and the patient dies. For years I focused on filmmaking. And I haven't lost sight of that goal yet. Directing films.

FROUG: You wrote a script at UCLA that was extraordinary, *Code Blue.*

DWORET: The one that won the Goldwyn Award.

FROUG: I gotta tell you I still think it's one of the best student scripts I have ever read.

DWORET: I appreciate that.

FROUG: What happened to that script? I thought that was a sure winner. Usually agents rush to get Samuel Goldwyn Award screenplays. This one was fresh, new territory—emergency room medicine. You were exploring the practice of franchising emergency rooms. You had a very fresh kind of a melodrama there.

DWORET: I got an agent relatively quickly on that, but I can't mention his name, because of what happened. He thought he could sell it very, very quickly for big, big bucks. He was so excited about it that he thought there would be a script auction. It was about the time that *Romancing the Stone* had been sold by Diane Thomas, and he was going to set it all up. And then, with all this excitement, he called me one day and said, "Listen. This is such a good script, I want you to pay me an extra five percent. I want fifteen percent."

FROUG: It's against the law, you know.

DWORET: I didn't know it was against the law. My wife hadn't been to law school yet, but I knew that I wasn't going to stomach it. I just told him, "I don't care how much money you're gonna make on the script. You're gone." I fired him instantly. [*Laughing*] My friends weren't sure I was right, but I knew I was right. I didn't go to medical school to curry favor with executives or agents or whatever. Fortunately, I can say "fuck you" to people, which is not always good because one can be too arrogant with that. But I have my own sense of integrity. I have to preserve that, which is difficult in Hollywood. It's a really tough battle. Continuously. And I wasn't going to lose the first battle, so I fired him. Then it was hard to get other agents. There was a lot of interest in the script, but nothing ever panned out. I don't know why. There's still interest in it now. I still have producers who are trying to sell it. James Egan is still trying to sell it. Actually, we just had a meeting about it yesterday. They were interested at Roger Corman's company.

FROUG: It should be an absolute winner. It's a wonderful script.

DWORET: Yeah. It's an exciting script. And now I'm thinking of taking some of the most exciting parts of it and putting it into a new, different kind of movie. Writers, I think, if they don't have something that sells, can borrow from another of their own scripts. But there are certain aspects of that script that are so wonderful I'd want to keep them.

FROUG: What did you do during this time that *Code Blue* was floating around and not getting the sale we all expected it would?

DWORET: I got together with a friend of mine, Bob Pool, a fellow student at UCLA. Bob and I met in a directing class with Delia Salvi, a course on directing the actor. A wonderful course.

FROUG: Delia is marvelous.

DWORET: I still study with Delia. Directing and acting. It's been so integral. When I go to her classes and see what actors have to do in a scene, it excites me about my writing. It reminds me that the process is the same—what's the actor's objective? How does he get what he wants? Why does he want it? When I do a scene now, I try to act every role. I've taken acting classes with her, and it's been a very important experience in getting inside the character. We met in this class, Bob and I, and I'd wanted to write a nuclear thriller. And he'd written a nuclear thriller, but it wasn't right. About a bomb in a plane. I said, "No, let's do it where there's gonna be a bomb in a city, and you have two days to find it. And together we decided to focus on a guy who's at a crisis in his own life, so the search for the bomb becomes in some way symbolic for his search for his own inner peace, his search for resolutions to the problems in his life regarding his marriage and his mistress and whatever. A man who's not sure where his career is gonna go, who's about forty, and he's just not sure what direction he wants to take his life." So we decided to write this together. At the same time, *The Fifth Horseman* had just come out.

FROUG: Did you read *The Fifth Horseman?*

DWORET: We hadn't read it, but we'd heard about it. We called Craig Baumgarten, and we were full of chutzpah. We were convinced that we should be the ones to write this major book. So I called up Barry Diller's office, and Craig Baumgarten, his vice president, called me back (this is 1981). Baumgarten said, "Listen, you know, people don't call Barry Diller, Doctor." I had used the name doctor because I wasn't getting any response. Laurence Dworet wouldn't get a response. He said, "I don't want you to appear weird. I mean, I don't want people to think you're insane. But people who are normal don't call Barry Diller and try to get work. The only reason I'm calling you is because you're a doctor, and I know that you don't know what you're doing . . ." [*Laughter*]

FROUG: That's wonderful.

DWORET: Yeah. I said, "We wanna write this movie script." And he just said, "You're not famous enough to write this movie script, and next week we're announcing a very famous writer to adapt the book and a very famous director, and it's all going forward. And don't call us again." Anyway, they never made their movie. It never even was announced. It never was written. Who knows what happened to it. Meanwhile, we went ahead and wrote what became a cult script in Hollywood. It's a very exciting script.

FROUG: What's it called?

DWORET: It was called *The Second Reckoning*. Eventually it became *The Ultimatum*, and it was sold in 1990. The same script we'd written in 1981, essentially. The 1981 draft was terrifying. I remember one producer who read it and said, "I had to have the cab driver keep the light on even though he wanted me to turn it off; it was so exciting." It was a real page-turner. Five years later we had to revise it, so I reread it and was scared stiff. It was that frightening. It came out of a real terror of nuclear bombs. A number of people were interested in it—Walter Mirisch tried to figure out how much it would cost to make. But the studios were too scared to deal with the issue of a terrorist nuclear bomb. They thought we would give the idea to Khadafi, as if he hadn't thought of it. It was amazing. They just didn't want to get into an issue that's so controversial. So we put it aside.

    Code Blue got us our first job—there was a producer named Pierre David, who wanted to do a story about medicine. His father was a famous cardiologist, and Pierre was the only one in his family who had gone into the movie business, which his father thought was insane.

FROUG: Well, it is insane.

DWORET: It is, of course, and his father was right. His father had had a turbulent career, checkered with a lot of unhappiness, but, eventually, he became a major force in cardiology in Montreal. Pierre never really said this, but it was obvious to me that he wanted to do a film that would justify in his father's mind that he was right to become a filmmaker. And a film that would pay homage to his father. He said, "I want you to write a script about a doctor who wakes up when he's forty and figures, 'I've fucked up my life and wasted it.'" That wasn't much to go on. But it was enough to spark an idea that I had about writing about professionals who were burned out, specifically, doctors who were burned out. I didn't want to get typecast as just a writer of medical shows. I avoided it, particularly after *Code Blue*. But here was a story that really interested me. In all the doctors I knew, even when I was around thirty, you could see the burnout. You could see the stress in their lives, the professional stress. It's very interesting to me, and I wanted to set it in another context, give it a bigger scope. So I spoke to some of my doctor friends, and we decided to take it into the realm of fraud in medical research. A particular doctor who's not evil, but who was our antagonist, was intent on winning the Nobel Prize in a race against other doctors, a race to discover a cure for heart disease. The drug that he had invented literally would prevent heart disease from ever developing. And he would fake his lab tests to get the drug approved in order to beat everyone else. This became *The Practice*. We centered the study on two doctors who were friends as well as partners, and one of them had gone wrong, taken the wrong course. He was a researcher who had participated in the scheme of this villain to alter the research. The drug would prevent heart disease, but on the other hand there was a cost you had to pay; there were terrible side effects which were covered up.

We found a wonderful hook into the story: these two guys were almost like brothers, and one of them had taken the wrong step, and the other was burned out as well. Basically, the protagonist became the other doctor who was trying to get a grip on his life. Salvage his life, salvage his integrity. Was he going to stand by when he knew the results? And if he didn't go along with it, his friend, his partner, was going to be destroyed. That became *The Practice*. We sold it and it was going to go ahead at Columbia. They were just about to make it in '84. Ted Danson was going to star in it, but got delayed a week on Blake Edward's *A Fine Mess*. Because of that, the whole movie was pushed back. They couldn't get insurance, and they were going to do it a year later. Then it fell apart. And the movie that was going to cost five point eight million dollars was canceled. They paid off on the director's contract and the producer's contract—over a million dollars—not to make the movie. We saw almost none of it.

FROUG: Did you get any money?

DWORET: Very little. It was our first real job. What you want to find in a producer is someone who has incredible tenacity, who *has* to make this movie. I felt we had that with Pierre David. He had to make this movie. You can't have a producer who wants to make thirty movies, and this is just gonna be one of them. David was driven to make this movie. He didn't give up for years. I mean, you need somebody to carry on that struggle. Unfortunately, after they paid off all that money, it made it prohibitive in turnaround. We had a chance to get it, but there was too much against it, and you're always competing with television. Medicine is an area that television thinks they own. And many studio executives say, "Oh, it's about medicine, it's television." Unless you could somehow attract major stars to the project, and we almost had Paul Newman at one point, which would have easily pushed the movie to a go status. And at the last minute, you know, Paul Newman wanted to do it, his doctor wanted him to do it, his agent, but . . . it all fell apart.

FROUG: Laury, what happened next in your career, when you're floating around with this screenplay? Does anything come of *The Practice*?

DWORET: No, *The Practice* is basically dead in the water right now.

FROUG: Because too much money has been poured into it?

DWORET: Too much money was against it, and the money's been increasing. It's not completely dead. There's a lot of controversy in the Writers Guild, the provisions aren't clear about the writer's ability to get a script back after a certain period of time. Five years is the period of time after which you're supposed to get a script back, but the terms that you're supposed to get it back at are very unclear. Nobody can agree on that. The writers take the position that we should only have to pay—to give back—what we were paid, which is minimal. The studio says, well, there's all these development costs that have to be paid. They could never agree. So, even though we were paid only sixty thousand dollars, somehow the studio felt that we had to pay half a million.

FROUG: Right. You have to pay for the director and the actors.

DWORET: Or just the other writers, and all these fees that they would attach. And by the time that this is resolved, the window of opportunity to reacquire the script essentially would be over. It's a very difficult situation. I hope that the Writers Guild is going to figure this out. Nothing is worse than writing an original piece of material and losing it forever. We're actually still trying to use our connections and producers who work through Columbia to say, "Look, you've spent all this money. You've got a great subject. Let's sell it, even for a cable movie. Try to salvage it." But this happens, at some point, to every writer who does anything original in Hollywood. So few scripts are actually made.

FROUG: In this case, you were commissioned to write a script, in effect?

DWORET: Right, we were hired to write a script based on this idea.

FROUG: Based on a one-liner.

DWORET: Yeah, a one-liner. And we were involved from the beginning. That's where I met Denise Di Novi, whom I later worked with on a number of scripts. She was working for Pierre David and Arnold Kopelson.

FROUG: She was the story editor?

DWORET: She was his development executive. She hired Bob and me to write a script based on white, teenage cocaine gangs operating out of Chicago before the Co-lombians came to power in the early eighties—how these kids would get hooked on the power and the money associated with this drug. How it would seduce them. It was called *Underground.* We were writing this script at the same time that we were doing *The Practice.* We were doing it at the same time I was also producing a movie. It was a real nightmare to juggle it all.

FROUG: What movie were you producing?

DWORET: In the early eighties, James Egan and I felt that we were sick and tired of the Hollywood system. We felt it didn't work. It was too difficult to get a movie made. After being told that we can't call Barry Diller and all the other things we couldn't do, we decided to just go out and do it. So we put together a limited partnership and made the film ourselves. It was called *In and Out.* Ellen Kesend had written the script. Ricardo Franco was the director.

FROUG: How in the midst of all this did you have time to practice medicine?

DWORET: It was hard. During weekends.

FROUG: Is that what you do now?

DWORET: I go in to the emergency room once or twice a week.

FROUG: Is this the franchise emergency room that you wrote about in *Code Blue?*

DWORET: Yeah, it's sort of like it, but ours is a democratic group of emergency-room doctors. *Code Blue* was *one* man owning all the franchises and basically screwing everyone else.

FROUG: Let's get back to this movie you and James Egan decided to make, *In and Out.*

DWORET: I put up the stake money to get this endeavor started. I took forty thousand in seed money and said, "Okay, we need to get a lawyer. We need to get accountants. We need to have a limited partnership drawn up." So we got this big law firm. We were great salesmen. We were able to convince these lawyers who'd never done this before that they should go in on the back end of the deal. [*Laughter*] That they should do all the legal work associated with this film—which we said would be modest, and, of course, turned out to be monumental—and do our partnerships and all our contracts. They should handle all our problems, and, this being our first movie, we had a lot of problems. And we convinced this huge accounting firm to go in the back end of the deal. Then we decided we'd raise the money for this script that Ellen Kesend had written for this Spanish director, Ricardo Franco.

FROUG: You gave it to me to read. I remember it wasn't very good.

DWORET: There were some problems with the script, but we were naive. The director is a wonderful guy and a close friend of mine, and more creative than anyone I've ever met. We felt that his genius would take a script that had some problems and make it into a work of art. [*Laughter*] Unfortunately, he'd never done an American comedy. And there were certain difficulties in making the film, which we eventually made in Mexico.

FROUG: Does it largely take place in Tijuana?

DWORET: Yeah, right in Tijuana. There were a lot of obstacles, a lot of problems we had to face, which was an interesting learning experience. Everything that could go wrong did go wrong, which is, I think, the way you want it when you make a first film. The only thing that was easy was raising the money. We raised four hundred, almost five hundred thousand in America, and then we got the Mexican government to be our partner.

FROUG: How did you do that?

DWORET: A real coup. A lot of that was because of Egan going down there and because the director, Franco, had won an award at Cannes when he was twenty-six. So he was very well-known. He made a film called *Pascual Duarte*, which was based on the book that later won the Nobel Prize. We got a good cinematographer—he's now one of the top cinematographers—for a thousand dollars a week. And we got some other good people. But we never solved the script problems.

FROUG: That's what I don't understand, a man of your intelligence building this empire on a weak screenplay.

DWORET: Unfortunately, I was writing two scripts for hire at the same time. Bob Pool and I even had to split up. I did a lot of the rewriting on *The Practice* while he was doing *Underground*. And at the same time Egan and I were trying to produce this movie. We were producing it, literally, in my office, doing the accounting on the computers that we had. I regret not going down to Mexico. In retrospect, it was a major mistake because maybe it would have changed the rhythm of the shooting and solved some of the script problems.

FROUG: What happened to the picture?

DWORET: The picture came out. We had wonderful music for the movie. We sold it to New World Pictures, and we eventually recouped most of our money in spite of everything. Unfortunately, the sound wasn't particularly great, and it was never one-hundred percent in sync. New World bought the movie because we happened to find a sales agent in New York, Walter Manley, who liked the film enough to sell it. He was very friendly with the people at New World Pictures, and they literally bought the movie just on their relationship with him. As soon as they gave us a check, we ran to the bank and cashed it because we knew they eventually would have to watch the movie. And when the chief executives watched the movie, they stopped it after about ten minutes and they said, "What the fuck's wrong! The movie's not even in sync. You didn't buy this, did you?" [*Laughter*] It was too late; we'd already cashed the check.

FROUG: What a couple of con men. Marvelous story.

DWORET: The movie taught us a lot—everything went wrong. We were going to make the prints in Mexico because we'd get them done cheaply there because they were our partner and they had to assume certain costs. So, this guy was cleaning the film, and he must have had to go to the bathroom awfully urgently because he put the film into the cleaning machine backwards, went to the toilet, and by the time he came out it was completely destroyed.

FROUG: A reel of film?

DWORET: A whole reel of original negative was gone. We then had to deal with our insurance company. Of course, they didn't want to pay. But our big, killer lawyers insisted. We spent tens of thousands of dollars trying to fix it, but the film was never the same. That was just one of the many problems that we faced. The film was a great learning experience. Everything went wrong that could go wrong. That's how you learn to make a movie. But we came in on budget and with a film that we liked. The music was by people like Los Lobos before they were famous. There were some wonderful elements in the movie. It's a sweet film. Didn't do much business.

FROUG: Did you get all your money back?

DWORET: We got almost all our money back, with the tax breaks, because back in the early eighties you had tax breaks to offer people. A lot of my doctor partners went in. I knew James Egan was going to be the producer, so I made sure that he raised most of the money from his friends so that he would be on the line and I wouldn't have to worry.

FROUG: How did Ellen Kesend come out?

DWORET: Ellen didn't come out particularly well because it wasn't a good movie.

FROUG: Let's go back to your screenplay, *The Second Reckoning*.

DWORET: Bob Pool and I were finishing *Underground*, and nothing happened to it. Warner Bros. brought in a writer who they were real keen on to rewrite us. He took a year instead of three months, and it was a terrible, terrible draft. The script just died. It died, to a large extent, because there was an anti-drug feeling among the studios.

FROUG: *Underground* was the white teenagers in Chicago selling cocaine?

DWORET: Right. And a teenager going underground as a

police informer, trying to break up this gang. It was an exciting movie.

FROUG: Where does it stand now?

DWORET: It went into turnaround at Warner Brothers, and we couldn't get it out. A lot of the film has been eclipsed by "Miami Vice."

FROUG: I think maybe we ought to take a second, Laury, and explain turnaround because some readers won't necessarily know the term.

DWORET: Turnaround is the time period in which the rights to a screenplay can revert to the writer or the producer or studio. The turnaround time and who holds that turnaround is agreed upon in the original contract. So you actually have a chance to reclaim your material.

FROUG: What it means, really, is get it back and sell it elsewhere.

DWORET: Right. You have to find someone who will pay the fees that were paid to you.

FROUG: Who will reimburse whatever expenses the studio had invested in it in the first place.

DWORET: Right. Which is a difficult thing, because most studios want only the freshest material and want it unencumbered by any fees.

FROUG: So that script, *The Underground*, is just sitting out there.

DWORET: Yes. Just sitting out there. There's still some interest in it, but nothing has happened.

FROUG: What are your thoughts about *Code Blue* sitting out there, *The Underground* sitting out there, *The Practice* sitting out there? Here are these major scripts, all of which are splendid, I'm sure, because I know your work.

DWORET: Well, I don't know. For whatever my makeup is, I don't really live in the past. Even though we've had a number of disasters. Even with this big sale of *The Second Reckoning*, which became *The Ultimatum*. I only think about the scripts in the future. Occasionally I'll think about scripts in the past, but there's so much pain and agony associated with those scripts that I have to move on. Otherwise I'll be paralyzed. There are too many paralyzed people in this town. And the movie business to me is a fantasy. I don't need it to make a living. That's the key.

FROUG: Thank God.

DWORET: I've only really written the scripts I've wanted to write. The stories I've wanted to tell. I've thought about writing novels. A lot of the stuff that I write really lends itself well to novels, but I've always been interested in cinema. It's that boyhood idea that I had that I was going to be a film director, which I still plan on doing. I don't really want to write novels. Films have to be seen by an audience. I want that. When they asked me how I felt about making all this money from *The Second Reckoning—The Ultimatum*—sale, I really was unfazed.

FROUG: Really. You and Bob Pool. At last you've hit a big one.

DWORET: Yes, we hit a real big one and last year at this time we were just about the hottest screenwriters in Hollywood. People said, "What does all that money mean to you?" And I said in *New York* magazine, "The money is irrelevant." It's completely irrelevant to me. I don't spend a lot of money. I don't live an ostentatious life. If I were only interested in money, I would have gone into plastic surgery, not into emergency medicine. To me it's seeing the movie made. All that work. The only validation you have as a writer is to yourself, that you've written something good that you really cared about, that you can look at it and read it and say, "This is my script. This is what I wanted to say." If your friends like it, then you're really pleased. What you dream is that an audience gets a chance to see your vision. I mean, that's why you write movies. But you have to come to grips with the reality that the chances of having a movie made are so slim. That it's so, so difficult.

Selling *The Ultimatum* script was a fluke of timing. Bob and I had stopped writing together for a number of years after I got involved with *In and Out*. Bob went off on his own and worked with a famous producer, who we will leave nameless. This producer was going to buy *The Ultimatum*. He told us, "I will attach elements to this movie that will make it impossible for any studio to turn it down. I can get Clint Eastwood on the phone in a minute, I can get Paul Newman on the phone in an hour. I'll get one of them before I go to a studio." And then he shook our hand, promised us all this money, and said, "We're gonna sell it." The very next thing he did, from what our agents later told us, was call all his studio chief friends and say, "Would you make this movie?" He didn't have any elements attached. They all said "You're out of your mind. We wouldn't touch it with a ten-foot pole." By Monday the deal was off. That's what it's like being in business with those kind of people. Unfortunately, there are a lot of them Hollywood.

FROUG: Did anybody advise you about this producer?

DWORET: Nobody had advised us about him.

FROUG: You should have called me. I would have advised you. His fans could fill the eye of a needle.

DWORET: Our agent was elated that this was going to be a big deal. People don't tell you the truth in Hollywood. They have their own secret agendas, whether it's agents, whether it's other people. It's a game. So there's such great frustration. Most people lie. There's a producer, a close friend of mine, who has to lie all the time, and she said it's just a game of lies. It's part of the business. You continually have to lie to get from first base to second base to third base, and maybe then the lie will become the truth or some semblance of the truth—i.e., the movie you wanted to make.

FROUG: What did you do next?

DWORET: I wrote a couple of scripts with Denise Di Novi. I've written with a lot of partners, three or four different partners, and I write on my own.

FROUG: You don't have a regular partner?

DWORET: No. Not anymore. I used to, because writing in partnership is interesting. Maybe we should talk about it.

FROUG: Yes.

DWORET: Some writers see themselves as writers from when they're very young—they're going to be writers. Some people can sit in a room and write. I think if I were writing novels, if I knew they were going to be published, I could sit there and just do it on my own, with my vision. That's not what happens in the movie business. More often than not, it's an uphill struggle, and the goal is never attained. It becomes very dispiriting to write movie scripts. You spend your life alone in a room, writing and writing, and there's very little chance they're going to be made. Somehow I saw myself as a director, as somebody visual. I wanted to be on the set. When I'm writing, I want somebody in the room to bounce ideas off of. I want to have some fun. Writing with a writing partner is having some fun and easing a painful experience. The pain is not the writing. The pain is what happens afterwards—the selling of it. So no matter what happens, I had a good time. I remember how one of my surgery teachers would always say, "You can easily look at one symptom and go down the primrose path," and you completely ignore the main problem. Having a writing partner, I often see things when I'm bouncing an idea off of them. So I can avoid the primrose path. Having a writing partner has a lot of pluses and certain disadvantages. It's not ever just your vision, which is why I have to write on my own now as well. It's trying to synthesize a vision, sometimes it's a difficult combination. You have to have a writing partner you can work with. It's like looking for a partner in a marriage. You're looking for the opposite, almost. Bob and I just happened to get along really well. We're opposites. He's a very low-key, easygoing Texan. I'm a very, you know, not high-strung, but certainly intense guy from the Northeast. I have a relatively dark view of life from the upbringing I had. He comes from a wonder-

ful childhood and has a very positive view. So between us
we can find a middle ground. We both like action. We
both like excitement. And we both have a lot of interests.
So, when we meet, we often spend more time talking
about world events and sports and things like that. It was
fun to get together. Even when we were writing the
nuclear script, we would spend most of our time in the
cafeteria. We'd go to this one particular restaurant where
we wrote most of the script, just talking about life and
sports, and do almost no writing. [*Laughter*] And a great
script resulted. And with Denise, also. It was a matter of
having a woman—I wanted to write with a woman. I
wanted to see what a woman would bring to a writing
relationship. It brings a whole different chemistry. Now
I'm writing with some other people. I'm also writing with
David Assael. We're writing a fantasy-action movie. My
only experience in TV was writing a show with him.

FROUG: How do you have all these scripts going with all
these different people at the same time?

DWORET: I don't. It's one at a time. I'll do one script with
David, and Bob and I will do another script.

FROUG: How long does it take you?

DWORET: It takes us about twelve or fourteen weeks after
we have the story. A typical example would be David and
I. Last August, David had an idea for a story that I liked.
We started writing notes once a week, a couple hours a
week. We started to flesh out the story. And now, eight
months later, we just finished the story, which we can
write in about twelve weeks. You've got to be juggling a
lot of balls at one time in Hollywood. Except, once you
actually get a job, once you decide to write, that becomes
all-intensive. Whenever that time comes, I do only that,
whether I'm writing my own script or not. Nothing else
comes in. But when you're in the story-structure phase,
there's a limit as to how many hours in a day you can
work productively until you get diminishing returns. I
found that for me it's about two hours. Two hours of

really intense work in the story and I'm done.

FROUG: But then who goes and writes the screenplay after you work out that story?

DWORET: We do it together.

FROUG: You sit in a room?

DWORET: The method is actually different for each person. David Assael and I sit in a room and write together. David's used to that. He's written with a number of partners. He's been a writer for sixteen years. Bob Pool and I don't do that. I'm more of an introverted person, and I like to fantasize on my own when I write. It has to be my own world. I'm inhibited by other people being in the room. I need to close my eyes. I need to write just whatever it is, to get into the characters. To fully feel the characters I can't have people watching me. I can't really be an actor on the stage in front of other people, particularly people that know me. Bob and I would know the story and the scenes, we would know the attitudes of the characters, we would basically discuss the characters so we both had a feeling for who they were. I'd write twelve pages; Bob would do the next twelve pages. We'd look at them, maybe make a few corrections, then go forward. And then, after we're all done, we would keep rejuggling. That way the script would move forward.

You can't work the same way with everyone. I once tried it with Denise where she wrote the first act and I wrote the second act. That was impossible. I didn't know enough about who the characters were, starting on page thirty, to know where to really go with them. I had to have an earlier feeling for who the characters were. Working in a partnership requires not just the right chemistry, but patience to see how you could really work with that person. Some people you can't really work with. And you have to decide if it's not working out for the best.

FROUG: When you're laying out your story, do you think in first, second, third acts?

DWORET: Yes, I do.

FROUG: Do you have in your mind a paradigm—that at the end of twenty, twenty-five pages, there's a major turn in the story?

DWORET: Usually. Though sometimes, unfortunately, it comes out a little bit longer than that. But I look for surprises in movies. Films have to be filled with surprises, reversals, character changes, story changes. Otherwise I get bored too easily. If a movie has anything I've ever seen before, it has to be thrown out. I look for subjects that have never been written about.

FROUG: Basically, if you're bored, you assume the audience is bored.

DWORET: Absolutely. And that's a little bit tricky with a partner. The partner may not be bored. You're bored, and it's a marriage, so you have to conciliate egos. You always have to be very positive in dealing with a partner. Yet, at times, you have to be blunt in terms of, "Look, this isn't good enough." And the partner may say, "Well, it's good enough. I like it." There's always a little bit of give and take, back and forth, and you have to be able to compromise.

FROUG: When you're working together, do you have about a hundred-twenty-page limit on a screenplay? What's your first draft?

DWORET: God, I had a script that went two hundred fifteen pages, a rough draft. I just ripped it off to see what would happen. That was to find out what the story was about. Typically, if it's a dramatic film, we'll run about a hundred forty pages on a draft. When we're making our step outline, we tend to end up with too many scenes (this is a problem I'm going to correct in the future). You know that when you're over seventy, seventy-five scenes you're going to run too long, almost absolutely. *The Second Reckoning* [*The Ultimatum*] was one hundred ninety-three scenes and one hundred forty pages.

FROUG: A hundred and forty pages is long.

DWORET: Yes. But this is a script that people said, and still tell us today, was the most exciting script they've ever read in their lives.

FROUG: This is the one you got the half-million bucks for.

DWORET: Yeah, this is the one that we were told Steven Spielberg said, "This is the most exciting script I've read in three years." Executives at Warner Bros. called it one of the best scripts they'd read in their lives. There's a funny story. A couple of years ago, Bob and I pitched a Paramount exec an incredible story about this jet called a "scram jet." We turned it into a really interesting story—a thriller. We went to pitch it and this executive wouldn't give us the time of day. Six months later he's reading a copy of *The Ultimatum*, which is what *The Second Reckoning* was called, and says, "Last night I read the most exciting script I've ever read in my life." His secretary laughed and laughed and laughed. She said, "These are the same guys you threw out of your office." [*Laughter*] It's very reassuring. It's not the money that's particularly giving me any real sense of satisfaction, but it's the fact that these executives have said you guys wrote one of the three best scripts they read in their life. That's nice. I mean, that's a good feeling, and nobody can take it away from you, ever.

FROUG: So why did they bring in other writers to rewrite?

DWORET: We sold it to Disney because we felt that they were going to make it right away. And they did put it right into a production track. The script went out immediately to directors, and they gave us just a few notes. For Disney, a few notes is rare. They gave us what they said were the fewest notes they'd ever given a script. They thought it was great. But there was an executive there, even at our first meeting, who said, "Look, I have a completely different take on this movie than anyone else in the room, but I'm not going to follow that, you know, obviously this is a great script and we're moving forward." Warren Beatty happened to get the script and wanted to do it. Disney felt at some level obligated to give it to Beatty because he was very involved with them on *Dick Tracy*. Beatty gave it to Spielberg. We were told that Spielberg said, "This is one of the greatest scripts I've read. Why wasn't it offered to me?" What happened then is that Spielberg took over the production. Essentially, his position in the industry is that he does whatever he wants to do; nobody will say no, nobody will say boo. He's basically God in the movie industry, as far as the studios are concerned. Disney lost complete control. They were upset, and we were upset. We never even had a meeting with Spielberg, which shocked us since he did say that he liked the script so much. He wouldn't meet with us, and he was going to bring in another writer with whom he said he had a shorthand, and he needed to move quickly. At some level we could understand that, but not to even give us a chance or the courtesy of a meeting was a little bit upsetting.

FROUG: A lot upsetting.

DWORET: That's the movie business, though. If good things happen, it's the unexpected. Our script only sold because this man Ron Hamady had been, in November of 1989, at a poker game with Bob Pool and said, "Do you happen to have any scripts?" Bob gave him *The Second Reckoning*. And Ron really loved it. He said, "I want to set this up completely independently." He knew the history of it. He thought he could sell it. Again, it was the greatest thing he'd read, you know, but he couldn't sell it. People were still too scared to do it. Hamady said, "I want you to make these changes, and I will find you independent money"— he'd been an independent filmmaker, made a couple of films—"and we'll go forward." On the basis that he was going to do it outside the studio system. We said, "Why not?" We made a few changes, and he brought in a director who read it and gave us a few more good notes. We made another set of changes. And then, in February 1990, *The Hunt for Red October* came out. It was a big, big hit. Suddenly, through this fluke of timing, high-tech thrillers were in. Our agents saw the writing . . .

FROUG: Who was your agent?

DWORET: My agent, David Wirtschafter, who read the script in 1983 as an intern at ICM, said, "This is one of the greatest scripts I've ever read. I fantasized eight years ago about getting involved in the sale of that script." We couldn't ask for an agent to say anything greater than that. He seized the ball, took the script away from the producers, and said, "We're going out with the script. It is going to be a major studio sale. You guys come along for the ride, or you're gonna be out." There was a big bidding auction, almost every studio wanted to be in on it. Eventually we made a deal with Disney because they said absolutely they would make this movie right away. Otherwise, we wouldn't have gone with Disney. They didn't make the best offer, but they included a multi-picture deal. They wanted the script that badly.

FROUG: The studio offered not only to buy this but a guarantee of other scripts?

DWORET: Another script, which they're paying for now, even though they haven't assigned us a project. We may never even write that second script for them. You get typecast in Hollywood. We're typecast as thriller-action writers. High-tech, thriller, action, whatever. They wanted to do a remake of *The Thief of Baghdad*. They had a script written by a good writer, but it wasn't what they wanted. It really wasn't the tone that we felt was right. We went in to them just recently with a step outline that they loved. But even though they loved it, this whole sixty-scene step outline, they're not sure they want us to do it because we haven't written anything like that. We're thriller-action writers.

FROUG: Absurd.

DWORET: It is absurd, but that's the movie business.

FROUG: So now let's go back into this. They make this deal with a half a million up front for what's now called *The Ultimatum*; they guarantee it will come to over a million when you're done with it, and then they give it to Steven Spielberg?

DWORET: They didn't give it to him. He just got it and said he wanted to do it. By September—six months later—he decided that he didn't want to do it. And he was out of it. Which we thought was a good sign. We then had to do a quick rewrite. But, during those six months, the executive in charge of the movie had decided that he wanted to change the movie to fit his vision. He wanted to structure the movie his way. It's a tight thriller that's about finding a bomb in forty-eight hours. He wanted to make it into a big love story. It didn't make any sense to us. If you've got forty-eight hours to find a bomb, the audience would laugh at every opportunity that you take to find your girlfriend and have sex with her, or whatever. Anyway, we wouldn't go along with those changes. We were let go of the project after that.

FROUG: You refused to make those changes?

DWORET: Yes. We made all the changes that we agreed to, that Disney asked for, but then had another meeting where they asked for another whole set of changes, changes they knew we weren't going to make. They weren't used to having writers or anybody simply say, "No." We wouldn't destroy our movie of eleven years of work. It made no sense. It would only be a failure. We wrote them a letter saying why it wouldn't work. They hired some big name writers to rewrite it—a husband-and-wife team. We weren't at the meeting, but they assured the producer that they basically were going to stick to our story line. Three weeks later, they delivered a draft that was different, completely different from our script, except for one page.

FROUG: What did they pay them?

DWORET: Almost three hundred thousand dollars for three weeks' work and an awful draft.

FROUG: Under the Writers Guild M.B.A. [Minimum Basic Agreement] you have to be shown that draft, don't you?

DWORET: No, I don't think so. We were shown it anyway. It was awful to the point that the studio wouldn't show it to anybody. They've now brought in other writers, and a major star has been attached to the project, Richard Gere. Disney's decided the version that this husband-and-wife team wrote was to a great degree an attempt to make the vision of the film that the executive had. And it didn't work. So we're hopeful that the executive, at this point, has seen the light. We think now he sees that he had destroyed a lot of the elements that he really liked, that made him be one of the people who wanted to buy the script in the first place. A producer's been attached ever since we made our deal, and the movie is back on track. It will be a highly controversial movie, if it ever gets made.

FROUG: But it's basically back to your script, more or less.

DWORET: It's basically back to our script for now, but they're bringing in another writer, and it may be something completely different by the time it reaches the screen.

FROUG: This is a typical Hollywood story, Laury. It happens often.

DWORET: Bill, being a movie executive is the worst job in the world. They've got to produce hits, and nobody really knows what will be a hit. Not even the writers. But I like what Barry Diller said, "It never gets any better than the script."

FROUG: Knowing the insanity of this business and the kind of madness and the frantic pace of it, why don't you stay more in medicine?

DWORET: Well, since I really love writing, I try to find a balance between both of these worlds. I sit in a room three or four days in a row and I get a little bit stir crazy. There's no sense of reality other than my life in my home and the fantasy world that I'm creating. And at some point after three or four days I need a respite. I need something real. I don't find anything particularly real in the people in Hollywood. I go to the hospital, I see fifty, sixty patients, or thirty or forty patients in a day. Each one of those patients is a real person whose life I can go into.

Gratification in Hollywood takes a long, long time. A very fine writer told me when I first came here that it would take ten years to really get established. That's the average. And I found that to be true. You have to be ready to persevere for that long. If you're really lucky, if things happen by some miracle, sure, maybe you'll make it sooner. But you really have to be in it for the long haul, and I'm this kind of guy who likes gratification much sooner than that. When I walk into an emergency room, I can save somebody's life in five minutes or a minute or thirty seconds. I can really alter someone's life forevermore. That to me is really gratifying. That's reality. Movieland is fantasyland. If our scripts sell, I'm delighted. If they make our movie, I'll be ecstatic. But I have to keep writing them my way. I've made the decision that all the sacrifice of going to medical school and continuing to be a doctor gives me the freedom to say what I want. So, if I like somebody's ideas, and often I do, I'll take them. But if I don't like their ideas, if I really think it's something I can't live with, I'm very fortunate in the fact that I can walk away. Most writers I know have to make a living writing. It's very, very difficult. I've done it once where I had to be under somebody's thumb. It was unbearable. It was the only moment where I hated being a writer. It was when I had to listen to someone tell me exactly how I was going to write, the characters I was going to write. So I came home and went to the emergency room and bought the freedom to write whatever I wanted. I'm lucky; no one can ever take that joy away.

Diane Frolov

1980	L.A.T.E.R. [TV Series] *(six episodes)*
1981	MAGNUM, P.I. [TV Series] *(two episodes)*
1983	HAVE A SAFE DAY *(Screenplay)*
1984	V [TV Mini-series] *(Shared Credit on Parts 1, 2, and 3)* HOT PURSUIT [TV Series] *(one episode)*
1985	SHADOW CHASERS [TV Series] *(one episode)*
1986	RAGS TO RICHES [TV Series] *(one episode)*
1989	ALIEN NATION [TV Series] *(six episodes)*
1991	NORTHERN EXPOSURE [TV Series] *(two episodes)*

"SEOUL MATES"

PROLOGUE

FADE IN

1   EXT. CICELY MAIN STREET - DAY   1

The town is being decorated for Christmas. Decorative
ravens are going up everywhere -- raven Christmas lights,
raven stencils, plastic raven figures lit from within. A
non-traditional Christmas SONG comes to an end.

                    CHRIS (V.O.)
                  (in Indian)
            Quviasugin Kraisimagzigmi...
                  (in English)
            Seasons greetings from K-BHR -- this
            is Chris in the morning, and from
            where I'm sitting I've got a great
            view of the yultide decorations
            going up all over town.

2   INSIDE RADIO STATION - CHRIS   2

is at the mic, whittling a little raven out of wood. The
room is also decorated with the raven motif. Maurice sits
in his office, behind Chris.

                    CHRIS
            Let me tell you -- there's nothing
            like the sight of a beautiful black
            as pitch raven to fill you with the
            Christmas spirit. Hey, that reminds
            me -- congratulations to our own
            Marilyn Whirlwind who's landed the
            part of Princess Susitna in this
            year's Raven Pageant. Break a wing,
            Marilyn.

3   CHRIS'S POV - THROUGH THE WINDOW - MAGGIE   3

crosses the street, tripping on the curb. Catching her
balance, she knocks into a pedestrian.

                    CHRIS (V.O.)
            Oops. I see Maggie O'Connell is in
            her usual Christmas mode. This time
            of year, you know, she gets a little
            accident prone.

*"A good script should involve me like
a well-written book."*

This summer, my wife and I decided to look in on a television series that had received a lot of favorable press and affirmative comments from friends, "Northern Exposure," CBS's recently launched one-hour series.

We watched and were enchanted. It was far better than we expected. It was also very funny with a delightfully wacky brand of humor. We fell in love with the show.

One night I found myself paying close attention to the credits and a name leaped off the screen at me: Diane Frolov, Supervising Producer. Suddenly all sorts of memories congealed in my mind. About fifteen years ago I had a very gifted young woman in one of my UCLA graduate screenwriting seminars, a Diane Frolov. Was this the same person? I vividly remembered her writing style because it was so unusual and it exactly matched what we'd been watching on "Northern Exposure." It was unmistakable.

I wrote Diane a fan letter in care of the Writers Guild. She quickly responded, "Yes, it's me." Then she recalled some of her experiences in my classroom. "You told us to never chase the marketplace, to write our own vision. There have been times in my life when that was hard, but I would force myself, just because you said it."

I phoned her at her office and asked if she would be willing to let me interview her for this book. It would have to be a phone interview, I was already far over my budget and, in truth, the book was already complete. I didn't know if there was still time to include another interview and make our publication schedule. With no assurance anything would come of it, she enthusiastically agreed to the interview.

Hearing her cheerful voice and infectious laughter, I now recalled the pretty but painfully shy young school girl coming into my classroom, timidly handing me her screenplay titled *Come Get Maggie.*

It was the poignant story of an unhappy little girl longing to be rescued from her painful life. Yet it had moments of off-the-wall humor and delightfully fey characters in wonderfully developed scenes.

I was enchanted not only with the screenplay but with its author. Diane was a delight to have in our graduate seminar, her tinkling laughter affected us all. In spite of her being her own toughest critic and having excessive self-doubts, she was a treasure.

I have difficulty remembering my own shopping list, but I can vividly recall every outstanding student or student screenplay ever written in one of my classes over a span of twenty years.

I phoned Diane and taped our telephone interview. I was not surprised to hear Diane offer important advice for the aspiring screenwriter that no one else in this book had suggested. Brief though this is, Diane's recommendations for the new screenwriter are important and well worth close attention.

Once again, I was struck by the fact that there is no place in the motion picture business today for gifted comedy talents of the ilk of Bill Bryan and Diane Frolov. But then moviedom's loss is television's gain.

Say hello to the richly talented Diane Frolov.

FROUG: How did you go from school at UCLA to writing successfully for a living?

FROLOV: I became a member of Theatre East. I was writing plays at the time. I was a playwright, you know, at UCLA. And a friend of mine there gave one of my scripts to an agent at Eisenbach, Greene & Duchow. They liked it and took me on as a client. You remember, I think, my first screenplay, *Come Get Maggie?*

FROUG: I certainly do remember it.

FROLOV: It was optioned but not produced. Ann and Ellis Marcus read it when they were staffing a late-night television show, a strip show (five taped episodes a week), "The Life & Times of Eddie Roberts." They took me on. That was my first staff job.

FROUG: That's great. How long had you been out of school?

FROLOV: About two years.

FROUG: And that came from showing them your *Maggie* screenplay?

FROLOV: Uh-huh. That screenplay, I think, got me a lot of work at first. Anyway, it got me a lot of attention.

FROUG: It's a wonderful screenplay. What's interesting to me is that you are a very offbeat writer. You don't fit the mainstream of Hollywood, and yet you came soaring in there.

FROLOV: Only initially. It was a short flight. That show was soon cancelled and I was out of a job. So I wrote for "The Incredible Hulk."

FROUG: [*Laughter*] It didn't seem to hurt you.

FROLOV: No. That's how I got into episodic TV—out of half-hour.

FROUG: How did you move into comedy?

FROLOV: Comedy was what I was always interested in.

FROUG: I know, but "The Incredible Hulk" is not very funny. It's funny, but it's not comedy.

FROLOV: I know. It's strange, but there are a lot of writers in hour dramatic episodic television who *are* very funny writers. It helps the heaviness of the form to have writers with a sense of humor.

FROUG: That's true, but since it's a genre that's easy to kid, did you allow them, in their episode form, to be funny or to make jokes?

FROLOV: No, not there so much. There were some funny moments but not joke jokes.

FROUG: How do you break out of episodic TV into comedy? Specifically, how did you do it? It wasn't through an episodic TV script, it was through your screenplay—your show script—right?

FROLOV: Right. The scripts that I wrote after that were all comedy scripts. I continued writing them, film scripts, while I was doing television and in between television work.

FROUG: Spec screenplays?

FROLOV: Yes. I wrote a screenplay called *Men* that has also gotten me a lot of work and attention. It, too, is a comedy.

FROUG: Is that going to get produced?

FROLOV: I don't know, maybe one day. It's been optioned. It was optioned by Arthur Cohen, but I don't know. It's in turnaround now.

FROUG: That famous ugly word.

FROLOV: Yeah. I don't know what will happen to it.

FROUG: Is your ambition to get out of television and into feature films?

FROLOV: Well, I did that for a while. I took off from TV about two or three years and just wrote film. The experience didn't really make me eager to get back to it again.

FROUG: You didn't sell any?

FROLOV: I had a script optioned by Michael Gruskoff—a screenplay called *Lowflyers*. Disney/Touchstone developed it with us but nothing happened.

FROUG: A lot of development deals, yes?

FROLOV: A couple. After *Lowflyers,* I did a script called *Men.* I worked on that with the director for about a year and a half.

FROUG: Who was the director?

FROLOV: Evelyn Purcell.

FROUG: Tell me, when did you meet your husband?

FROLOV: I met him right after I lost my first job, "The Life & Times of Eddie Roberts."

FROUG: With Ann and Ellis.

FROLOV: Yes. Right.

FROUG: They're old friends of mine, by the way. Weren't they great to work with?

FROLOV: They were wonderful. Working for them was a dream job. There was just the three of us. We were like a family. We used to drive around the lot with Ellis in one of those little golf carts. I'd look at all the stages, the sets—I was in heaven *and* I was getting paid to be there.

FROUG: Marvelous. Tell me, Diane, were these spec screenplays kind of sustaining you financially? Option money and that sort of thing?

FROLOV: Yes, they did—I made enough to get by. I went back to TV for other reasons. It was always so heartbreaking to work on something for a year and a half, two years and then have it die—not to ever see it done. In television you have the opportunity to see your work produced— often within weeks of writing it. Also, you have a lot more control over what happens to it.

FROUG: I'm hearing this more and more, Diane, from writers who're saying that in television they get to see their work—it's up there—and they have more influence than in movies.

FROLOV: Yes, yes, you do. I think a writer's best position right now is in television as a writer-producer.

FROUG: Which is what you're doing.

FROLOV: Right. In film you have the director who really runs the show. In television it's the opposite. The writer-producer runs the show—he or she is there for the whole season. The director comes in for two or three weeks and then moves on.

FROUG: That was my experience. How many staff writers do you have on "Northern Exposure."

FROLOV: There're just four of us.

FROUG: Well, you sure turn out great work.

FROLOV: We spend a lot of time with our scripts. They're developed and written over months. With some TV shows, the staff conceives an idea on Friday, gang-writes it over the weekend, and preps it on Monday. Also, we have a great staff, an educated and well-rounded staff. It's unusual for TV because all of us are what you would call "older writers." We're all in our late thirties, early forties. That's unusual right now.

FROUG: That's older writers? [*Laughter*] That's older writers, my God.

FROLOV: Other shows have much younger staffs. That's my impression—it may be wrong, I don't know.

FROUG: Are you astonished by the success of "Northern Exposure"?

FROLOV: Yes, I am . . . I am.

FROUG: Why do you think it's so successful?

FROLOV: I don't think there is anything like it. "Northern Exposure" is really different. It doesn't have to conform to any specific genre—i.e. detective, sci-fi. You see things on "Northern Exposure" you will not see on any other show. Also, it's intelligent.

FROUG: Yes, it is.

FROLOV: We never write down to our audience. I think that's exciting. We touch on everything from quantum physics to Franz Kafka. Sometimes the network thinks we over-intellectualize, but we believe our audience appreciates it. On another level, our town, Cicely, is a place that you want to go to. It's what Josh Brand calls a nonjudgmental universe. There are no bad guys in Cicely.

No one is consciously mean or hurtful.

FROUG: Is that a real place? Is that what Alaska is really like or is it what you imagine it's like.

FROLOV: It's what we imagine it's like. Or rather, we consider our Alaska more a state of mind than a location.

FROUG: None of you writing the show have spent any time in Alaska?

FROLOV: No. Josh Brand and John Falsey, the creators, went up there to visit after they had created the show. Cicely is a place in our heart, really.

FROUG: That's what makes it so beautiful.

FROLOV: Yes.

FROUG: I think the audience senses that. It's where we all would like to be. Paradise. With snow. [*Laughter*]

FROLOV: Yeah.

FROUG: Did you get a two-year pick up or a full-year pick up.

FROLOV: Originally, it was for thirteen, but we just got a pick up for a full season of twenty-two episodes.

FROUG: Is this the same staff as last year?

FROLOV: We had one writer move over to Josh and John's other show, "I'll Fly Away," and so we brought on another writer. The staff changed by just one person.

FROUG: And all the producer titles are, as usual, writers, yes?

FROLOV: No, we have two line producers—one in L.A., one in Seattle.

FROUG: Well, somebody has to do the producing around there. Somebody has to cast it, somebody has to get out there and get sets and stuff.

FROLOV: Yeah. And we're split up. We have production offices in Washington. That's where we're filming, up near Seattle. The writing and the post-production is done down here in L.A.

FROUG: Have you been up there?

FROLOV: Yeah. It's great. It's so *fun.* As a writer, you're in a little room all the time. [*Laughter*] You don't get out. When you go up there and see the sets, you realize that the writing is actually for something.

FROUG: You see it coming to life.

FROLOV: Yeah, yeah.

FROUG: I love that kid who plays Dr. Fleischman. Are you going to get him together with the pilot?

FROLOV: I don't know. That would be way down the line. Once that happens, what do you do? You put them together, and then you have to get them apart again.

FROUG: Well, you may be milking the "Moonlighting" storyline a little long if you're not careful.

FROLOV: Yes. That's a good way to anger your audience.

FROUG: And "Moonlighting" went on until it lost its audience.

FROLOV: Yeah, we're running into that problem. We're starting to have to construct our stories to keep them from interacting romantically. We don't want our audience to say, "Enough, already—Why don't they go to bed!"

FROUG: Right. I love your story of the four or five boyfriends who were killed. Delightful.

FROLOV: Yeah, it's fun. It's the kind of show where you can do that stuff. That's what makes it a great show to write for.

FROUG: Your results are beautiful. This is very much Diane Frolov kind of writing.

FROLOV: Yeah, it is—twisted. That's what I have an affinity for.

FROUG: Is your husband on the show, too?

FROLOV: Yes, he is.

FROUG: As a producer?

FROLOV: Yes, he is the co-exec producer.

FROUG: He's a co-exec producer and you're a supervising producer?

FROLOV: Right. So far we've kept our titles separate.

FROUG: Separate but equal, I hope. [*Laughter*]

FROLOV: Yes.

FROUG: As supervising producer, what are your functions?

FROLOV: The role of supervising producer varies from show

to show. On "Northern Exposure," my primary responsibility is script—hiring writers, story development, editing for content and production, plus developing and writing my own scripts. To a lesser extent, I'm involved in casting, prepping the directors for tone and intent, editing and the selection of music.

FROUG: What kind of response do you get from the network? Are they high on the show?

FROLOV: Yes, they are. They love it. They don't always understand it.

FROUG: I know. I loved that running-of-the-bull sequence. That was delightful.

FROLOV: We got into a lot of trouble with the town for that.

FROUG: With the town?

FROLOV: Yeah, because some of the actors decided to really do it.

FROUG: [*Laughter*] Great, that's wonderful.

FROLOV: So the men took off their clothes and started running down the street, and, just then, the mayor came out of his office and saw this.

FROUG: Is there a real town?

FROLOV: Yes. It's a real town.

FROUG: It looks like that?

FROLOV: Yeah. And it behaves like Cicely, in a way. You know how we have town meetings on the show—well, after the "Bulls" incident, they had a town meeting. Our Seattle line producer had to go and apologize and promise it wouldn't be shown on television as it was.

FROUG: Are they angry about these "Hollywood characters" who come up there?

FROLOV: No. They were just angry about the nudity. It's probably annoying having us up there all the time. I know some people moved up there to get away from the city.

FROUG: Where is this town?

FROLOV: It's in the Cascades.

FROUG: In Washington State?

FROLOV: Yeah.

FROUG: Do they really get all that snow?

FROLOV: Normally, yes. Unfortunately, last year was very dry and that snow you saw was trucked in.

FROUG: Do the actors live in Seattle and commute?

FROLOV: Yes, they do. They stay in the Seattle area while we shoot. Roslyn's very close—about an hour and a half drive. Sometimes they spend the night.

FROUG: That's the real town, Roslyn, Washington?

FROLOV: Yeah.

FROUG: Well, I just hope they don't kick you out. You have a great show.

FROLOV: I think they basically like us. The show brings a lot of income into the area.

FROUG: Do you think new writers, ambitious to write movies or television, should go to film school?

FROLOV: Yes, I do. I wouldn't say that about everybody. Film school in conjunction with leading a lot of lives. I mean, having life experiences. I think *just* film school doesn't give you everything you need. You need to go out and have a lot of different jobs, and a lot of different relationships.

FROUG: Did you find that film school shortcut your entry into the marketplace?

FROLOV: Yes, it did. Besides learning a craft, it gave me energy and it gave me hope. I was surrounded by other writers, and I had teachers like you who said, "Go and do this." And, you make contacts from school.

FROUG: Which carry on into your career.

FROLOV: Right.

FROUG: Do you run into a lot of people, now that you are a full-time working person, whom you knew in school?

FROLOV: Quite a few, actually.

FROUG: Hollywood is a small town, isn't it?

FROLOV: Very. Yes, a very small town.

FROUG: When you approach a screenplay, do you use a paradigm? Do you, for example, say: "my first act ought to be around page twenty-five, my second act around seventy-five or eighty," and so forth.

FROLOV: No. I have that in the back of my head, but it's really something that you feel rhythmically, about the sense of story—where it peaks, where there is more complication, and where it resolves.

FROUG: What do you think is the most important thing you need to know before you sit down to write a screenplay? What's going to really make it work for you?

FROLOV: I would say theme. You really need to know what the piece is "about" and you have to make sure that all plot turns and character arcs elucidate and project that theme.

FROUG: What do you look for in a good script?

FROLOV: A good script should involve me like a well-written book. That is, I should be so caught up in the characters and the story that I'm unaware of the disengaging script format, i.e., INT., EXT., CUT TO, etc. When a script is so engaging, we like to say it is "a seamless read." Within that context, I look for story and character turns that are "fresh," surprising, yet still emotionally grounded and motivated.

FROUG: What is your advice to the current generation that's coming out of film school? How would you advise these kids who want to be writers?

FROLOV: I see a lot of writers who have been brought up on television. They know television. They know film. But they're limited. They don't read much and they haven't had a lot of life experience. They've only been experiencing the media. So, I would say, read as much as you possibly can and do many different things. I'm always interested in writers who bring something else into the writing than *just* film school and *just* having watched TV.

FROUG: That's excellent advice, believe me. I don't think enough young writers are aware of that. They think that, if they've seen enough late-night movies, then they can write movies.

FROLOV: Right. And the detail in which they know those movies. I'm always astounded.

FROUG: Yeah. They know all those movies from the thirties and forties from AMC, but they don't seem to have had much life experience. Do you think students should set out to write TV or film?

FROLOV: If you mean, should initial spec material be for TV or film, I'd say definitely film. Not because film is in any way a superior medium, but because the writer must create from whole cloth—that is, he or she is not borrowing characters conceived and established by someone else. Also, the writer must structure a longer piece—a hundred and twenty pages as opposed to sixty or forty-five. That is much more demanding, but much better training. Finally, a good filmscript is a continually useful calling card, whereas even the best "thirtysomething" is still yesterday's news.

FROUG: So, now that you are settled with a ten-year-old son, a home, and a husband, life is good, what is your next career move?

FROLOV: Well, we would like to create and run our own show. I'd also like to write again for film. I think the thing that's lacking in television is that you never get the experience with the audience. You don't get to sit in a darkened room . . .

FROUG: And hear how they react.

FROLOV: Yes. I miss that.

FROUG: Jeff Boam talks about the thrill of being in the audience and watching reactions. He says he's pretty sure exactly where they're going to laugh or where they're going to snicker or where they're going to move restlessly in their seat. He says he's always upset when they don't do it where they're supposed to. And he's surprised sometimes when the big laugh comes in places he didn't anticipate.

FROLOV: That's right. Everybody perceives things differently.

FROUG: All you get in television is a rating service. Do you trust a rating service?

FROLOV: Well, it's not really a matter of trust. Valid or not, the ratings determine the show's future, so they have a tremendous influence on our lives. If the ratings are good, it means the network will probably pick us up, we'll probably have a job, and we'll probably be able to pay the mortgage. With bad ratings, the reverse is true.

FROUG: Is your show high-rated? It's up there, isn't it?

FROLOV: Yeah, right now. We've been in the top ten. That's unusual also for a ten o'clock show because less people are watching—it's bedtime.

FROUG: Is there anything you would like to add? Any thoughts you'd like to express?

FROLOV: To have courage and really love what you do. But not to lose sight of the life around you. You'll find, as you go through the process, there will be so many people who will tell you that it is impossible and that you can't do it. You'll have your heart broken so many times, and you just have to sustain yourself with your vision. And, as I said, your love of what you do.

FROUG: That's perfect. That's beautiful.

Ronald Bass

1985   CODE NAME: EMERALD *(Based on his novel)*

1987   GARDENS OF STONE *(Screenplay)*
BLACK WIDOW *(Written by)*

1988   RAIN MAN *(Shared Screenplay)*, Academy Award

1990   SLEEPING WITH THE ENEMY *(Screenplay)*

RAINMAN

FADE IN:

EXT. DOCK, SAN PEDRO - DAY

Soft focus on a blur of shapes and colors. SOUNDS of a major
HARBOR working full-tilt. A green shape slowly moves into frame.
And as MAIN TITLES begin, we snap to SHARP FOCUS on...

...an apple-green FERRARI. Suspended from a towering crane.
Cradled in a net all its own. A polished, gleaming treasure,
lofted gracefully above...

...a teeming customs DOCK. Three cranes working to unload cargo
from a freighter's hold. As CREDITS CONTINUE, we...

...PAN the dock slowly. Containers being opened for inspection.
A pot-bellied man in a rumpled tie methodically checks cartons of
patio furniture against his manifest...

...a customs inspector in shirtsleeves stands with a worried lady
before a small cluster of antiques. She is tailored and hard.
As the inspector talks, her fingers stroke the cracked surface of
a broken armoire. She doesn't know what the hell she's going to
do. And down the dock...

...our Ferrari has settled gently to earth. The net falls away,
and we see that it stands next to another vintage Ferrari.
Cream-colored, different model and year, just as exquisite. PULL
BACK slightly now to see there are...

...six of them. Side by side. Gleaming black, silver, Ferrari
red. An elegant line, aloof somehow from the common bustle
surrounding them. And with the customs inspector stands...

...CHARLIE BABBITT. Mid-twenties, with dark good looks and a
restless intelligence behind the eyes. His clothes show a trace
of flash, but they are expensive. Then again, they would be if
it took his last dollar. He pulls some papers from a slender
briefcase. But even as he hands them to the inspector, Charlie's
eyes are riveted on his shipment.

He stalks the apple-green. Very slowly. Fingers absently
tracing a polished fender. Stops now. The inspector is
talking, but Charlie doesn't hear him. Sinking to his heels,
Charlie gently releases the latch. Lifts the hood.

He stands now. Lights a Lucky straight. With eyes experienced
beyond his years, Charlie stares down every inch of the gleaming
engine. And as CREDITS CONCLUDE, we hold on his appraising gaze
and...

...DISSOLVE to black.

EXT. QUONSET HUT, SAN PEDRO - LATE AFTERNOON

A street of junkyards and warehouses. The quonset hut sits with
its corrugated roof, peeling paint. The sign says HOLLYWOOD
IMPORTS.

[Handwritten margin note:] The emotional core of this story which depicts 2 brothers, each in his own way emotionally walled off from others) is to explore how difficult it is for one human to actually reach another, and yet how essential that process is for us all. *[signature]*

"So much of it is letting go and letting it happen."

I met Ron Bass at his office in Pacific Palisades, an upscale bedroom suburb of Los Angeles overlooking the Pacific Ocean. It was a rare pleasure to make the long drive out Sunset Boulevard early Saturday morning with no traffic in sight. Suddenly it was the Los Angeles I knew and loved in the forties.

Though I had never met Ron, my wife, Christine Michaels, had when she was Vice President of Business Affairs at ABC Motion Pictures. She and Ron had been involved in negotiations a decade earlier, and she told me, "Ron is a good man, very bright, a tough negotiator, but fair and honest." When a lawyer has high praise for the lawyer across the negotiating table, it gives special credence to the compliment.

I believe you will find no more insightful view of what goes on in getting a film made than Ron's description of the tortuous journey involved in bringing the Oscar winner *Rain Man* to the screen. The film swept the Oscar field in 1988, with Oscars for Ron Bass and Barry Morrow (Best Original Screenplay), Barry Levinson (Best Director), Dustin Hoffman (Best Actor). I can not imagine a more labyrinthine creative process with writers and directors moving on and off the project like passengers on a subway. For a while there you could not tell the players without a scorecard. There is also the extraordinary role of Mike Ovitz, co-founder of Creative Artists Agency, who held the project together with singular zeal and determination. Only a man of Ovitz's extraordinary power and skill could have pulled it off. Perhaps he should have gotten an Oscar.

When Ron and I finished our talk, I realized that my wife was right in her assessment of him: honest, very bright, and, no doubt, tough, but I would also add modest.

Beyond Ron Bass' description of the Byzantine machinations that are sometimes required to get a movie made in Hollywood, you will find as good an explanation of the creative (as opposed to the mechanical) aspects of screenwriting as you are apt to see in print.

Welcome to Hollywood, friends, where what goes on off the screen is often more interesting than what goes on on screen.

FROUG: The obvious question is, being a very successful entertainment lawyer, what drove you to become a screenwriter?

BASS: Well, the truth is that I'd always written when I was younger. I wrote stories when I was a child, and I actually wrote a novel when I was a teenager. I'd always wanted to be a novelist. My heroes when I was growing up were Dostoyevsky and Faulkner, Fitzgerald, and so on. And then the world sort of convinced me that that was an impractical goal. It was kind of like wanting to be the centerfielder for the Yankees or something. It wasn't going to really happen, so I should be realistic and get a paying job. Start to study something in college that could earn me a living. I could always write, sort of, in my spare time. So I became practical and realistic. I abandoned my writing and went eventually to law school. And I really never started writing again until the mid 1970s. When I started to write novels, I had no idea that I'd ever want to write for the screen. It was nothing that was ever even remotely in my mind. I wanted to write prose, and I wrote three novels in the late seventies and early eighties, all of which were published.

FROUG: That's remarkable.

BASS: Yeah. All of it was while I was practicing law full-time. Writing at home, writing in early mornings, writing on the weekends, writing on vacation. This was my hobby.

FROUG: The West Coast Scott Turow.

BASS: Well, no. He is real successful.

FROUG: Didn't at least one of your novels sell to the movies?

BASS: Well, yeah. The last one of them became this awful movie.

FROUG: *Code Name: Emerald?*

BASS: *Code Name: Emerald,* yeah, which was my third novel. It was called *The Emerald Illusion,* and it was bought by a terrific guy named Jonathan Sanger, who wanted to make it his directing debut. He's a very famous producer—he produced *The Elephant Man* and other films. He was so supportive and so wonderful; he allowed me to write the screenplay. I'd only written one screenplay before, once upon a time, just for fun. So this was my first really serious screenplay. When the screenplay was done, my then-agent, a woman named Melinda Jason (who's now my manager and one of my oldest friends), copied the script and sent it around to everybody in Hollywood. And people liked the script and started to offer me writing assignments. Robert Cort and David Madden, who were then with 20th Century Fox and now run Interscope, gave me my first studio assignment. I started to get a lot of studio assignments, and so I started to write. I would get up every morning at three o'clock and write from three to six. Then my daughter would wake up, and I would hang out with her until I went to the office at eight o'clock to be a lawyer all day long.

FROUG: As a lawyer, did you represent any screenwriters?

BASS: Oh, millions. I mean, this is what the firm did. I was a theatrical motion-picture lawyer. That firm still is, I think, the most successful feature-film legal firm ever. Our clients were directors and actors and producers and writers. That's all I did all day long.

FROUG: Did anybody know you were a closet screenwriter at the time?

BASS: Yeah, it wasn't so much in the closet. When I was just writing novels, people didn't know about it because the novels weren't wildly successful. It was kind of secret. When I started writing screenplays, they were getting bought, and everybody in town was now reading the first one that I'd written. So it became very amusing. Sort of like a gorilla driving a car—the fact that he can do it at all is amazing, but that he can do it even remotely well is astonishing. So I was getting a lot of kidding. But a lot of people were kind and interested and really supportive. I felt like an idiot because people were so amazed that I could do it that I wondered, "What did they used to think of me? They must have thought I was a moron."

FROUG: Are you still practicing law?

BASS: Oh, no, no. Although they're kind enough at the firm to still keep me on the letterhead as of counsel, they haven't actually tapped me for of counsel advice in many, many years.

FROUG: The first really big screenplay for you was your Oscar-winning *Rain Man*, yes?

BASS: Well, it certainly is the biggest. Though there were two major-studio films made before that. One was *Black Widow*. And I usually consider that sort of the first substantial thing.

FROUG: That was an original?

BASS: Yeah, absolutely.

FROUG: It was very good.

BASS: Thank you. And there was one for Francis Coppola called *Gardens of Stone* that followed *Black Widow* almost immediately.

FROUG: In *Black Widow*, how did you get along with Bob Rafelson? How was the writer-director relationship?

BASS: Well, it's always different. On that particular project, I'd written the script speculatively, and I wasn't developing it with anybody. We sold it to Fox, and then we did some rewriting for them. Then Fox brought in Bob. Every one of my experiences with directors has been different. Every one's been unique, and that was no exception.

FROUG: Any of them good?

BASS: All good in lots of ways, but not all of them perfect. Bob is a fascinating guy. He's a brilliant guy. He's really a challenging guy, and he put me through a lot of hell. We did nine or ten drafts of it, and he would rewrite some scenes and give them to me. We would have fights from time to time, but all the way through the process, I really respected him. He's just a smart guy.

FROUG: He really is. I know him.

BASS: Everything he wanted to do, even when I didn't see the sense of it at the time or I didn't see where he was going, it all did make sense and it was all going toward a vision that was his vision. It was my first time working that closely with a director. I had worked with Sanger before, but this was really different. This was my first lesson in trying to let go of my vision of the piece and understand that there comes a point when the director's the guy who's got to make the movie, and you really have to be servicing his vision, not in a subordinate way, but in a way where you . . .

FROUG: It's a collaboration.

BASS: Well, it's definitely a collaboration. It was collaborative, but I'm trying to say something a little more than that. There's a moment where you have to sort of get on board as his partner and not just be working for him in collaboration but really say, "I've got to make his vision my own in some way. I've got to find the thing in the director's vision that I'm not just willing to help him with, but that really excites me, so that I can get inspired along his track of thinking, rather than just be more workmanlike and obedient." This was, sort of, my first experience in trying to do that. It was more successful in some areas of the script than in others, but it was wonderful for me. The thing that I will never forget and always be grateful to Bob for is that he was the first guy who actually took me into the editing room. He showed me all the cuts and I gave him millions of notes, and he used a lot of my notes. I sat with him and John Bloom and sort of rewrote the film. There were pieces of film that were meant for totally different scenes that wound up getting placed somewhere else. We'd look at it and say, "You know something? I think you could really put that moment over here." It was a fascinating process. He was so generous to listen to me and to treat me like a collaborator at that stage. It's the most special thing I'll always remember about him.

FROUG: *Black Widow* was your first spec screenplay?

BASS: I guess it was my first fully written spec screenplay because I basically work only on commission and believe in that. I've written very few spec screenplays in my career. Sometimes I'll write a spec script with an actor or somebody I want to collaborate with, but I don't normally believe in that process. A lot of writers feel that they have more creative freedom when they're writing for spec. I don't feel that way. I feel that if I'm writing speculatively, then I'm sort of trying to guess what would sell. I'm trying to guess because I want this script to be commercial. I want to make a living from it. Whereas, once I'm commissioned I have a vision that squares with my studio executive's and my director's—whomever I'm working with—and then I'm relaxed. I'm on this job, I know what we all want to do, and I just go ahead and write that first draft the way that I want to write it.

FROUG: In *Black Widow* you had what I've told my students are the best possible characters. They're obsessed. Find a character who's obsessed and you have a real driving line. You had both characters—both the Debra Winger character and the Theresa Russell character—obsessed. It made for a fascinating film. What was the origin of that particular story, do you recall?

BASS: Yeah. It was very, very funny. I was sitting with David Madden, and I was pitching him. At the beginning I used to have fifty different ideas, a carpetbag; I would go and I would pitch six or eight things at a time. I pitched him, over the course of one day, about six or seven ideas and two different main ideas. One idea was about a female Bluebeard, and the other idea was a cop story about a woman cop. And there was a point in the conversation where David said, "You know, the thing I don't like about your cop story is the villain. It would almost be better if you married the female cop story to your female Bluebeard story." David Madden actually invented the idea.

FROUG: He planted the seed for it.

BASS: Yeah. He put that together, and then, when I developed the whole thing and presented it to them, they didn't like it enough to buy it.

FROUG: [*Laughter*] That's marvelous.

BASS: I wound up selling it to an Italian producer who never paid me. Never really finalized the contract—he kept fooling around and fooling around with the contract. I'm a very trusting soul, so I kept writing and writing and writing, and by the time I was done there was still no contract and no money. My lawyer said, "You can redo the contract his way or you've written the script for nothing." And I said, "Well, I like this script and I'm going to bet on myself." So we terminated negotiations with those people and we went ahead and sold it to Fox. The very studio that hadn't bought it as an idea turned around and bought it as a finished script.

FROUG: You used a key phrase that I think every new writer's got to know: "I'm going to bet on myself." Ultimately you have to bet on yourself, don't you?

BASS: You always bet on yourself. Every minute, every word that you're writing is betting on yourself, unfortunately. [*Laughing*]

FROUG: Do you think it's fair that *Black Widow* should be called a Bob Rafelson film as opposed to a Ron Bass film?

BASS: Absolutely. One-hundred percent fair. First of all, the film is very different from my vision. There are lots of things in every film, including *Rain Man* and films that were very successful, that weren't at all the way I'd have wanted them to be. I see the film and I say at the end of it, "Boy, he's a lot smarter than I was and smart enough to realize it." Or I see the film and I say, "As successful as it is, I still would have preferred it the other way." So the director is, with all apologies to George Kirgo [at the time of this interview, Kirgo was President of the Writers Guild of America, west] and the Writers Guild, the director is the author of the film.

FROUG: The author?

BASS: In my mind, he's the author of the film. The screenwriter's the author of the script. And there's a lot more in a film than the script.

FROUG: George, I'm sorry he said that. [*Laughter*]

BASS: But it really is how I feel. I think any writer who wants to have the final creative decision as to what goes into the film that is made out of his work should direct. I've written novels, and a novelist has the final say. My editor sent me eleven pages of notes, and I used five, or something, five notes out of eleven pages worth. That was my decision. On the dramatic stage, the Dramatists Guild's regulations are such that you can't change a word of the playwright's work. To the extent that having control is what you want, film is a bad medium for a writer who wants control. You have to enjoy collaboration and enjoy the other aspects of it. And you have to understand that what's going to get made is going to be the final decision the director has in his mind.

FROUG: Are you planning to be a director?

BASS: Not in the slightest. The farther I go in my writing career, the more I enjoy what I'm doing, the more sympathetic and admiring I am of directors. I think directing is the lousiest life in the world.

FROUG: Ten hour, twelve hour days.

BASS: Well, I work very long days, but, despite the control that writers envy and think that directors have, the directors are the victims. They are controlled by the movie. They are the victims of the flaws in my script, of the actors' problems, of the money, of the studio. They have to cope with everything, and they're the guys who have to deliver. How those people keep a family life and how they deal with young children and how they're there to watch their kids grow up . . . I mean, to me, I have such a perfect life. My time is my own. My schedule is my own. I work on eight or nine different projects a year instead of only one project in eighteen months, and I love that diversity. We go away and we travel a half dozen times a year. We own a home up in the Napa Valley. It's like being in heaven, creatively and personally, and what you sacrifice for that is that someone else is making the final decision on the film. But, for me, my scripts and particularly my first drafts, they're my work. And I'm proud of them. I don't know why it's considered by some writers to be a disgrace to work collaboratively with a director and help him realize his vision of the story.

FROUG: I haven't heard that.

BASS: I know a lot of writers feel that way.

FROUG: I've heard writers' egos get bruised, but I haven't heard anybody say it's a disgrace, really.

BASS: I think there are writers, very famous and successful writers whom I won't name, who really feel that you're a sellout if you're not dogmatic about your vision, who believe that if you want to be collaborative with a director and help him realize his vision that you're somehow being untrue to yourself. That's a version of things I don't understand.

FROUG: Tell me about *Rain Man*. That was a very troubled project.

BASS: Sure was.

FROUG: You came in to save it, didn't you?

BASS: Well, I don't know if I was part of the problem or part of the solution or both. When I came on the project, Barry Morrow, who was the original writer who conceived the idea, had been let go by Guber-Peters and United Artists. They were looking for another writer, and my friend Roger Birnbaum, who's now the head of production at Fox and was then the head of Guber-Peters's company, called me. At that time I had the chicken pox, terrible adult chicken pox I had gotten from my kid, and I was really sick and miserable. Do you want the long story on this?

FROUG: Absolutely. Not many writers get a shot at an Oscar,

and you got one and made it.

BASS: Yeah, there is no question that it was the luckiest thing that ever happened to me in my career. In January '87, Roger Birnbaum called me and said there's this Dustin Hoffman and Tom Cruise thing with a start date of March 27. "You've got to be available to start immediately." And I said, "No way that I can, even for Dustin Hoffman and Tom Cruise and Marty Brest," who was the director at that point. (I work in this very strange way where I book myself way, way, way ahead. I'm usually booked for two or three years in advance; that's the way I work. I have a lot of things going at the same time—I'm usually writing six or seven things at the same time, different drafts at different stages.) I said I would have to go to nine different people and beg them to step aside, and that's a big thing to ask. So he said, "Well, let me tell you the story." He told me the story idea, Barry Morrow's wonderful idea. The story was so mesmerizing. I said, "Boy, that's a story I would love to get a chance to work on." So Michael Ovitz, who's now my agent, was the agent, of course, for Dustin and Tom and Marty and was very active in trying to help me get these other commitments to wait, to give me some time to do this. They were all, with only one exception, very understanding and very generous. So I started work. I could only work with Marty Brest by telephone because I had the chicken pox, and both his wife and Dustin's wife were pregnant. Apparently it's not great for pregnant women to be in contact with chicken pox. I never got to meet anybody face to face during that period of time. I was only working on the telephone. I'm very actor-oriented—I love to develop things directly with actors and get input from actors. I wanted more input from the actors. So I had some phone conversations with Dustin and a few with Tom. Marty really was in the driver's seat and he said, "Let me interface with the actors." Marty and I worked out an entire version that we really loved. I still think it was a wonderful draft. And I got it all done in time. After that, I had to leave town because I'd promised my family a vacation, and I never break those kinds of promises. My family always comes first. I gave some of the money back to United Artists so they could hire a writer behind me to work on my pages and to be the guy on the set. They hired Richard Price, one of the best writers around, and I went off to Hawaii with my family. I just felt great that I'd worked on this great project, this wonderful story, and I was sure that when I got back Richard Price would be writing for Dustin Hoffman on the set. I got back and the movie was off. There was no movie. It didn't start. There were creative differences between primarily Dustin, I think, and Marty. Dustin had a different vision of it.

FROUG: Dustin has a reputation for having a different vision than almost any director he works for.

BASS: Well, it's great that I have a chance to tell you about my experience with Dustin. It was as positive an experience as I've ever had working with anyone, anywhere, in any walk of life.

FROUG: Amazing.

BASS: It was unbelievably positive and supportive. This is what happened. Marty was off the picture because he and Dustin disagreed. I wasn't even given a reason. Then I just sort of forgot about the project. Immediately the rumors were that this picture would never get made, the picture was dead, and all that stuff. I go about my business, and take my family away to Paris that summer. We rented a flat, and I'm writing something else. Then I get a phone call from Mike Ovitz saying that they got a new director, and the new director was Steven Spielberg. He said that Spielberg liked my version and wanted to talk to me about continuing. So we finished the Paris trip and came back. I met with Steven and he said, "Dustin has a lot of problems with the thing that you wrote for Marty, and I think Dustin is right. We think you did a great job writing it, but it's a different character. The Barry

Morrow version of Raymond Babbit was retarded, like the guy that he knew, the guy that he modeled it after. If he's sweet, lovable, cuddly, then there's no conflict there. He's too easy to love. Dustin wants to play this guy autistic, difficult, and cantankerous; not lovable, but weird and eccentric—the kind of guy you just hate, who just puts your nerves on edge, a character you can't stand to be around. Put that guy up against Charlie Babbit, a self-centered, egotistical guy who's autistic in his own way—emotionally autistic—because he doesn't want to share or reach out. Both men are living inside a wall that they've built. Neither of them wants contact with the other. Now if you can give me those guys and make them fall in love, you've got something." I wasn't smart enough to get it right away, but Steven was extremely patient with me. He talked with me until I started to realize this was not only something to get behind but was really a much better way than I'd been going. Then we started to meet with Dustin and Tom. There were four-way meetings at Steven's house at the beach. Tom was in many of them and Dustin was in all of them. They were co-writers. It was just unbelievable. We invented scenes together; we invented the characters together. Dustin brought this guy out from the East Coast who was the brother of the real model for our *Rain Man,* not the Morrow version. We talked about his brother and his very idiosyncratic way of speaking. He became the character in the film. It was inspired by this guy's brother. Dustin and I walked on the beach and "improv-ed" this speech to each other. I can't tell you how much Dustin contributed and how much Spielberg contributed. Then I went away and I wrote this long draft. Dustin really liked it and Tom really liked it. Steven liked it, but he felt it needed more work than the actors did. So we continued to meet and talk about what it needed. And then we reached a moment in time when Steven realized that he wasn't going to be able to do the movie and keep his commitment to George Lucas to start the *Raiders* sequel that he had a firm commitment to do. So Steven withdrew and has, he told me subsequently, always had second thoughts and regrets because he really loved *Rain Man*, and he brought so much to it. It's a shame that people who are involved with a film in its interim can't have their name connected with it. Spielberg really did a tremendous amount but, when he left the project, it was dead again. Then the whole town said it was never going to get made—"Forget it, my God, they've lost two directors; it's ridiculous." But Dustin Hoffman and Tom Cruise wouldn't let this thing die. They wanted to play these guys, and Dustin in particular was completely the champion. He was the guy who never gave up. It didn't matter how long it took; he turned down many other movies. At this point, he hadn't made a movie in a long time. This is the movie he wanted to make, so he went to Sidney Pollack, obviously one of the great directors who's ever directed. Sidney decided he wanted to take a crack at it, and didn't want to use me because he always used Kurt Luedtke and David Rayfiel. These are writers who've won Oscars with him, and for him, in the past. And he's a very gracious guy. There's a film I did called *Gardens of Stone* that was originally going to be with Sidney, before it went to Francis Ford Coppola. I was all these guys' lawyer. Sidney's lawyer, Coppola's lawyer, Redford's lawyer.

FROUG: And now you're suddenly their screenwriter.

BASS: Either I am or I'm not; I'm the guy they use or the guy they fire. So Sidney and I met for a day. He was very clear that he was going to use another writer, but he wanted to get my ideas on some of the things I was trying to do. And then I was off the project. I felt very sad, obviously, in a selfish sense, but I was glad it was going to get made. Then Sidney and his writers didn't find a way to do it that they liked, and Sidney left the project.

FROUG: At that point Dustin and Tom Cruise wouldn't go along with what they found?

BASS: No, I don't think that was it. I could be wrong because

I wasn't on the project. I don't think it was a disagreement with Dustin and Sidney; I think it was that Sidney never found a way he liked of solving what he considered the story's problems. I don't think his writers ever wrote anything or turned anything in. They never found a way of putting together a story they wanted to do. Obviously they disagreed with Dustin's version, but they never had their own version. They worked on it, but it never came together. So Sidney Pollack was through. Now, in January or February of 1988, Barry Levinson comes into the scene. He really had come in to kind of talk to Dustin or talk to Sidney and try to help out. Suddenly he and his wife Diana, a terrific lady, decided he ought to take a crack at it. Everybody else had. So Barry was into it. Barry liked my version and I got hired again.

FROUG: Each time you got hired, were you getting paid anew? You'd worked on it now about a year.

BASS: The answer is no. There was some additional money at one point beyond the original money, and I think that was it. It really wasn't about money at that point. I'd been paid very nicely; it was just about wanting it to happen. So now Barry Levinson and I (I had been Levinson's lawyer, also) . . .

FROUG: Amazing.

BASS: So I knew these guys a little bit from my other life, not well because Barry Hirsch was the guy who had the day-to-day talks with them, but I knew them a little. These are like the nicest guys, these directors. They're not only great directors, they're also really great people to work with. So Levinson has his own take on it, which is very idiosyncratically his. And then I meet Mark Johnson, his producer, for the first time and he became a real friend. He's a wonderful, wonderful guy. He's Barry's partner. They work as a team. They come in together. But now we're four or five weeks away from the Writers Guild strike of '88. And Barry, of course, who's a wonderful writer, an Academy Award-level writer, and I both have tremendous respect for the Writers Guild, so we're not going to do anything to violate the strike. We start working around the clock, hoping the strike will get settled but knowing that they practically never do. I'm working around the clock; I'm sleeping four hours a night. Barry's got a million other things to do—pull together a whole movie and cast the girl (we've only got two roles cast). And he's so calm, so unflappable. You never even see that he's nervous. And he's so respectful; it took me a while to get in the rhythm of his low-key style. If Barry Levinson says to you, "You know, that's really great, but I was just thinking that it might be interesting to do it this way," the English translation is "This is the way I think we really ought to do it." It's worded so diplomatically, it took me a while to realize that what he was saying was, "Come on, pal, let's get with it. This is what we want to do." He was a joy to work for, and I actually delivered the last set of pages handwritten in pencil on yellow paper on his doorstep, I didn't even wake him up. It was early in the morning of the day of the strike, and I hand delivered the pages on his doorstep before the strike started. And then we had no communication during the strike. I didn't get a chance to be on the set of that movie because I didn't want even the appearance . . .

FROUG: Of breaking the picket line.

BASS: Yes. Although you were permitted to be on the set of the movie. But I didn't want people to get the wrong idea. I thought it might just make people think that there was writing going on, and there wasn't. So I was pretty nervous the first time Barry invited me to see a cut of the movie.

FROUG: How did it measure up to your drafts and your expectations?

BASS: It was the same and it was different. It was very uniquely Barry's version. Barry had added his personality, his vision, to it, which is one of the most successful things about the film. It was Barry's determination to always go against the sentimentality, to be extra careful not to be overly sentimental. And I'm a very sentimental guy. I usually write very sentimental material, and Barry's restraint was enormously successful. It was praised in all the reviews, and I'm sure it was a major part of the film's success.

FROUG: You got the Oscar. Did you share the Oscar with Morrow or anybody else?

BASS: Well, they gave us two. They gave us each an Oscar. We shared writing credit on the film. There was a Writers Guild arbitration on that, and so we both got Oscars. I had never met Morrow before the award season, and we got to be very friendly. We went to all the awards together and our wives became friends. He's a really sweet guy.

FROUG: Did Mike Ovitz bring Barry Levinson into the project?

BASS: I don't know if he brought him in, but it was certainly Mike Ovitz' dedication that made the project work.

FROUG: He brought this film together, yes? He brought in all the parts and held it together somehow.

BASS: Yeah. He was always in that mix. He was the guy who was working along with Dustin and Tom to keep it alive.

FROUG: Did you always, from the very beginning, know that your theme was "Yes, you are your brother's keeper"?

BASS: Well, there's more than one theme in the movie, and I'm not sure that being your brother's keeper is the way that I would shorthand the theme of it. But it's certainly a valid one.

FROUG: How would you shorthand it?

BASS: I sort of think the film is about how hard it is for human beings to connect with each other and how necessary it is. It's the most important thing we do in life and maybe the hardest thing. That's the theme that's in a lot of the stuff I write. Once Steven and Dustin got me squared away to see that that's what this film really should be about, then I got really excited. Yes, they're brothers metaphorically, they're brothers biologically, and, yes, that adds a lot. But Raymond gave at least as much to Charlie as Charlie gave to Raymond. And since Charlie was better able to receive, you come out at the end of the movie knowing Raymond can't really change. Or he can only change in very, very tiny increments. Raymond's benefit from Charlie may be his experience of getting out in the world. But his real benefit is that Charlie will always be in his life and be there for him. What Raymond did for Charlie was change his whole life, give a man who had no real inner life a humanity and a personality and an ability to fall in love and to relate and to live a productive, emotionally satisfying life. And, of course, the goal was for each one of us to walk into the theater and identify with Charlie Babbit and come out with that point of view about what really counts in life and what really is important.

FROUG: I think that came through beautifully. The interesting thing is that you managed to have both of the brothers come to the realization that they were connected at the hip. The movie evolved the way you put it, that you have to find ways to somehow get along. Beautiful film.

BASS: Thank you.

FROUG: When you're writing a screenplay, do you use a paradigm? Do you say, "I have to have a first act around page twenty or twenty-five and a second act written around eighty, eighty-five or ninety"? An Aristotelian approach? Three acts?

BASS: Yeah. I always see things in terms of three acts. That helps me. There are exceptions where there'll be a four-act piece or there'll be a two-act piece or something. But generally I start off with three sheets of paper and I sort of know where my act breaks are going to be, and I build each act forwards and backwards toward the center of that act. I certainly don't think that each of my acts are forty pages, but my prejudice is toward keeping the three acts close to equal in length. That's my instinct. My instinct is for a first act of forty pages, a second act of forty pages, and a third act of forty pages. It's not a bad goal to start from. And if the story starts to tell you differently, starts to inform you that it should be a little different, then it is.

FROUG: Do you use index cards or scene cards?

BASS: I use no index cards at all.

FROUG: Legal yellow pads, I'll bet.

BASS: They aren't legal size. They're notebook size, looseleaf notebook; that's what it looks like.

FROUG: Do you write in longhand?

BASS: I only write in longhand. Now my assistant has a computer, and every day she gets the pages and types them up on the computer and I proof that. It gives me a second chance to see it. Typed words look a little different than handwritten words, so I get a little different feel for it.

FROUG: When you approached *Sleeping with the Enemy*, originally a book, did you think in terms of three acts?

BASS: *Sleeping with the Enemy* was a rewrite. It was written first by another writer, a very good writer named Lloyd Fonvielle, and I was the middle of three writers on that. Bruce Joel Rubin, who won the Academy Award for *Ghost*, came on at the end and redialogued some of the love scenes for the director. He did some very nice work. I was originally given Lloyd's script by Fox, the studio. They wanted a different writer at that point. Lloyd scripted it extremely faithfully to the novel, a very skillful adaptation of the novel. There were just a lot of things about it that the studio and Leonard Goldberg, who became the producer of the film but at that time was head of the studio, didn't think was the best way to tell the story on film. What works in a novel isn't always the best way to tell the story on film. So I had some ideas, and Leonard had some ideas, and we had a meeting of the minds. I went off and did a series of rewrites, and at a certain point Joe Ruben was brought in as director. Joe had his own vision, so I wrote six or seven or eight drafts for Joe.

FROUG: Your general process of writing is rewriting, yes?

BASS: Well, it's everybody's process. The first draft of anything is really yours. I'm always amazed that they pay me for the first draft because the first draft is just pure joy and fun.

FROUG: That's when you're being the auteur, I guess.

BASS: Yeah. It's like there is nobody else in the film but you at that moment. You're seeing it all in your mind and you're writing the film for yourself, for an audience of one. Then reality intrudes and the guys who are going to pay thirty million dollars to make the film, the guy who's going to have to direct it, the star who's going to have to say the lines, and all these other people say, "I don't like that idea, Ron. How about doing it this way?" And then you start to work collaboratively and, hopefully, always improve it.

FROUG: Have you seen a film based on your screenplay that caused you to say, "God, this is nothing like I wanted. This is just totally different"?

BASS: Each of them have been different in many respects from what I wanted, even films like *Rain Man* that are very successful films and films I think are wonderful. And a lot of the time they're different from my vision in a very positive way that I really admire. The guy did it so much better than the way I was doing it. But lots of times you feel you would have done it very differently. *Gardens of Stone*, a Coppola film, was a film where I would have done many things differently.

FROUG: That didn't do well, did it?

BASS: It didn't do well, and at the box office did very, very badly. It's, I think, my wife's favorite film, one of her two favorite films I've ever written. And many people have told me how much they respond to it. Working with Coppola was really an honor and really a treat. He took me up to his house in Napa Valley. (I now own a home in Napa Valley because I so fell in love with the area in the ten days that he brought me up to his house with his family.) He went through an unbelievable personal tragedy during the making of that film. His son Gio, who I'd met while I was living up there, died in a boating accident during the preproduction of that film. And *Gardens of Stone* is about fathers burying their sons. That's what the whole movie's about. So the heroism of Francis going on with that project—with any project—in that situation was beyond the call of duty. To go on with a project in a cemetery where the Jimmy Caan character is burying his surrogate son. That's what the movie's about, this older man looking on with sorrow and regret at the courage and impetuousness and idealism of youth that's cut down before its time. I get chills saying it now, the idea of this guy going on the set every day and doing that film.

FROUG: Incredible.

BASS: Beyond incredible. Beyond belief. He is such a thorough professional. He didn't want Tri-Star to suffer any more due to the film. And, again, he's one of the greatest screenwriters who ever lived; I think he owns three Academy Awards for screenwriting or something, one of only two men alive who do. So he had his own version of it, and he said to me the day we parted, "You know, don't be upset, don't take it personally, but it's going to be different from what you wrote. You can't reach out there from Malibu." I said, "I don't live in Malibu." He said, "Well, wherever you live, you can't reach out from the grave and grab the director by the neck." And I said, "Well, I couldn't be in the hands of anyone more talented than this guy." He made his own vision of the film, and we have not actually spoken since that time, but I would love to have a chance to work with him again. I don't really know how much of the film that was on the screen was Francis' vision and how much was affected by the unbelievable trauma that he was going through at the time. But for me, certain parts of the film are enormously successful, and certain parts are less.

FROUG: Now that you've reached this lofty status, what are your projects ahead, not as a lawyer but as a screenwriter?

BASS: Writer is not a lofty status. Writer is a real down-home status. You don't make the final decisions; you're just one of the members of the team and you're just glad to be there. It's a real team-player role.

FROUG: It's true. Probably the writers that can't accept that, being part of the collaboration, struggle the hardest, don't you imagine?

BASS: Well, I don't know. I see a lot of these egotistical statements from a lot of these guys who don't look at it that way. Some guys are very successful in being icono-clastic, but I think you're always in for a lot of heartache if you don't accept the fact that the final vision of the story is going to be the director's.

FROUG: Like it or not.

BASS: And it does bother you. For instance, *Sleeping with the Enemy* was an enormously successful film at the box office. I knew exactly what Joe's vision was. I collaborated considerably in reshaping it toward Joe's vision, and he executed his vision. In the last twenty minutes of the film, I knew what was going to happen every minute because I wrote it with Joe. We pieced it all together over weeks of figuring out exactly how every moment should go. And it just scared the heck out of me. I know that Julia screamed the first time she saw it, and she performed in it. So he did a masterful job. Nonetheless, my vision of that film was different from Joe's vision of that film. My vision of that film was more about men and women in a more generalized version of how this psychotic guy, who wasn't really like anybody that any of us knew in real life, had connections and similarities to non-psychotic men who look at women a certain way, not nearly as dominating or as possessive. There are threads there that I would have liked to have brought out and made women in the audience sit and think about the man in their life and wonder if they should have a talk. [*Laughter*] About how they see each other and how they relate to each other as human beings. But that element of the film was of less interest to Joe than the thriller aspect of it and the pace and excitement of it.

FROUG: Did you know going in, when they cast Julia Roberts, that you were going to have a hit because she's so hot in the box office right now?

BASS: First of all, when Julia Roberts was cast in the film, *Pretty Woman* had not been released, and Julia Roberts was not at all a movie star. She had success in *Steel Magnolias*, and everyone in the industry felt she was going to be a movie star. There was a terrific, as they say, "buzz" about *Pretty Woman*. I had met her. There was a script that I'd written called *Heart's Desire* that Julia liked. I had written it with a collaborator named David Field, a wonderful writer, and we were going to produce it together. Julia wanted to play that role.

FROUG: Do you think screenwriters ought to go to film school?

BASS: Speaking strictly from ignorance, I have an enormous prejudice against screenwriting classes. It's completely my own prejudice. When I went to Stanford University, I had a professor of literature named Wallace Stegner, a famous American novelist. Stegner taught a course in American literature, and I went up to him after class one day and said, "Can you help me in terms of taking a writing course?" He said, "Never take a creative writing course. Never take a writing course. Why would you want to listen to someone who you are going to invest with the mantle of authority telling you how to write? Even if the person doesn't want that mantle, you're going to invest him with that mantle. They're going to tell you the way they write, their rules. If they don't call them rules, they're still going to be perceived as such by you. It's a straitjacket. Never take a course in writing. Read every great book that was ever written, steal everything you can steal from the best. They want you to. Anything that I've ever written that you can use and that helps you learn how to do something. That's what you learn from. Learn from watching people who are the best, who have done it, whom you admire, not from someone who's teaching you to do it." And I took that advice to heart. I never did take a screenwriting course, and I am always approached by people who say things to me like, "Well, Mr. Fields says," or "This person says on page sixty-five and on page twenty-five," and I just laugh. Not because I'm right and they're wrong. I don't have a clue. But to me, writing is autowriting. The story tells itself, and you are just kind of privileged to be the thing it's telling itself through.

FROUG: You're the vessel.

BASS: And, boy, when I talk to other screenwriters whom I admire and respect and I say that to them, I get a lot of response. A lot of people feel the same way. They really do. It's a process that you just have to not try and control very hard. You have to let it happen. Of course, the rewriting process gets to be more rational in places and there is intellect, but so much of it is just letting go and letting it happen.

FROUG: Out of your guts.

BASS: Yeah, that's one way of saying it. But it almost doesn't feel like it's coming from your heart or your guts. It just feels like the Michelangelo quote, "There is a statue inside this block of marble somewhere, and it's talking to you as you're chipping away at it."

FROUG: He said something like, "All you do is chisel away everything except David."

BASS: Yes. That is, a little bit, what it feels like. When I'm writing dialogue, I'm seeing the people, I'm hearing the people, I'm there with them, and I'm just sort of writing down what they say. I try to prepare, I think about it beforehand, I look at some notes. And then, when I get into the scene, I just let the scene happen (I usually write in the park or some place where other people aren't around). After that, I may edit it or I may change it and so forth, but I'm always hearing the woman's voice or the man's voice and I'm seeing them in my mind. I'm watching their faces and their bodies and really just trying to describe them.

FROUG: How much do you have to know about your characters before you sit down to write?

BASS: I probably wind up knowing less than other people. I don't find it as necessary as other people do, and I'm faulted on this a lot. An executive will say, "Well, I don't know anything about Peter. Don't know anything about him." What I know about him is what I needed to know. I knew how he felt in that moment. I knew what he'd say, I knew what he'd do, I knew what he wanted, I knew where the conflict was, so I'll wind up inventing this story. You know, the single most interesting story of that was Bob Rafelson sitting at a blackboard and saying, "Why does Katherine kill? Was she raped when she was a child? Did her father abuse her? Did her father beat up her mother? Why did she do it?" I said, "I never stopped to think about that, Bob. It doesn't matter." He said, "Well, it matters to the actress. It matters to Theresa Russell. She's got to know why." I said, "Bob, if I tell you why, you're going to wind up putting it in the goddamn film, and then it's going to be like . . ."

FROUG: Boring.

BASS: It's just like a snap, you know, kind of TV instant psychoanalysis that now we understand this woman in a nutshell because someone's given an easy two-line explanation. He said, "I swear to you"—and he kept his promise—"it will not be in the film. I promise you, but let me sit down with Theresa and tell her something." I said to myself, "Okay, I'll have to learn how. Katherine will have to sort of tell me how. But I know she wasn't raped. And I know she wasn't abused, because she loves these men." That's the important part about Katherine, she loves the men she kills. It's not about revenge. And sitting right there, I said, "Well, now I know what it is. Katherine's father was the best person in her life, not the worst. She adored him and she worshipped him. They were the two closest people in the world and, when she was nine years old, he died of cancer. She was so enraged and frustrated and abandoned at that leave-taking that something inside her determined, in a way that became ultimately psychotic and twisted, that no man she loved would ever leave her again. No man would ever make the leave-taking within his control. And so she finds these men, these father figures, whatever age they are, and she makes them love her as her father loved her, and she loves them the way she loved her father. And it has to end in death to repeat the experience that she had, that she's trying to work through. She causes the leave-taking. She is now in control of it when it ends and so she can't be hurt or left or abandoned anymore. She's the one who decides." Well, he loved that and Theresa loved that, and that became her internal model. It enabled her to love these guys the way she should love them. It wasn't about someone who was after their money or something like that. She didn't need to keep doing it.

FROUG: That film deserved a better audience than it got, didn't it?

BASS: It actually was, I think, reasonably successful for its time. For what it cost, and in those days, it was considered by the studio as a success. It had an incredible life in video and it's still on cable today, six years later.

FROUG: It's an excellent film, an excellent original idea.

BASS: Thank you.

FROUG: Thank you for this chat. Would you like to add anything?

BASS: The only thing that I would say, in brief, is it's such a difficult life, being a screenwriter. It's so hard for most screenwriters to be successful at it. The major distinction I make to people who ask me about being a writer is whether they are in love with writing or in love with the idea of being a writer. Write only if you love writing, if you get that joy every day that I'm going to get in fifteen minutes when I go to the park and I sit down with today's scenes and I do it. That's what makes it all worthwhile. If what you're looking for is the money and people to hang out with and the contact with celebrities and all that stuff, you're going to be miserable.

Jack Epps, Jr. and Jim Cash

1986   TOP GUN *(Screenplay)*
            LEGAL EAGLES *(Screenplay)*

1987   SECRET OF MY SUCCESS *(Shared Screenplay)*

1989   TURNER AND HOOCH *(Shared Story and Screenplay)*

1990   DICK TRACY *(Screenplay)*

FADE IN:

EXT. AT SEA - NIGHT

It's a moonless night in the heart of darkness: the carrier
U.S.S. KITTY HAWK is tossed like a toy in the angry waves of
the stormy Indian Ocean.

Thick clouds have blacked out the moon, and lightning rips
the sky like jagged electric ropes. The sea shifts and
swirls, lashing the Kitty Hawk with walls of wind; the ship
plows into the waves that spill over her deck like oozing
black lava.

Above the crashing waves and the howling winds, we hear the
VOICE of the TOWER, filtered over a radio.

                    TOWER
          Ghost Rider One-One-Seven, you are
          cleared to land. Conditions stormy,
          very turbulent...

EXT. CLOUD COVER

Above the storm, we find two Navy F-14's, floating in close
formation. Outlined majestically against the full, white-
moon, the F-14's exude a raw and lethal power with their
long tapering noses, erect tails, and the streaks of
moonlight that splash off their silver surfaces. There is
no sensation of speed -- not yet -- these two spectacular
planes drift like they were in a dream.

                    TOWER
          Approach at vector two-four-nine. Winds
          at 19 knots with crosswing swirls...

INT. F-14

The pilot of the first F-14 is LT. PETE MITCHELL (call sign
"MAVERICK"). In his flight suit and oxygen mask, we can
only see his eyes -- they are young. At twenty-three, he is
lean, hard, athletic. If we read nothing else in his eyes,
we read the supreme arrogance of the fighter pilot: poise,
confidence, a refusal to recognize failure or fear.

Behind Maverick, in the back seat, is his RIO (Radar
Intercept Officer). LT. JOSH BRADSHAW ("GOOSE") is angular,
hawk-nosed, and straight out of Alabama.

                              (CONTINUED)

"We have a words and music relationship."

It was an eerie experience for me to drive onto the busy studio lot in Culver City where Jack Epps, Jr., the Hollywood-based half of the highly successful screenwriting team of Cash and Epps, worked. The four-story parking structure was on the site where we filmed several segments of "The Twilight Zone" when this acreage had been one of MGM's two backlots. I had produced the final season of that exceptional show some twenty-eight years ago. Now MGM's town square with its facade of a small-town city hall, bank, real estate office, ice cream parlor, etc. was no more. In their place I saw giant soundstages, huge set-construction shops, scores of workmen busily moving skiploaders, scenery, etc. The location for countless movies and as many TV shows was no more. It gave me a chill, chicken skin. I felt as if I were in an episode of "The Twilight Zone" myself. But this brave new world was real enough, and whether I liked my jarring time leap over almost three decades was of no importance. The future, so it seemed, was here and now and I was stuck in it.

My queasiness was not assuaged by the knowledge that I was about to interview two screenwriters who were most certainly of a younger generation. This team collaborated by modems (whatever they were) and used all the high-tech gadgets of the late 20th century. I feared they would overwhelm me with their whiz-bang technological expertise.

It turned out that nothing could have been further from the truth. I was greeted by Jack Epps, Jr. in his office doorway, a smiling, handsome young man with a warm, welcoming handshake. Jack could not have been more gracious.

He explained that his partner, Jim Cash, was standing by in East Lansing, Michigan, to enter the discussion via a speaker-phone whenever we needed him. Jack also set me at ease by telling me how much my first book, *The Screenwriter Looks at the Screenwriter,* had meant to them. Suddenly I felt like the celebrity, which was fun but was as uneasy for me as what was happening outside to the sacred ground of "The Twilight Zone."

We settled in to tape our conversation in his large, plushly furnished office after Jack cautioned his secretary not to interrupt us.

What follows is surely the most relaxed and thoroughly enjoyable interview to which I have ever been a lucky participant. I hope you enjoy reading the comments on these screenwriters' work as much as I did listening to them.

FROUG: How long have you and Jim Cash been collaborating?

EPPS: We started working together sometime around 1976. We started trying this process of writing long distance, and we sold our first script in 1978.

FROUG: What was your first script?

EPPS: The first script was a spec script that took us about two years to write called *Izzy and Moe.* It was based on two prohibition agents in the 1920s. Later on, a Movie-of-the-Week was made based on the same two characters, but not on our script.

FROUG: Did you always plan to write by computer or phone or . . . how do you work this, by the way? Technically, I'm an ignoramus.

EPPS: Well, it's interesting. The relationship—we've been writing together now, as of this interview, somewhere around twelve, thirteen years. So it's evolved. At first, Jim and I tried writing by cassette, sending it back and forth, and sending just a page here and a page there and telephoning. We didn't really have the money to talk on the phone a lot at that time. It's evolved now to where we have computers and we have modems and we have fax machines and all sorts of stuff like that. We have a very words and music relationship. I think that's why Jim and I've been successful. I think for any good partnership to be successful the partners should have different strengths and weaknesses.

FROUG: Absolutely.

EPPS: So you're not competing with each other.

FROUG: Right. Has Jim opted not to move to Hollywood? Obviously you can't operate out of Michigan. Somebody's got to be here.

EPPS: You know, in a sense, if you're a writer, you can write anywhere you want, fly into town and do your business and leave. There's nothing that keeps me here except that I like to produce—I like to be involved in it. Jim likes East Lansing, Michigan. I mean, he loves small-town America; he loves being there. There's just something very nice and pleasant about it. And he's the only screenwriter in East Lansing, Michigan. [*Laughter*] That makes him very special.

FROUG: When he goes into the store, they know Jim Cash.

EPPS: That's right. As opposed to here, you know; just another guy.

FROUG: Does he also teach or is he a full-time screenwriter?

EPPS: He does teach at Michigan State University, and this is something you should really talk to Jim about, because he can describe his situation better than I can. He teaches at the University and enjoys that. You know, as a writer, it's such a solitary job; you need to get out. Teaching is something that's great for him, because it gets his mind off the work and gets him into something else.

FROUG: That's what I did for a number of years. Taught at UCLA and wrote. It was a very good way to live. Now, let us start with you guys. You have so many super hits, let's start with the most popular, which I guess is *Top Gun*.

EPPS: Yes.

FROUG: Whose story idea was *Top Gun*?

EPPS: Well, it's interesting, *Top Gun* was originally offered to us from Paramount. Simpson-Bruckheimer, the producers, had found this article in *California* magazine about the Top Gun School. And they said, "Jeez, there might be a movie in this Top Gun School. Guys, go down and see if you can find a movie there." The article had a terrific photograph in it. It showed this jet up at twenty-eight thousand feet with the white, billowing clouds flanked by two jets off to each side. In the center plane was a pilot wearing a helmet. When I saw that picture, I suddenly got a vision of the movie. It was, as we say, "That's the movie." So I said, "Well, if we can write a picture that has the same impact as that photograph, we will have succeeded." So I went down to the Top Gun School and spent about three weeks at the school. I interviewed the pilots and took a flight ride.

FROUG: You rode with them?

EPPS: Oh, absolutely. And that, in fact, changed the movie. We knew about the competitiveness, the whole fighter-pilot mentality—that comes out within five minutes of meeting these guys. But once I flew, I suddenly found out that this was an amazing physical event. It wasn't just going fast. To do it and do it well, you had to be strong, and it was an endurance test.

FROUG: To fly this plane.

EPPS: Because of the G forces involved, and the speed you're flying at, and the size of the turns. See, what *Top Gun* is really about—it's a sports picture. It's not a military picture; it's a sports picture. It's about this sport called ACM, aerial combat maneuvering. And that's really what we tried to get into because Jim and I are ex-jocks. I played hockey at Michigan State and Jim was a football star in high school. So, for us, it was bringing that sort of athletic competitive mentality to *Top Gun,* and that's what we keyed into.

FROUG: Did you write it with the idea that Tom Cruise was going to be in it?

EPPS: Absolutely.

FROUG: You knew it.

EPPS: From the beginning—well, actually, I didn't know he was going to be in it. When we were writing the picture I saw *Risky Business,* and Tom appeared to me as the character. What I call the young American. He just looked like the fighter pilot.

FROUG: The jock in the jet plane.

EPPS: That's right. So Jim and I wrote the picture aiming it towards Tom—that character, that mentality. He became Maverick to us, and when I gave the script to Don

Simpson, the producer, I said, "Think Tom Cruise." And Don was able to think Tom Cruise and also . . .

FROUG: Tom Cruise was able to think Tom Cruise.

EPPS: Don did a terrific job in terms of bringing Tom to the picture. I mean, that is something in itself, to get the actor to see the movie. And Tom was terrific.

FROUG: He was terrific. It was a wonderful movie, and it's still a marvelous movie.

EPPS: And you think about casting, how important casting becomes for the script of the movie. If it's cast with somebody else, it's a totally different picture, because Maverick is a character. He's cocky, he's a bit of an asshole, I mean, he's really over the top. To me he's sort of the young American presenting himself, waiting to get his block knocked off. So if you take an actor who's not instantly likable, and you put him in that role, suddenly it changes the whole movie. Suddenly you don't like this guy, you're not rooting for him.

FROUG: He managed to bring off the cockiness and still be likable, which is quite remarkable.

EPPS: Absolutely. I think that for me that cockiness—it's a little touch of Joe Namath. I mean, Joe Namath as a football player was cocky, but he always delivered the goods.

FROUG: Yes, he did.

EPPS: He could pull it off.

FROUG: Right. I think the only criticism I ever saw of the film was about the love story. Was that something conceived from the beginning, or did you kind of add it in?

EPPS: The love story was disappointing to Jim and me, too. We had written a different love story. We had written a love story that involved a girl (and I'm not so sure that what we wrote was correct) who was a world-class gymnast. She was physical, and she had had a major injury that had pulled her out of world-class competition. Therefore, at some point, she could share in Maverick's loss. His loss with Goose. So we tried to link that up. The studio wanted to basically keep it contained in the military and created this sort of love story that was then revised by somebody else. So we're not too pleased with it either.

FROUG: Also, it held up the movie.

EPPS: I fast-forwarded through those parts, too.

FROUG: [*Laughing*] The woman who was cast seemed to me a bit older than Tom Cruise.

EPPS: Yes. That casting would not have been my choice.

FROUG: Kelly McGillis is a good actress, but there was no chemistry with Cruise, was there?

EPPS: There wasn't. She's a terrific actress—in *Witness* she was just unbelievable. But here I don't think she fit the role. I think there was some sort of deal because of *Two Jakes* falling out. They had a deal at Paramount. I think they put her in the picture because of that.

FROUG: So, in fact, once you delivered the script, which got Tom Cruise and which got a go, you lost control of it.

EPPS: Well, what happened was that the studio didn't green-light it when we first delivered the script. They didn't see the movie, and it wasn't until later on, through a lot of circumstances, that they green-lit the picture. At that time we were away working on *Legal Eagles*, so we couldn't break away to do the revisions, and they brought somebody else in to do some of the revisions.

FROUG: Did somebody else get a credit?

EPPS: No. We got the sole writing credit.

FROUG: The second writer has to contribute an enormous amount in order to come in and get credit, doesn't he?

EPPS: The second writer on an original screenplay has to write more than fifty percent. The concept there is to protect the original writer. To get fifty percent of screen credit and fifty percent of the residuals, you have to do fifty percent of the work.

FROUG: At least.

EPPS: Yes.

FROUG: In the old days, it used to be seventy-five percent, and then they cut it back to fifty percent. In *Turner and*

Hooch, it's unusual—there's a whole gaggle of credits there. How did that come about? Story by Dennis Shryack and Michael Blodgett, screenplay by Shryack and Blodgett, Dan Petrie, Jr. gets in as executive producer and gets a credit, then come you guys. That's really strange.

EPPS: Actually, I'm on the screen credits committee of the Writers Guild. We looked at some Writers Guild documents on credits, and I think that's the only film released in 1989 that received that kind of credit, because three writers were involved. So it was very unusual. What happened there was a situation where Shryack and Blodgett had written the first draft and original screenplay. It was then heavily revised by several writers along the way. Then Petrie became involved, and he heavily revised it. Then Petrie hired us, and we heavily revised it. I think the situation was that there were many hands in the pot and that we were the three who had the biggest impact on the script.

FROUG: I would hate to have been on the arbitration committee for that one. I've been on a number of them, but that would have been a mind-boggler. *Turner and Hooch* was a successful movie, wasn't it?

EPPS: It was very successful.

FROUG: With Tom . . .

EPPS: Tom Hanks.

FROUG: . . . who was very funny in it.

EPPS: Tom was terrific. One of the things that we love doing is writing for actors. We knew Hanks was in the picture because when we were hired we were going to shoot in six weeks: "Guys, come on, and please, you know, do magic on the script." And Tom was heavily in on the development process. Which was very unusual.

FROUG: Jumping ahead to *Legal Eagles*. It seems to me that that was one of your most successful films. Was it?

EPPS: No, it was not.

FROUG: Why do you think it wasn't?

EPPS: Well, there are lots of things. I think it was a picture that, in many ways, never jelled properly. It's interesting enough, but one thing that happened, in terms of box office success, was that the critics nailed the picture. They just really came out loaded for bear.

FROUG: Do you think that was because of Redford and Winger?

EPPS: Because of Reitman—he'd just done *Ghostbusters* . . .

FROUG: Which was a supersmash.

EPPS: That's right. And here's Bob Redford's first picture in a long time. There was a CAA package involved, and there were rumors about the size of the budget. So they just came out and lambasted this picture. They really did a job. It showed that critics can really hurt a certain type of picture. But the funny thing that's happened is, since that time, people have seen it on video, and I've had more people tell me, "Hey, I really liked that picture. I don't know what all the problem was about. It was really a lot of fun."

FROUG: Very interesting. I've seen all the films of the writers I'm interviewing, most of them I'd seen in the theatre, but some I went back and saw again on videotape, and they often played better on videotape. It's strange.

EPPS: Well, I think because you have fewer expectations— it's in your house—you're more relaxed. In the theater, you've paid the money, you're sitting there with the anticipation—it's a whole different type of thing.

FROUG: Tell me about CAA's involvement in *Legal Eagles*.

EPPS: Well, that's difficult for me because I'm one element of that. All I can say is that they represented Ivan Reitman, they represented Bob Redford, they represented us. So they represent the people and then it becomes a package. I'm not involved on that level, in terms of their packaging and that sort of thing.

FROUG: When packaging motion pictures, does CAA get a piece of the budget as they do in television?

EPPS: You know, I can't tell you. I really don't know. I'm not involved in those sort of things.

FROUG: As a CAA client, do you find that they generate the jobs, like agents are supposed to?

EPPS: Well, I think for Jim and I, we've been successful for long enough that we pretty much generate our own jobs. At this stage, we tend to create our own pictures. They don't send the package to us.

FROUG: How long have you been with CAA?

EPPS: I think it's about eight years.

FROUG: That's a long time with one agency.

EPPS: It has been. I've been with my agent, Rand Holston, since Jim and I began. He's terrific. He's like the third partner.

FROUG: On to *Dick Tracy*. That film seems to play better on videotape, too. Why do you think that's so? It gets a lot of play; it's hard to get it in the videostores.

EPPS: I don't know. I think that with *Tracy*, it's one of those things where we wonder, was there too much hype? Did it turn people off and therefore it was the type of thing they felt was being pushed down their throat? I mean, the machine got very big there, promoting that picture. And maybe people just waited for the video to see it. I think it's also one of those things in which the color plays good on television; it's a very colorful movie.

FROUG: It's a very unusual film. The set design and the kind of surreal approach, I've never seen anything like it in any other film. Did you have any input into that?

EPPS: That's really Warren Beatty and his art director. We basically wrote a movie without thinking of that sort of stuff. What Warren wanted to do was make it look like a cartoon. He talked about this early on—make it look like one frame at a time, you know, like a cartoon. The same coloring, the same feeling, the same setup, and, in many ways, the same starkness. *Tracy* for me is a little too stark at times. There's not enough life in it.

FROUG: In writing it, did you envision which actor was going to be normal, a human being with makeup, and which actor was going to be this exaggerated cartoon character?

EPPS: No, because we were writing the comic strip. We basically were working off of Chester Gould's original comic strip. So we were going with the concept that these people were real. Flattop was real. I mean, he just looked like Flattop. Pruneface was Pruneface. He just looked like Pruneface. In terms of writing it, I don't think you can think of the cartooniness of it. You have to think more of just the characters and try to give them the characteristics you want them to have.

FROUG: How about Madonna? Was she always conceived to be a key role?

EPPS: The way the script began, interestingly enough, was we were hired by John Landis in 1982 or '83 to do *Dick Tracy*. And John's sort of orders were, "I want this script set in the thirties, I want it set around Big Boy, and I want a big finish." So we went off and then, going back to the original comic strip, wrote a draft.

FROUG: You read all the "Dick Tracy" comic strips?

EPPS: I read about ten years of them and became a huge fan. I love it. The old Tracy stuff; the stuff in the golden age from about 1939 to 1944 is the best. Mumbles and Measles and the Blank and the Brow and all that stuff; that's just terrific stuff.

FROUG: And the Kid was in the comic strips.

EPPS: Oh, the Kid was there from the beginning.

FROUG: He's wonderful. I love the actor you got, don't you?

EPPS: Yeah, he was terrific.

FROUG: After you delivered a draft, did Beatty come in and do a rewrite?

EPPS: What happened was this: we were hired by Landis and did two drafts for him. Beatty was not involved at that time. Then, we understand, there was a budgetary disagreement with the studio. John wanted to do a bigger picture; they wanted smaller scale. Walter Hill became involved as director, with Joel Silver as producer. We then did two drafts for Walter and Joel.

FROUG: Were you paid for these drafts all along the way?

EPPS: Oh, yes, of course. Anyway, Walter and Joel had a disagreement with the studio about the size of the budget. It was going to be a bigger picture than they wanted. Then Dick Benjamin was brought on board, and the project shifted from Universal to Paramount, and we did two drafts for Dick Benjamin, who was going to sort of play it down, a more limited budget type picture. But the problem was always casting. Who was going to be Dick Tracy? At that time, like 1983, '84, they really couldn't find the proper Dick Tracy. Beatty was getting close to it but wasn't sure, so that sort of all dissolved. And then, years later, Beatty ended up becoming very involved. He got the script from Paramount, secured the rights himself, and put together his own project. We were never involved with Beatty in the picture.

FROUG: I see. Does it bother you a lot when these projects stall and stall again over the years? Or are you already off onto something else?

EPPS: Well, at that time it was very difficult because Jim's and my history was that we had written six unproduced screenplays. Our first produced screenplay was *Top Gun*. We had written for years, trying to get a picture shot. And everyone would say, "Hey, boy, we love your script," but they just didn't get made. *Tracy* was the one that came the closest. They were building sets, they were hiring crew, and it was moving ahead. And suddenly that one stopped. It's very hard. I think at that time they didn't have the cast they wanted. They weren't happy with it.

FROUG: That's a point I'd like to talk a little about with you. All of my students and all the young writers, I always encourage them to generate their own jobs. They write script after script, and sooner or later, one of them gets attention and they get started. How many did you say you wrote?

EPPS: Well, Jim and I, we wrote six screenplays before anything was produced. Our seventh script was produced. Then *Tracy* was produced; then a lot of things. Suddenly we had a floodgate. We had three films released in eleven months. So we went from absolutely nothing to unknowns to then being thrust into the spotlight.

FROUG: Tell me the progression for new writers. What kind of money can you start out with on your first script, for example?

EPPS: In terms of?

FROUG: Your sale. Your first sale.

EPPS: Well, for us, it was a spec script. Our first two scripts were spec scripts. In this day, of course, spec script prices have gone through the roof. So the sky's the limit, whatever you can get at auction.

FROUG: I've heard that. Do you think that's going to keep going, or do you think it's going to fall off.

EPPS: No, I think it's going to fall off. I think, like any auction thing, there's a cycle with periods when people pay the high price, then the lower price. But there seems to be an area between a half a million dollar and a million dollar price range that a very attractive script falls into.

FROUG: For an original.

EPPS: For an original spec screenplay.

FROUG: But now that you have this kind of track record, which is extraordinary, you guys have to be over the million dollar range, right?

EPPS: We command a pretty good price.

FROUG: That's as far as you want to go?

EPPS: I think so.

FROUG: Okay.

EPPS: You know, you do it because you love the movies. The money gets in the way. I think that if you're a good writer, the money will follow. But if you're writing for money, I don't think it's going to work. I think that very few people can make that happen.

FROUG: I'm so glad you're saying this. Every writer I've talked to said that. Even CAA said that.

EPPS: Well, that's true, though. If it doesn't come from your heart, and if you don't really want it for the writing, then your motives are wrong, and it's going to show up on the paper. Jim and I had a lot to prove. We had some times when we were not successful, so we got together and said, "Look, we want to make this work. We want to make this happen." We were hungry. When you write from hunger—hungry to show that we could do it, to prove ourselves—that's the most interesting. And the money follows.

[At this point in our interview we brought in Jim Cash from East Lansing, Michigan, via a speaker phone.]

CASH: I have a question for you, Bill. Of all these guys you interviewed in your first book, who was your favorite?

FROUG: Oh, gosh. Walter Newman, of course. And Lew Carlino. Let's talk about this book, Jim. Let's talk about collaboration. How does it work for you? Do you guys work on scenes together or just your step outline and script together?

CASH: We've done it just about every way possible; there's no way to honestly say this is the way we do it every time. Usually, Jack works ahead of me, planning scenes. His story instincts are exceptional, and I give him all the room he needs to develop the main body of the work. He'll pitch several scenes to me at a time, and we'll talk about each one of them for a few minutes, turning them inside-out a couple of times, reshaping something, adding something else. His job during this is to make sure the story stays on track. My job is to make the scene interesting. He's looking at the whole sky; I'm looking at the incoming bogey. I write the first draft of the scene, working very fast, like throwing paint at a canvas. After it's all out, I structure and polish it—that's the fun part. Emily Dickinson called it "gem construction." Then I send it to Jack, and he does his own gem construction and sends it back to me. Then we move on to the next set of scenes.

FROUG: So in effect you kind of rewrite each other.

CASH: "Why'd you take out that line? That was my favorite line in the scene"—a lot of that.

EPPS: What's interesting is that we do have a words and music relationship, like I said earlier. I think the key to collaboration is knowing what your strengths are and knowing what your partner's strengths are. And not trying to compete with each other. I've been in several partnerships. Some were not as successful as this one, of course. And I learned from those. I learned you've got to park your ego at the door, that basically the partnership has got to be the thing. Jim likes to say, and it's true, there's three egos involved here: there's Cash's ego, Epps's ego, and then there's the ego of Cash and Epps. And that's the one. When we get together, we try to let the team be the important thing.

CASH: We're writing our best when the third personality takes over.

FROUG: I understand that. How often do you guys actually get together, face-to-face?

CASH: Too often, wouldn't you say, Jack? [*Laughter*]

EPPS: Yeah, too often is right. And the last time was about five years ago.

FROUG: Really?

EPPS: Yeah. We've been working twelve years, and I'd say Jim and I have seen each other, what? four times? five times?

CASH: Yeah, I'm very entrenched here in the northern midwest.

FROUG: Like me, you're a college teacher, yes?

CASH: I've been teaching at Michigan State since 1970. I donate most of my money back to the university in the form of scholarships and awards and the rest of it I give to high schools for scholarships. Technically, I teach for free because I enjoy it so much.

EPPS: The real reason he does it is to get the campus parking sticker.

CASH: Hey, that sticker's worth at least forty thousand dollars a year.

FROUG: Oh, I'm sure. That's great. Did you guys meet in college?

CASH: Yeah.

EPPS: At Michigan State. Interestingly enough, fate really was involved in Jim and I getting together and working together, because he was actually teaching screenwriting at State. I was making films. I figured, well, if I'm going to learn to make films, I should learn to write the damn things and applied for his class, but I couldn't get in because the class was full. So I had to go and sort of beg this guy to let me in his class.

FROUG: Marvelous.

CASH: At the time I was the producer at the local PBS station.

FROUG: That's a wonderful thing to be doing. Something I'd love to do, by the way.

CASH: It was a lot of fun. I was there for three years in the beginning and then took a year and went to commercial television. And I ran back as fast as I could to public television because all my time was being taken up with making commercials and meeting impossible deadlines, and I loved PBS. Public television gave me so much room to do it any way I wanted to. I loved it a lot.

FROUG: You could do stuff you believed in?

CASH: Yeah. Plus, I was the special projects producer, which meant that, any grants we got, the money came to my office and I got to have all the fun, really. Everybody else was doing weekly shows. I just did special productions.

FROUG: You don't have an urge to get together and hash out this stuff in person?

CASH: Well, we have great times whenever we do. You see, I don't fly worth a lick. I just don't fly. That's a big part of it.

FROUG: Ah, now we get to the root of the problem.

EPPS: But it's also the great irony. Here we are writing this big jet movie . . .

CASH: But I'm not going to get in an airplane.

FROUG: You didn't go up in *Top Gun*?

CASH: No, I just went on a few thrill rides at the fair. That taught me all I needed to know. Jack went up in *Top Gun*.

FROUG: That's a great irony. Here's a guy who doesn't like to fly but was involved in writing the definitive flying picture, right.

EPPS: But of course, that shows . . .

CASH: I wrote it with fear. Jack did go up in the . . . it wasn't an F-14, but it was fast enough.

FROUG: I think anything faster than a motor scooter's fast enough.

CASH: Yeah. A bicycle is about my top speed. But think about that for a moment. Isn't that what writing is all about? You can write about jets without flying in one because sometime in your life you've experienced sensations of speed, fear, competition, freedom, confinement, rage, and dozens of other things, even though you didn't necessarily experience all of them at the same moment. You draw on them collectively, paste them together like a mosaic, and you've written a pretty good scene about flying jets. To me, writing all comes down to four things: imagery, emotion, rhythm, and structure. You write pictures that capture emotion, and then you discipline it with rhythm and structure. Of course, when you're doing it right, it all happens with a flow that you don't even think about.

FROUG: Do you get together in the very beginning, to work out the theme, for example? Do you have a theme to start out with?

CASH: We usually have a character or an image. It took us six months to find the character we wanted to write for *Top Gun*. Four months? Something like that.

EPPS: Well, actually, we found the character fairly soon. We had a sense of Maverick. It was the story in that one that eluded us for about three months.

CASH: Okay, I guess I was thinking of *Old Gold*, where we

finally found the character, and it took off.

EPPS: Right. And that's important because, for Jim and I to take off, we have to have a voice. And until that character has a voice and talks to us on paper and starts telling us who he is . . .

CASH: The actual writing of the screenplay is a lot faster than the *discovery* of the screenplay.

EPPS: Yeah, it seems to be. But the uniqueness of voice is essential for us to have a successful character for a screenplay.

FROUG: About how long do you spend writing your first draft?

CASH: I can give you extremes in both directions. *Legal Eagles* was about a year for the first draft, wasn't it, Jack?

EPPS: Yeah, but that was because the process was also very unique.

CASH: But the fastest was *Secret of My Success*, which was about four weeks.

FROUG: In that, did you already have Michael J. Fox when you started?

EPPS: Yes. That was a unique situation. Universal Studios came to us and said, "We're shooting a picture on June 1. We have Michael Fox for ten weeks. We're shooting it with whatever script we have in hand. We would like you guys to deliver us a better script."

CASH: We had an idea that was similar to it that we sort of put into the framework of the script they had.

EPPS: So we sat down and did a total page-one rewrite, top to bottom, in four weeks. But knowing we had Michael, knowing that this is the actor who's going to play these scenes and these lines, gave the script incredible energy. And he just nailed it. He really did.

CASH: We could write forever for Michael Fox or Tom Hanks. They're inventive and energetic and they always bring something extra to a good scene without ripping apart the material that's already on the page. Jack and I tend to write about winners—jet jocks and top cops and characters who have specific goals, a sense of humor, and no unnecessary baggage or angst. Michael and Tom project a natural enthusiasm for life that fits with that kind of character. It takes a fearless actor—and fearless writers—to look in the face of the human condition, draw some laughs, and declare that life can be won.

FROUG: Did it hamper you to know that there'd been this successful Broadway show and a movie called *How to Succeed in Business Without Really Trying*?

CASH: Well, neither one of us had ever seen it.

EPPS: Actually I had seen it . . .

CASH: Did you?

EPPS: Yeah, because when Universal turned down *Jobs*, which is the idea that we then married with *The Secret of My Success, How to Succeed in Business* was one of the reasons why we changed it. But Jim and I love to tackle things that people say can't be done. There hadn't been a successful flying picture in how long?

FROUG: God, since *Wings*?

EPPS: "Flying pictures? No one goes to see planes up in the air." But we said, "No, as a movie, but we see a vision." And the same thing with business. They said, "Oh, you can't do a business picture. No one wants to see business because business people are villains." And we said, "No, there's something good here."

CASH: If you look at the original script for *Top Gun*, you'll see that all of those flying sequences were very carefully choreographed on our pages.

FROUG: Really.

EPPS: Absolutely. We were proud of that, and we never got credit. Everybody figures they just went out there and shot a bunch of planes, but each one of those flying sequences has a story progression. Something happens to Maverick's story each time. So each flying sequence progressed him a little further down the way and created situations that then fed into the main story.

FROUG: I was struck by that, and I've seen it now three

times, by the way. I saw that progression the first time. Each one had an effect on his character, which is marvelously done.

CASH: The toughest one was that we had to have Maverick win his first encounter at Top Gun School, because Iceman was going to win ultimately. But, at the same time, Maverick had to lose in some way. It was a simple solution when we finally got to it, that he wins by breaking a minor rule. So, therefore, they count it as a loss.

EPPS: Breaking the rules of engagement.

FROUG: Very well done, by the way. You created a villain who wasn't a villain, which I really loved in the film. Iceman is a pilot wanting to be better, but he's never villainous. That was an excellent take on the character.

EPPS: Well, it's about a competition. Like I said, Jim and I being athletes, we wanted to deal with the competitive nature of one American's life and the flying school. It's not really quite as competitive down there, because you can't be a fighter pilot and compete against your fellow pilots. There's much more camaraderie.

CASH: I think a lot of it, too, was that there was some good casting on that picture. Val Kilmer was a good Iceman. He looked like an Iceman.

FROUG: He was excellent.

CASH: And Cruise was Maverick. Jack was the first one to come up with the idea of Cruise for Maverick. He was Maverick in our minds as we were writing it. Jack saw him all along, and I grew into him, because I hadn't seen that much of Tom Cruise. People don't remember, but, before *Top Gun*, Tom Cruise was not the major star that he is now. He'd just done *Legend* and before that was . . .

EPPS: *All the Right Moves.*

FROUG: And *Risky Business.*

CASH: But, jeez, there was star written all over him, really. He just needed the right vehicle.

FROUG: Jim, you're largely handicapped—you're in East

Lansing, Michigan. I doubt if they show many movies up there, do they?

CASH: [*Laughing*] Well, I don't know. Every now and then we get one that comes in by Wells Fargo.

FROUG: Saturday nights, right?

CASH: That's a very cosmopolitan small community. You have to realize it's a university town. Big university at that. It's one of the ten biggest in the whole world. And there are theaters all over the place. I, personally, don't like the modern-day movie theaters, because they seem to be located in malls, usually. But there are a couple of old theaters that still have the big screen, with the ornate railings and surroundings. That's what I like to go to.

FROUG: That thirties architecture.

CASH: You bet.

FROUG: I agree with you. I find that you can hear the sound of the film next door reverberating, banging against the walls, in these mall theaters now.

CASH: One of the courses I teach is a history of motion pictures, and I show my kids about thirty pictures a term—about three a week. I show nothing but American movies, which is highly unlike most history of motion-picture courses. I figure they can see the foreign films in the foreign-language departments. Nobody who teaches film, I guess, has the daringness to try to look at Hollywood films as something very special. And I consider them far more special than foreign films, if you really want to know the truth.

FROUG: I used to be a foreign-film nut in the sixties.

CASH: So was I.

FROUG: And now I've discovered, Jim, much to my surprise, that most of them don't hold up when you see them today. They were better then than they are now, whereas Hollywood movies tend to have a lasting power.

EPPS: Yes.

CASH: Even the ones I thought were incredibly great at the time, I mean, I thought *The Seventh Seal* and *The Magi-*

cian were the greatest things ever done.

FROUG: I felt the same way.

CASH: They're still awfully good, don't get me wrong.

FROUG: Yeah, but they're not as powerful as they were then.

CASH: I wonder if I was just very susceptible to something because it was so new and so mystic—I don't know. But they don't thrill me like they did.

FROUG: *Singing in the Rain* is still as good as it ever was.

EPPS: Absolutely.

CASH: Well, I show it every term.

FROUG: Good. You use my buddy Arthur Knight's textbook, I hope? *The Liveliest Art*?

CASH: I change textbooks about every three years because the students start to get onto my test questions after about a year. I have used Knight's book. It's a terrific book. And I've used a number of them.

FROUG: What do you see as your future plans? Now you've piled up hit after hit, and you're up in the big bucks market. How about team direct?

CASH: Well, the big bucks—Jack sends me a hundred bucks a week [*Laughter*], so he gets a hundred, too.

FROUG: I love it. That's probably all he gets after taxes, after paying CAA.

EPPS: That's about it.

CASH: Jack is much more ambitious about this than I am, in terms of wanting to direct and produce. I spend most of my time raising my kids. It's been our lives, really, just raising our kids.

EPPS: Jim and I are involved as producers on virtually everything we write these days. At this stage of the game, for us to write a script and then walk away from it makes no sense. We also feel that we should be in there when the decisions are being made and have a say in more than just the words on the page. In addition to that, we have a production company, Cash & Epps Entertainment, where we have several projects in development. We're working with good young writers who show a lot of promise and talent.

CASH: But the great thing, hopefully, about having your hand in the production is that the thing will come out looking like you wrote it. At least closer than it usually does. You know, it's a great frustration to pick up a review, because, if the picture's not liked by the reviewer, it's always the screenwriter's fault. And if it's great, it's always the director.

FROUG: Absolutely.

CASH: There's something that's just not right there. They should require all critics to receive a copy of the first draft of the screenplay when they go in to watch the movie. And then they can make the judgment on whether the script was good or not. Because it is collaborative, and it gets just plain changed. And that's it. That gets a little frustrating at times, and so you just learn not to read the reviews.

FROUG: I agree with that one-hundred percent. Case in point: Jack was just telling me you guys got slammed for the love story in *Top Gun*, which is widely acclaimed as a great movie but a dumb love story. And Jack tells me it wasn't your love story.

CASH: That was the major change in *Top Gun*. We had a totally different woman.

FROUG: And somebody else came in and imposed a love story with a different character that you had no idea of using, right? Didn't want to use.

EPPS: We wanted her to have a purpose in the picture, which was to sort of soothe his pain and to be somebody else he could be attracted to off the base. Sort of a San Diego story. But, you know, that's just part of the process.

FROUG: It is part of the process. If you're the producer, you have a little more influence, but the truth is, only the director really can kill you.

CASH: Yeah, I think so.

FROUG: The producer is kind of somewhere between.

CASH: Jack wants to direct so he can kill us. [*Laughter*] At least they'll know who to blame.

FROUG: That's good. Listen, Jim, I love the idea that you're a professor. Are your students aware of your super success in this alter ego?

CASH: One of the great things that I love about living in Michigan is that people generally treat me about the same as they used to. There's a little more recognition factor in a restaurant or something like that, but nobody makes too special a deal of it. I happen to like that. Our lives here are centered on our family. I think they know me more as the dad of my kids and the husband of my wife than they do as a screenwriter. They know I'm a screenwriter, but I don't wear it. I drive Fords.

FROUG: They forgive you, right?

EPPS: What does it mean, being a screenwriter, anyway? Nobody can figure out what it means to be a screenwriter. What does it mean you do? Nobody can figure that out.

CASH: Well, the question they usually ask is, "Do you write the words they say, or what?"

EPPS: That's right.

CASH: Yeah, we do that; we do a little of everything. You can't explain to them, especially when some of the words have been ad-libbed by an actor or something. You say, "No, wait a minute; I didn't write that word there. I didn't write this word over here."

FROUG: It underscores the collaborative nature of it all, doesn't it?

CASH: Yeah, but there is an alternative to wanting to be in a collaborative art, and that alternative is to sit in an attic and write poetry that nobody ever reads. But I've always wanted to write pictures that people see. And I mean millions of people. People all over the world. There's a great kick in that for me, to know that there are people in Japan who sit there and watch *Top Gun* or *Secret of My Success*, or whatever. I'd love to see those movies in Japanese. It'd be great. They sit there and they are entertained by them, amused by them, they enjoy them;

and that's a great kick to me that that level of success has come to us.

FROUG: I can tell you firsthand—this is a first report from Tokyo—my son is married to a Japanese girl, and they live in Tokyo, and yes, they love *Top Gun*. [*Laughter*] When you're teaching, does what you read influence your writing? For example, do you guys follow the paradigm that's often talked about: the first act should come somewhere between pages twenty, twenty-five, second act roughly between pages eighty, eighty-five, with rising action, etc.? Do you lay out a screenplay in that kind of form?

CASH: Let me start the answer on that, Jack, and then you pick it up. Jack is really the structurist. He's the best story structurist I've ever seen. But part of what we do (this always takes a little explanation, but you'll probably understand it right away) is go for mistakes. We make mistakes. We take a story where it doesn't necessarily . . . where our instincts tell us it shouldn't necessarily go, and we take it there just to see what's going to happen. For *Top Gun*, a hundred and twenty page script, hundred and fifteen page script, we wrote at least twelve hundred pages and maybe more. So a lot of what we do is exploration, just going into the wilderness to see what's behind that tree.

FROUG: Writing and rewriting and rewriting?

CASH: And, again, exploring. Just taking it another direction. I do a lot of that on my own, too. I'll just send Jack something new, and he'll say, "Oh, curve ball. Nice job." Or, "A curve ball. Terrible job."

EPPS: Right. "And what do we do now?"

CASH: "You got us in a great predicament here now. How do we get out?"

EPPS: That's right. "I love it, but what do we do with it?"

CASH: Yeah. So, we've always got Jack's cards. He's always got scene cards with an idea of where we're going, but we take a real roundabout way of getting there, I think.

FROUG: I used to use scene cards. How many scene cards do you figure, Jack?

EPPS: It's about fifty to fifty-six.

FROUG: Fifty to fifty-six for a full-length screenplay?

EPPS: We tend to write long, so it probably should be less, probably about forty or forty-five.

FROUG: Is each index card a scene?

EPPS: Each index card is a scene with a heading of what each scene is about and then little details on the scene. It gives you a sense of the overview. You can see the movie in one fell swoop. If you're going page by page, you can't do it.

FROUG: I used to do that. I'd assign my UCLA students to do sixty scene cards before they started a screenplay on the idea that they could improvise, you know. That just gave them an outline, but they were free to develop the story in new directions. Do you give yourself freedom to improvise?

EPPS: Oh, absolutely. What happens (it's part of the give-and-take Jim and I have) is that if I sketch something out, and then Jim is doing a first draft, we'll be talking back and forth about what's working, what's missing, how do you feel here. We'll be talking about the places it's working or isn't working or "Hey, this is working great. Let's have more of this." We don't always know where we're going when we start, and we don't want to know, because I can write formula all day long; it's very easy. But part of the fun is having the movie go in directions you don't expect it to—the unpredictability.

FROUG: Surprising yourself.

EPPS: That's it. Letting the character take it somewhere. That's the importance of the character finding his voice and letting him decide for himself.

FROUG: You guys are in a unique position to answer this question. You are a former film student and now a film teacher: should an aspiring screenwriter go to film school?

CASH: I've got an answer, but you go with yours first, Jack.

EPPS: That's a tough one. We're talking about a beginning screenwriter. The most important thing you should do is write. That's the most important thing.

FROUG: Everybody I've asked has said that.

EPPS: It just is. You can find all the excuses in the world not to write. If you're writer, that means you love to procrastinate anyway, so you don't want to do it. Film school is something that has to be chosen carefully. You can spend so much time studying the things that aren't important when what you really should do is write script after script after script. Jim wrote four novels before we started working together. That's a lot of pages.

FROUG: A hell of a lot.

EPPS: I wrote several solo scripts and spec scripts that didn't go anywhere. But in the process of writing, that's how you learn.

FROUG: Absolutely. Jim, what's your view?

CASH: My greatest growth as a writer came when I was about twenty-two years old. I was just about to graduate from Michigan State after having dropped out a couple of times. I quit school; I had about eight credits to go to graduate. I went back to my home town of Grand Rapids, and I took a job on a night shift in a factory. I worked for two years in that factory, from four in the afternoon to about midnight, and when I'd get home I'd start writing, and I'd write till about six or seven in the morning, when the birds woke up. I'd go to bed for about four hours or so and get up and write until it was time to go to work. I did that for two years almost every day with occasional time off to drink a beer or watch a ball game or something. I kept everything I wrote during that period and I stacked it all up, and at the end of those two years it came more than three feet tall—all the pages—and the pages were very thin pieces of paper. It takes a lot to make a stack three feet tall, three and a half feet tall. I looked at the first stuff and I looked at the last stuff, and it was a different writer. It had nothing to do with taking writing classes, even though I'd taken as many as possible in college. It had nothing to do with asking somebody or writing letters to famous writers and saying, "How do I write?" It just had to do with sitting down and putting pen on paper and learning what works and learning what doesn't work. It's not the easiest way. I'm sure there are shortcuts you can pick up in the film schools.

FROUG: I don't know; learning by doing is about the best way, don't you think?

EPPS: Yeah, I don't think there are any shortcuts to writing. I think it's a long, hard, lonely process. It's a very solitary thing. And that's what's difficult. Jim's saying you have to sit in a room doing it and doing it and doing it. That's really hard. The other thing that's very hard, I know Jim faced it and so did I, is getting rejected.

CASH: Yeah, that's a lot of fun.

EPPS: Rejection is something we faced early on in our career. It's easier to face it together. But, we're lucky; as a team we've never been rejected.

CASH: I was going to say, Jack, we haven't done that in screenwriting. Mine was all with novels and short stories.

EPPS: That's right. Jim and I faced rejection; we came together, and that's part of the wonderful thing of collaboration.

FROUG: You created that third persona.

EPPS: That third persona, and did it together. What's also wonderful about collaboration is that it's good to have a partner to sort of weather the storm with, because the business is very difficult. It's a hard-hitting business. Let's face it, it's the major leagues. Very competitive; there's a lot of pounding going on. You get it from the directors, you get it from the studios.

CASH: It helps a lot that you like each other, too.

EPPS: That's right.

CASH: Jack and I happen to like each other.

EPPS: I have a great admiration for Jim Cash; he's tremendous as a writer.

CASH: Now, don't get too carried away.

EPPS: It's true.

FROUG: You're not Gilbert and Sullivan; you speak to each other.

EPPS: Absolutely, yeah, absolutely. I have wonderful admiration for him and enjoy working with him. And, although we don't live in the same city, I know he's a decent guy. He's a family man; I'm a family man. We're both Midwesterners. I'm transplanted; I envy that he lives in the Midwest right now. I keep trying to trade places. We'll trade houses and do the whole thing if he wants to. But you can see, he's not going to take me up on it.

FROUG: No. [*Laughter*]

CASH: Well, not in the spring; it's beautiful here now. Talk to me in February.

FROUG: Well, do you have anything you'd like to add to this very excellent interview? Are you ever going to run out of ideas?

CASH: The thing that you run out of sometimes is energy, just because, truthfully, we overwork our work. We take too many turns sometimes. We think too much, and by the time we finish our first draft, it's really what you could call a sixth or seventh draft. And at that point you feel so good, I mean, you really feel like this is the way this story was meant to be written, and this is it. This is the story. And the energy starts to sap when the inevitable changes occur. That's just part of it.

FROUG: That's when you take the punishment.

EPPS: That's right.

CASH: You take it or you don't. You can get on to something else. But it does wear your energy out a little bit and your enthusiasm. So, I say, the best thing you've got at all times as a writer is your first draft. And after that you'd better accept the fact that you're a hired hand, and that's it.

EPPS: That's one of the fun things about production rewrites. Because you have a deadline and they're going to shoot the picture, there's no time for rewrites. The fun thing in

Secret of My Success was that we knew that they had to start the picture in eight weeks, so . . .

FROUG: They had to shoot.

EPPS: They had to shoot this. We handed them the script, and they had to shoot it. They couldn't play with it. Actually, funny enough, it's one of our favorite pictures because it represents our style so cleanly, so few hands in there. And Herb Ross was the right director for our theatrical style. So that the whole staging and playing and tempo and timing and all that, it's just all there.

FROUG: When you get these last-minute overnight rewrites, are you able to reach each other and collaborate, or do you just have to do it, Jack, because you're here?

EPPS: No, no, no. We always write as a team.

CASH: I just bought a fax machine. Jack finally talked me into it.

FROUG: Great.

CASH: Yeah, and next I'm going to read the instruction book and see if I can figure out how it works.

EPPS: We have a program that allows us to have the same page on the screen at the same—simultaneously across the country. So I can make a change here and Jim sees it in three seconds. Or he makes a change and I see it in three seconds. We have the speaker phone on while we're working, so, in essence, we're there together.

CASH: But in the beginning we used to do it by writing the scenes out and sending them by regular mail.

FROUG: Oh, my God.

EPPS: We used to do cassette tapes. We used to talk in cassette tapes.

CASH: It took weeks, sometimes, but what the heck?

EPPS: Our first script took us close to two and a half years, I think.

FROUG: How much is your phone bill?

EPPS: Well, that's one reason we have a studio office . . .

FROUG: Because the studio pays the phone bill, right?

CASH: You notice I didn't call you. [*Laughter*] But it can be pretty expensive anyway.

FROUG: The results are extraordinary.

EPPS: Thank you. We hope so.

CASH: The results are great fun. I have no complaints. You know the great thing is to sit in the theater when people are watching one of your pictures. And in those moments when you say, "Gee, I wish I could stop the film and tell them what we had in this point that was a little better," they don't notice that. They're sitting there, and they're entranced. They're either watching jets in the sky or they're watching Michael run around being funny in secret; they're just totally entranced in the picture. And that's a terrific feeling, sometimes, to look around you at the audience. The best feeling, of course, is when they laugh at the right time, and you remember when you wrote the line, you remember the moment. You even chuckled yourself a little bit; you say, "I can't wait till Jack reads this one." Jack calls up, he says, "You know, the funniest thing in here is this line," and all of a sudden the audience is there, and boom! Laughing. There is a payoff there. It takes a long time coming around. It's not like music, where you can sit down at the piano and play and you're getting instant gratification for yourself, at least. It takes a while before you suddenly say, "Well, nine months ago I wrote that line, and you're laughing now." It's a great feeling.

EPPS: It's a terrific feeling.

FROUG: Jeff Boam describes that in his interview, the feeling of: they're laughing where you hoped they would laugh, and they're silent when you hoped they'd be silent. It's that reward, I guess, of connecting to a lot of people, don't you imagine? It's almost a spiritual thing.

EPPS: Absolutely.

CASH: Well, so much of it is silent until that moment. You're writing it, but it's still just words on paper. Then it's a director reading it and responding or a committee of people reading it and responding. And by the time the picture comes out, there's a certain deadness, at least for me. I'm exhausted by the story, by the whole thing. It's very difficult for me to sit and watch it. If it wasn't for the fact that there's audience reaction, I wouldn't.

FROUG: You know, it occurs to me that what we're really talking about on another level is the true meaning of the word "entertainment." The French derivation of entertain is "to hold." It's communication on an intimate level. When they share your laughter when you wanted them to laugh, that's really a moment of intimacy, don't you think? Even though there are a thousand people out there.

CASH: Yeah, absolutely. It's that connection. As I say, it's that payoff of everything you did. I like that quote you had by I.A.L. Diamond in your first book. "Chaplain set out to entertain and he created art. And the guys who set out to create art don't even entertain."

FROUG: That was a great quote.

FROUG: *Top Gun* will be around as art, I think, longer than some of the films that are paraded before us as art.

CASH: Well, one thing they can't ever take away is that it was the number one picture of 1986. I mean, it's like winning a batting championship.

EPPS: Yeah, that's exciting. It's a great feeling.

CASH: It's there, it's in the record book and they can't touch it. And the other ones have all been right up there, too. Most of them in the top ten, but that one was number one. We may never do it again, but it's great to know you can do it once.

FROUG: You know, the nice thing is every time out you might do it.

EPPS: You might. That's the fun thing, seeing your picture released and going there and watching it happen and seeing the box-office figures and being involved. That's very exciting. It's a lot of fun.

Fay Kanin

FADE IN:

1 EXT. THE PIGPEN, MULLENS' FARM - THE HOGS - DAY   1

as they run toward the fence, squealing, pushing.

                    MICHAEL'S VOICE
          Pig! Pig! Pig!

2 MICHAEL MULLEN   2

enters the pen, carrying a bucket of feed. The hogs
mill around him as he fills the troughs. He likes it.

3 A LONGER ANGLE   3

as Michael finishes the feeding. The end of summer is
in the air, in the foliage of the trees surrounding
the barn and pen. Near them is the house built by
Michael's father on the site where his great-
grandfather first homesteaded over a hundred years
before.

4 INT. PEG'S WORKROOM - PEG MULLEN - DAY   4*

at the sewing machine, concentrated on the T-shirt
seam she's reinforcing. She snips a loose thread
getting up.

5 EXT. THE PIGPEN - DAY   5*

Michael is hammering a sagging fence post loosened by
the hogs' pressure, drawing the wire fencing taut
against it. He tests it, satisfied.

6 INT. MICHAEL AND JOHN'S BEDROOM - DAY   6

Peg comes in, crossing to a partly-packed barracks bag,
places the folded shirt beside it. Her eyes are unable
to avoid the neatly-pressed Army uniform hanging on the
closet door, the shined shoes on the floor. She moves
quickly past them.

7 EXT. NEAR THE FRONT DOOR - DAY   7

Michael finishes planting the second of two evergreens.
After a moment, Peg comes out, smiles.

                    PEG
          They look nice.

                                              (CONTINUED)

*"Writers will always prevail because
they tell the stories."*

Fay Kanin must have spent the last twenty years in Tibet in that paradisaical village James Hilton called "Shangri-La." Meeting her again in the doorway of her and Michael's Santa Monica beachfront home, seeing absolutely no signs of aging, not a hint of change, and still exuding the same quiet yet forceful charm and poise, was a bit unnerving. But, then, you ought to expect miracles from this very feminine screenwriter who has, in the interim, won three Emmy Awards, the acclaim of her fellow workers, and been elected president of the Motion Picture Academy of Arts and Sciences for four consecutive terms. No ordinary work-a-day screenwriter here.

As we settled into the same living room, the same book-shelves displaying Michael Kanin's Oscar (for co-writing *Woman of the Year* with Ring Lardner, Jr.) and Fay's Emmys, the feeling that time had stood still almost overwhelmed me, until I noted that the old TV had been replaced by a giant-screen TV now that's viewable from anyplace in this very large living room. That great blank silent screen said a great deal about the changes that have taken place these past twenty years.

As Fay makes abundantly clear, technological advances have only helped the cause of the film writer. There is a new moon on the writer's horizon.

Fay Kanin is not a new writer, obviously. But no screen and/or television writer can come closer to giving us an overview of the filmwriter's life in 1991 than Fay can.

All of that notwithstanding, no writer in memory has brought more honor and dignity to our profession than Fay Kanin.

For those of you who met her in *The Screenwriter Looks at the Screenwriter*, say hello again. For those of you who missed that opportunity, now's your chance.

FROUG: Well, here we are, sitting in the same seats, in the same room, twenty years later. It's a miracle. The real miracle is that we haven't aged a bit. [*Laughter*] Since our twenty-years-ago interview, you've done some astonishingly good work. *Friendly Fire* was, for me, one of the best TV movies ever made. You won an Emmy for that, didn't you? And for *Tell Me Where It Hurts?*

KANIN: Yes.

FROUG: You won two Emmys and a third one as Writer of the Year, and then you became president of the Motion Picture Academy of Arts and Sciences.

KANIN: The Oscars.

FROUG: How in the world did a screenwriter find herself in this lofty position?

KANIN: There have been maybe two screenwriters ahead of me who were presidents of the Academy: Dan Taradash and Charlie Brackett. I was elected to the Academy board by the writers' branch, maybe fifteen or twenty years ago, and have been on the board and an officer all that time. So, at the Academy, writers do get that sort of recognition.

FROUG: And if you just endure long enough you become the president?

KANIN: Maybe they just thought, "Well, we may as well make her president."

FROUG: You know, that's an easy explanation, but I don't buy it.

KANIN: Okay, I don't either. I said to them, "Now, no election because I'm a token woman. I don't want that." A curious thing—you're elected to the Academy presidency for one year only. You're allowed to hold that office for four consecutive years, but you have to be re-elected every time. I consider the ultimate compliment not that I got the office but that I was elected four times.

FROUG: That is an incredible compliment. A man can wear the same tuxedo, but you had to keep buying a new dress for every Oscar?

KANIN: Every one. I don't have to buy evening clothes for the rest of my life.

FROUG: Those were the days of a thousand dollars, at least, for each dress.

KANIN: Oh, those dresses were gorgeous.

FROUG: In '71 you said, "There are fewer people going to the movies than at any time since the talkies." What is the situation in 1991?

KANIN: I can't quote figures, but there are certainly a lot of people going to the movies these days. At the Academy, for instance, we figure an audience of a billion people, and you don't tune in to the Oscars unless you're in some way interested in the movies.

FROUG: You said a *billion*?

KANIN: A billion is our worldwide audience now.

FROUG: As the former president of the Writers Guild, what is the state of the Writers Guild today?

KANIN: I'm former president of the Screen Branch of the Writers Guild. As a matter of fact, the last president of that branch before they amalgamated.

FROUG: You mean, combined the screen and television branches?

KANIN: Yes, they were once separate entities. What's the state of the Guild now? Stronger than ever, I believe. The value of writers was proved during the last strike. The companies kept saying, "We're not really being hurt by this. We've stockpiled scripts. We can hire writers from other countries." In truth, they couldn't because our colleagues supported us magnificently—the Australians, the British, the Canadians. Only now do the companies concede the degree to which they were crippled by the strike. Only now are they willing to admit that writers are valuable. That is, until they get into production. Once there, everybody wants the writer to get lost.

FROUG: I interviewed Jeffrey Boam. He just signed a deal at Warners for four and a half million dollars for three years. When he sits in the story conference with the producer and director and he throws out ideas, they say, "Oh, no good. It doesn't work. We don't want it." But if the director comes up with an idea, they don't even question it. It's still going on, isn't it?

KANIN: Unfortunately, yes. But, as a result of the strike, we now have a couple of active committees (on which I sit) working with the top level of studio and network executives to try to increase communication between writers and producers and to explore some voluntary guidelines that will defuse the director's fear of having the writer on the set. I think we're making some progress there. You know, too, that the Guild has just signed a four-year extension of our Minimum Basic Agreement with the AMPTP [Association of Motion Picture and Television Producers].

FROUG: What do you think about that?

KANIN: There are some understandably mixed feelings among Guild members, though it was voted in by a sizable majority. There are many members who think we've sold out our bargaining power. On the other hand, the advocates, including George Kirgo, the present president, feel that the Guild can use a time of peace to strengthen it financially and to work on some of its ongoing problems and challenges. Rather than walking a picket line, I guess.

FROUG: Which God knows we've done enough, haven't we?

KANIN: Yes. But what has made us the best union in the town has been our guts, our willingness to take a strike when it was necessary.

FROUG: It seems to me that we walked a picket line every four years.

KANIN: There's something to be said on both sides. I guess only time will tell us whether the extension has been a boon or a bust.

FROUG: Let's talk about what it's like to be on the board of the Writers Guild, in terms of the different temperaments of the writers.

KANIN: I'm not on the board of the Writers Guild right now. But there are people who hold strong and often diverse views and they're not afraid to argue them. Strangely enough, writers like to talk—maybe because so much of our working life is spent in a room alone.

FROUG: What do you see, looking back, that the Guild provides screenwriters? No one can join the Guild, can they, until they've sold a screenplay or a television script?

KANIN: That's right. What the Guild provides a writer, particularly a beginning writer, is muscle. Right now we're working on a handbook to be circulated among members acquainting them with all the remarkable advances we've won through the years. A lot of us don't appreciate what strengths we have to negotiate our deals, strengths provided in the Guild contract that we often don't even realize are there.

FROUG: A lot of the new writers just don't see that at all. They don't understand that without the Guild they'd have no residuals, no right to arbitrate or decide credits.

KANIN: Everything this generation of writers takes for granted was won by this Guild. My husband Michael's grandmother always used to say, "A cow doesn't give milk. You have to take it from her." That's the way it's been in our industry. All the benefits this generation thinks have always been there were won by past generations of the Guild.

FROUG: Our version of solidarity, basically.

KANIN: Yes. Our health fund, credits, minimums (which at the very least establish a floor for beginning writers) have all come through Guild negotiation. It behooves anyone who's coming into the industry to read, if not the contract (which is admittedly difficult), certainly this handbook we're preparing.

FROUG: Whatever happened to that rump group in the last strike who sued the Guild?

KANIN: There are always dissidents; they appear at almost every strike. Some don't want to lose work or money; some have other disaffections.

FROUG: They're shortsighted, I must say.

KANIN: I think we have often lost important gains because a dissident group worked to try to break a strike. In video-cassettes, for instance, if we'd held out a bit longer, we might have won a really significant participation. I just read the other day that there is now more money made by the studios in video than in theatrical release. The Guild saw that coming and went on strike for it, but, because of the internal pressure, we didn't stay out quite long enough.

FROUG: It concerns me that people who read this book understand the importance of the Writers Guild and what it's doing for them. Now let's get back to you. What are you doing?

KANIN: At the moment I'm developing films with a production company, and I will produce the things I develop. Someone said you should change your career or your job every five years. Well, I've had a lot more than five years at the typewriter (I haven't joined the word-processor contingent yet), so this is fascinating for me. I find that I can use my craft in working with other writers. And many writers seem to enjoy working with another writer in the development process, probably because we talk the same language.

FROUG: There is somebody reading this book who wants to sell their screenplay. How do they go about it?

KANIN: Oh, Lord, that's always the toughest question. The market for spec screenplays has been phenomenal, although we're beginning to hear some resentment from the studios about the amount of money being paid for these scripts. We're hearing, "No more million or two million dollar screenplay deals. It's a monster that's gotten out of hand."

FROUG: I heard that from CAA, of course.

KANIN: However, if it's a monster, it's one they created. The competitive bidding pits the ego of one studio executive against another. "If he wants it, I want it—whatever it costs." Listen, that competition benefits actors, directors— why shouldn't it happen with writers?

FROUG: True. But let's go back to this person who's reading this book and says, "I have this screenplay. I'd like to get somebody to read it. Do I have to get an agent?"

KANIN: A lot of companies, including the one I'm with, won't accept unsolicited scripts unless they come through an agent or a lawyer.

FROUG: Because of potential lawsuits?

KANIN: Yes. We live in a very litigious time.

FROUG: How many screenplays do you get a week?

KANIN: We have someone reading for us, and she seems to be reading from morning to night. She's never without a pile of scripts on her desk. We must get ten, fifteen a week—screenplays, plays, books. Very few people do treatments anymore or stories, because there's almost no market for that. A lot of the time there's a pitch, where you tell your story and get a development deal.

FROUG: Do you accept pitches?

KANIN: Only from writers we know. If a writer with whom I have some relationship comes in and has a wonderful story that he or she can communicate, we're willing to take the chance that a good script will come out of it.

FROUG: How many films do you have in the works?

KANIN: Right now we have three in the writing stage. And a couple of finished scripts at studios, ready for directors and casting to come together.

FROUG: If the screenwriter has a screenplay and wants to give it to the company or to Fay Kanin, what is the process? He gets it to an agent; the agent gives it to you?

KANIN: Yes. Then we have our reader cover it.

FROUG: Cover—you mean they do a report on it?

KANIN: A summary of the story and the reader's comments. If there is something in the story that interests me, I read the material.

FROUG: If you like it, what then?

KANIN: If I like it, I will ask some of the others in the company to read it. If enough of us think it has merit, we talk about where would be the best place to take it. We have access to all major studios; we also can go to any network and to cable.

FROUG: Is that a market now?

KANIN: TNT and HBO are very big markets. Some cable companies have specific interests, like Lifetime, for instance, which is very interested in women's themes.

FROUG: There are buyers who are looking for women's stories?

KANIN: The networks are all interested in women-oriented subjects.

FROUG: Really; that's interesting.

KANIN: In big-screen movies, you will hear "a woman can't open a movie"—meaning that there's no woman star they feel can make a movie take off by the power of her presence. Maybe, just lately, that phenomenon Julia Roberts. But there are a half-dozen male stars they feel can "open a movie."

FROUG: I love this lingo.

KANIN: On the other hand, in television a woman protagonist is by no means a liability; it is a plus. Television feels very strongly that women's themes and a woman star can command an audience.

FROUG: Some women think there's a prejudice against woman writers. Do you think so?

KANIN: I don't know that there's a conscious prejudice. It doesn't quite work that way. In the action cycle, for example, there's the feeling that men can write those movies better than women. Some men can, but I think there are also some women who can do them very well. Differently, perhaps, but well. I can't, because I'm not interested in them. I would say that the majority of women writers don't have an interest in the hard-edged action piece. And since there's so much of that lately, women have had slim pickings. But I read all the time now about spec scripts sold by new, young women writers.

FROUG: I interviewed Anna Hamilton Phelan, who wrote *Mask*. Lovely woman.

KANIN: And a good writer. Anna has no trouble getting assignments; I think she turns down a lot. I never had that trouble. I am sure there were films I would not have been considered for, though no one ever said that to me directly. And certainly that happens with men writers, too. But it is harder for women to break in all the way along the line. That doesn't mean it's impossible. We just have to work twice as hard as men to accomplish it.

FROUG: Do you think we are out of the action cycle?

KANIN: Unhappily, I don't think we'll ever be completely out of it. All you have to do is watch the nightly news on television, and you know there's an appetite for violence and guns and murder and mayhem. And the European market, which grows more and more important, loves action movies.

FROUG: Car chases don't need subtitles.

KANIN: Exactly. The theme of *Driving Miss Daisy* is more or less a local phenomenon, although I'm sure it has some worldwide appeal. But an action movie is understood in every language.

FROUG: Car chases and guns and explosions and all the rest are big box office in any country. It's a sad comment on the human condition.

KANIN: And the more of it we see, the harder it becomes to excite an audience. So graphic depiction of violence keeps escalating. I find that very dangerous.

FROUG: It's frightening. I would assume you are not particularly looking for stories in that direction.

KANIN: Not particularly, or ever. Every movie is almost a

year of your life, from the beginning through the development and production. I don't want to spend a year of my life on any of that.

FROUG: I don't even like to spend two hours watching it. And they have to come up with thirty, forty, fifty million dollars to make these ultra-violent movies. Is it because of the recent, big box office for a *Driving Miss Daisy* or *Ghost* that studios are starting to open their minds to the intimate story?

KANIN: Undoubtedly. Let's not forget that the movies are a business as well as an art. Love stories are coming back— romance. *Ghost* and *Pretty Woman* are refreshingly old-fashioned movies. *Green Card*, which I saw the other day, is charming, absolutely a "forties" movie—the situation, the way it develops.

FROUG: Interesting; it's written by an Australian who probably saw lots of American "forties" movies.

KANIN: You'd imagine that would say to producers, "Let's make a lot more of those." You hope so. But I don't think we'll be flooded with them.

FROUG: They're probably more secure when they put a ten-million-dollar star in a fifty-million-dollar picture, whether it's Schwarzenegger or Bruce Willis or whomever.

KANIN: Right, even the ones that fail. The truth is that nobody really knows what's going to make it with the audience. So it's futile for a writer to play that guessing game. My advice is to write what you like, to please yourself, and then to be a bulldog about trying to get it made. Don't give up. Someone once reminded me, "All you need is one buyer." There are a lot of studios out there, independent companies, three primary networks, Fox Broadcasting, cable. There are a lot more buyers out there than there used to be.

FROUG: Do what you love; the money will follow?

KANIN: Yes. If you do it well.

FROUG: That's wonderful advice. Frankly, I'm happy to see it's a theme running through every interview.

KANIN: And there will probably be new markets that we haven't even thought of. The one thing that will never change is that people want to see a story. They want to be taken out of their world into another world or to see their world illuminated for them in a way they can understand. So writers will always prevail because they tell the stories.

Bill Haber and Rowland Perkins

"If they're only writing it for the money, they shouldn't bother."

Creative Artists Agency is unquestionably the most powerful talent agency in Hollywood since Lew Wasserman folded MCA (at the government's request) and took his entrepreneurial genius to Universal Studios. It wasn't until twenty years later that five young William Morris Agency agents left their jobs and took off on their own to form a new company: CAA. My good friends and former agents Bill Haber and Rowland Perkins were among those five founders. "We got a line of credit from the bank," Rowland recently told me, "but from the first day forward we never needed it. We made more money our first month in business than we ever made at William Morris." Today, CAA may be more powerful than MCA ever was.

Bill and Rowland and I had had a relationship for more than five years, both as friends and as business associates. During the time they represented me as a writer-producer, I was never a day out of work. They invited me to come along with them to CAA, but by then I had been terminally bitten by the teaching bug and was bored to death with television. "Teaching is a good way to go broke," they laughingly assured me. Many times during the following years, first at USC's School of Cinema and later at UCLA's Department of

Theatre Arts, Film & Television, I came close to proving them right. However, producing and/or writing an occasional TV pilot during the summer months out of school paid me more in a single summer's work than three years of teaching. So, while I survived, Bill and Rowland thrived and became what they are today, mega-power brokers, operating out of their own sixty-five thousand square foot, I.M. Pei-designed, multi-million dollar, state-of-the-art building in Beverly Hills.

It's hard to think back to only a few years ago when Diane Perkins and Carole Haber worked at the CAA switch-board answering phones to help their husbands get started.

Today, I can't think of two more knowledgeable people to advise screenwriters than Bill and Rowland. In all our years together they were never less than straight with me, and I was confident when I approached them to do this interview that they would be just as straight with you.

There's excellent advice in abundance here from two of the top professionals in the business. Avail yourselves of it.

FROUG: What are the movie stories that are hot right now? What do you think is a hot sell right now? Is there a current trend?

HABER: Well, at the moment, *Ghost* has led everybody to believe very romantic, wistful movies with love affairs are in. Some of them with some topspin are hot at the moment.

FROUG: What does topspin mean?

HABER: Well, *Ghost* had a ghost in it. That's different than a normal love story.

FROUG: I see. That's what they call topspin?

HABER: Something that makes it a little unusual.

PERKINS: They used to call them gimmicks.

FROUG: Okay, let's say I'm a new screenwriter. I've just gotten out of film school, and I have a show script. How do I get an agent?

HABER: The best way to do it is to know somebody who's in the business, any part of the business whatsoever. A gate guard—it can be from a gate guard to Lew Wasserman.

PERKINS: It's really anybody who knows an agent who will call up on your behalf and say, "This person is legitimate."

HABER: It's not so difficult, really, to know people who know people. You, as a totally unknown person, can go to any of these screenwriting seminars that they have and meet young screenwriters. All of them have agents. So you simply say to them, "Would you put me in touch with somebody at your agency?" And most of them will always say yes.

FROUG: The next and toughest question beyond that is, as an industry professional, how do you get anybody to read your material?

HABER: Well, there's one thing that you shouldn't do. I've been reading an article in the *New York Times* about an agent in New York who charges people to read material. Never pay anybody to read your material. Never.

FROUG: Under no circumstances?

HABER: You should never, ever do that. Don't ever pay anybody for it. It's just a question, really, of who you know. Hopefully, an agent that you get to will have some young people working for him, or young agents working for him, and they'll always read material. Depending on who you know and who that person knows, you can even get high-level senior agents to read material.

FROUG: A lot of these folks who are going to read this book are out of town, they're not in Hollywood. What do they do?

PERKINS: They write. I frequently get letters from people asking us to read scripts. If the letter sounds articulate and the person sounds intelligent, I'll usually send it to one of the younger literary agents. Surprisingly, most of the scripts are for motion pictures. They're not for television.

FROUG: Not surprising.

PERKINS: Usually the ones that are smart tell you, "I have a screenplay. This is what it is about."

FROUG: Not a synopsis of the screenplay—just a couple lines.

PERKINS: Not a synopsis. Then they ask you, "May I send you a synopsis. If you're interested in it, then I'll send you the script." This is a very intelligent approach. I read every letter. I won't throw anything away. If it sounds interesting, I pass it on to one of the literary agents and ask them to answer it however they want to answer it.

FROUG: Do you think it's a good idea for new writers to send a synopsis of the screenplay, or does it kill the surprise in reading it?

PERKINS: No, I think you shouldn't synopsize it. I think you should tell what it's about in maybe a good, solid paragraph to pique your reader's interest. If the writer can write an interesting paragraph, I say maybe they've got a chance of having written an interesting screenplay.

HABER: If somebody has a screenplay, doesn't live near Los Angeles or New York, doesn't know anybody in the business, and they want somebody to read the screenplay, they should go to New York or Los Angeles. They ought to go spend two or three weeks there.

FROUG: Pushing to get someone to read it. Do you think that beginning writers are better off trying to write a TV episode that they've seen on the tube, or a screenplay?

PERKINS: I would think the screenplay. Television's basically all written by staff. They buy only a certain limited amount of freelance scripts.

FROUG: Not a good idea to spec for TV.

PERKINS: Not a good idea. Particularly if you're out of town.

HABER: Unless somebody wants to be in the television business and wants to be producing television. You sometimes can do a sample of a television episode and get somebody to read it. They'll know whether you can be on the staff of a television series, though they won't buy your script. That's happened often.

FROUG: Nine out of ten of the students I've had want to be in features. They don't want to be in television. Do you find it true of your clients, the writers?

HABER: Yes.

PERKINS: It's true, for some reason. Except, after a while, a lot of them realize the necessity of making a living. There are too many of them who have written six or eight or nine screenplays. All I can say is, I hope that they keep on writing.

HABER: To some of them you suggest television and they say, [*whispered*] "No."

FROUG: I understand there's a general feeling that television is inferior.

HABER: Well, there's always been a desire to be on the big, silver screen, where your script that you've worked so hard on gets made for twenty-five million dollars. You can't make a movie and distribute it anymore for under twenty million dollars.

FROUG: Twenty million bucks is the bottom line now?

HABER: Pretty much.

PERKINS: Adding production and distribution.

HABER: So, if you're going to do that, if you're going to spec something, you might as well hope that a theatrical movie happens rather than a television movie that will never be heard of again.

FROUG: If you do the world's best television movie, as a writer, it doesn't do a hell of a lot for your reputation, does it?

PERKINS: No, not really. And that's why a lot of our motion picture/television people who work as producers in television will only write theatricals. As writers they're repeatedly offered television movies, and they won't do them. They say, "No. If I'm going to take the time to write a hundred and eight pages, I'm going to write a theatrical film and take my shot."

FROUG: Do you think it's of any value for young writers to go to film school? Do you think it helps writers?

HABER: Yes, it's a good idea because you get to meet members of the industry that way.

FROUG: Especially in L.A.

HABER: That's the best way to get material bought. Aside from L.A., there's NYU—there are many people from our industry who were involved there.

PERKINS: Bill, it's true. I think they learn more about making films. A writer, in my opinion, has to know how all aspects of the business work. He or she has to know how directors work. They've got to know how actors work. By going to film school, they have to participate in those classes. I think it will help them as writers.

FROUG: Okay, let's assume that I'm a graduate of a film school, and I have this show script. It's gone through the various readers at CAA, and you've decided you like the screenplay. How do you go about marketing it? What do you do? Do you first have to tie up a director or star, or get the "elements?"

HABER: No, sometimes if you know a company that's looking for that particular subject matter, you can send it to them without elements.

FROUG: So you don't have to tie up somebody for it?

HABER: No, not always.

FROUG: Suppose somebody's written a spec script for a TV series. Let's say he happens to like the number-one sitcom, whatever the number-one sitcom is.

PERKINS: "Cheers."

FROUG: He's got a "Cheers" script. I hear they get them by the truckload. My understanding is they have a skiploader come out once a week to haul away the unsolicited scripts that are submitted.

HABER: They don't read any of them.

FROUG: But let's say, by a miracle, our writer knows somebody who knows somebody who knows the doorman at "Cheers," and it's read. As a comedy writer, is he an easier sell than the drama writer?

PERKINS: Oh, sure. Because of staffs. Comedy shows operate totally on staffs. Not that they don't have them on dramas, but some of the comedy shows have as many as eight writers on staff. So I think there's a bigger demand. And it's somehow considered a tougher craft to be able to write jokes and humor than to construct a normal story.

FROUG: Well, I can tell you, during my tenure at UCLA I don't think I saw four really good comedy writers. It's a rare gift, a very rare gift. Do you see very many talented comedy writers?

HABER: Mostly in television. They don't make a lot of theatrical comedies. And the theatrical comedies that you see are actually done by a half dozen people. Comedy is for television, if you're breaking into the business, and drama, action-adventure, romance, is for the theatrical market.

FROUG: So what can you hope to get for a beginning writer in television? What kind of money can he hope to make?

PERKINS: Scale.

FROUG: Writers Guild scale?

PERKINS: Writers Guild scale.

HABER: But you actually get paid more per week than you get as a freelancer.

FROUG: You mean if a writer's on staff?

HABER: If you get a staff position.

PERKINS: Otherwise you're writing on spec. Otherwise you could get minimum on a script. You could give the writer an assignment that would not be lucrative.

HABER: What is staff minimum? Eighteen hundred dollars a week for thirty weeks?

PERKINS: Right. There's a Writers Guild minimum on staff.

FROUG: But that's approximately it?

HABER: Yes, that's it.

FROUG: Let's say this guy has this show script. You guys like it, you shop it around, and you've got a studio that likes it or a producer who likes it. What kind of money can this beginning writer hope to get for his screenplay?

HABER: A theatrical screenplay?

FROUG: Theatrical.

HABER: If somebody wants it, three million dollars.

FROUG: Sky's the limit.

HABER: Sky's the limit if somebody, a major company or a company with a lot of money, wants it. It doesn't make any difference if it's a first script or a tenth script.

PERKINS: You try to get into a bidding war. If you get into a bidding war—more than one person wants it—the sky's the limit.

FROUG: Okay, you've got this script. And you, CAA, represents the writer. How do you engineer a bidding war? An auction situation?

HABER: An auction situation is out in the open—everybody knows about it and they have a certain amount of time to make offers on it. And whoever pays the most for it ends up getting it. But most of the time it doesn't happen that way. Most of the time the script is leaked out to many people, even though each person thinks they're the only person getting it. They're all out to make offers on it, and you build heat on the project. Actually, it builds its own heat. It's like a firestorm.

FROUG: So you get a lot of people saying, "This is a good script. We ought to get it."?

HABER: Right.

FROUG: Meantime, you're saying to this studio or that producer, "I've now got three hundred thousand. Will you go more?" Do you do it that way, or do you let them make an offer first?

PERKINS: You just say, "No, the client won't accept that."

FROUG: I see.

PERKINS: That's when they'll say, "Well, what do you want?" Avoid that if you're waiting for a lot of people. Just say, "That's not enough."

FROUG: How long can you keep juggling the balls in the air with a screenplay?

HABER: A couple of weeks. Sometimes two days, sometimes two weeks. Usually not more than two weeks.

PERKINS: After a while, people start losing interest, nobody wants it.

HABER: It cools off.

PERKINS: They feel they're getting hype.

FROUG: So they keep bidding and they finally buy this thing for a million, three million. This doesn't necessarily mean they're going to go forward with it, does it?

HABER: No, not at all.

FROUG: I can't understand that, can you?

PERKINS: It probably will be more likely that they will make it if they paid a hundred thousand for it.

FROUG: I had a student who sold a screenplay for three hundred thousand, his first screenplay, and they immediately brought in rewrite people and paid them three hundred thousand more. Now they've got six hundred thousand in it, and they haven't decided to make the picture yet. Is there an explanation for this insanity?

PERKINS: Well, you can ask Mr. Eszterhas when you interview him. That's what happened to his script. They paid him three million, they paid the producer a million. Then they took them both off the picture, hired somebody else to rewrite it, and now they're going to bring him back in. They're committed to Michael Douglas for fourteen million, so now there's, twenty million dollars, and not a camera has rolled.

FROUG: That's incredible, really. Does CAA ever get involved in the financing end of films?

HABER: You mean, do we put our own money into it? No, we're not allowed to under Union Franchise Agreements.

FROUG: Do you recommend that new screenwriters take development deals?

PERKINS: I think that when they're starting out they should take any kind of deal they can get.

FROUG: Just get started, right?

PERKINS: Get started.

FROUG: A lot of these new, hot scriptwriters get themselves three or four hundred thousand dollars for a screenplay and then the wheels come to a grinding halt. Nothing after that. Sale of a screenplay is no guarantee you've got a career, is it?

HABER: No, but it is a guarantee that your material will be read seriously.

FROUG: Do you accept outlines or ideas or treatments? If somebody sends you something, do you want a complete screenplay?

PERKINS: From an unknown writer, certainly.

FROUG: Do you have release forms?

HABER: Yes. We always have to have literary release forms signed by anyone we don't represent. Incidentally, here's an interesting point for new screenwriters. They have to understand that there are hundreds and hundreds of thousands of scripts that flow in unsolicited to agencies and to producers and to studios in the city. Hundreds of thousands. Not ten thousand. *Hundreds of thousands.*

Everybody wants to be a screenwriter. Everybody has a script some place. And out of those come ten thousand lawsuits for reasons that are totally unjustified.

FROUG: My own experience in the industry is that there's a great deal of student paranoia, but there really is very little plagiarism. Do you find there's much plagiarism going on in Hollywood?

HABER: Well, you have to understand that there's very little that's new. To use an example, had *Ghost* been written by a new young writer, which it wasn't, somebody might have thought it was their own idea. But since movies began they've been writing ghost stories.

FROUG: Ghost movies with a ghost lover—I can name ten movies that have a ghost lover.

HABER: And so somebody somewhere will think that they've been plagiarized.

PERKINS: Particularly if you've sent your script unsolicited. Even if it comes back to you, supposedly unread, and they make a movie that's on your subject, you're gonna say, "I mailed that to them. They stole it and sent mine back."

FROUG: But you log a script in, and log that you returned it immediately, right?

HABER: Yes.

FROUG: Do you recommend that new writers register their material with the Writers Guild?

PERKINS: Yes. Absolutely. I'm finding, even in some of those letters that I get, that people are getting astute enough to say, "If you are interested in my treatment, please send me the proper forms." I mean, they know they have to sign releases.

FROUG: Do you find that TV networks readily accept new writers?

PERKINS: They say they do, but not really.

HABER: They accept them in spurts. When they get in the mood. [*Laughter*] Every other year they get in the mood and decide they want all new, young writers from all over the country. It lasts for about a month. Then they get out of the mood.

FROUG: I've heard that with a lot of these hot, new screenplays, the heat's generated by a great idea. The studios get hot for it, but as soon as they get the script in, the director or the producer begins to reexamine it and sees all the things wrong with it. Then they bring in an old pro to fix it up. Do you find that so?

PERKINS: That's true, though the definition of an old pro these days is hard to define.

FROUG: It's forty, right? [*Laughter*]

PERKINS: That's right.

FROUG: Do you still find much age discrimination in the industry?

HABER: Mostly in television. I don't believe that there's the ageism problem that many older writers believe there is. I think that oftentimes what happens is that older writers become less patient and less pliable to the needs of the business. It builds on itself, and they begin to think they're being discriminated against because of age. Really they're being discriminated against because they don't have the flexibility that new writers coming into the business have.

FROUG: And, maybe, they're not as hungry. Or they're hungry, but they're not beginning writers.

HABER: They don't have the patience.

PERKINS: Also, if you remember back in the old days when you and Bill and I were originally in television, you'd go to CBS and there'd be, say, Alan Wagner running all of the development. There was only one guy. Now you've got layers of people that get in the process, and it takes a lot longer. And the younger these studio people get, the less they seem to know people. It's understandable. Sometimes somebody asks about, for instance, I'll pick a name out of the air—Reggie Rose—and says, "What's he done?" Well, you have to realize, they might have read it somewhere if they were really prepared, but, nevertheless, there's no law requiring them to know that. And they ask you, "Is there something to read?" You say, "Well, maybe I can get you something." We're faced with that. We have to deal with that.

FROUG: There's a great story I've heard about that. Jack Neuman—my old college roommate, who created a half dozen TV series—is a multiple Writers Guild Award-winner, a long-time veteran, a writer-producer with enormous credentials, went into a meeting with a development guy at NBC. This executive, a young guy, says to Jack, "I'm sorry I don't know much about you. Tell me what you've done." And Jack said, "You first." [*Laughter*]

HABER: Television is like a paper shredder. Television is something that shreds up the creative people that work in it. It's an industry where you have to become successful quickly, financially, and in terms of your stature. Or, eventually, it will chew you up and move on to younger people.

FROUG: When you get a guy who's hot in television, do you prefer to have him set up his own company to package him? Is it better for him and you both?

HABER: Yes.

FROUG: We should explain. This packaging process means you put him together with an actor, usually, for a lead in the series, and maybe other writers and directors? As many elements as you can bring to the project?

HABER: Sometimes.

PERKINS: Or maybe even a joint venture with another company.

HABER: Sometimes he can just stand on his own.

FROUG: Are there any television people, like Steven Bochco, who can stand on their own?

HABER: Yeah, but even Bochco has somebody distributing his products. He had to make a deal with Fox.

FROUG: So when you talk about the package, you're not talking about distribution. You're talking about the production end.

HABER: Right.

FROUG: If you're going to take on a new writer, screen or television, what are you looking for? What quality are you looking for in this person?

PERKINS: I think, in my case, I first look for general writing talent—if their writing is stimulating and exciting and if the writer has some knowledge of his or her craft. If they're submitting materials specifically, I want to know that the writer has some idea of what the marketplace is all about and what the particular medium they're writing for is about. I think television, by nature, is more exacting and has more of a formula than motion pictures. You can read rambling motion picture scripts that just need editing, fine. But if the writer doesn't know how to write the TV form, it's very difficult. You can find that with playwrights who can write good Broadway comedy or theater comedy. They'll try to write a half-hour show, and, if they've not aware of the form, they're at page thirty and just getting started. It's not just a student's game. So I think that's the value, as you asked earlier, of being at a university or having a training ground—I don't care how you label it, but you need some training ground.

FROUG: I was just asking Bill Haber about a bio for CAA, because I believe this is truly a great American success story.

HABER: Bill Haber says that we don't do bios and promote ourselves because we are both legally and emotionally agents. We are thereby employees. Our clients are our employers, and we are only interested in our employers, not in ourselves.

FROUG: It's history that will be written by somebody.

PERKINS: They can do what they want. We hope they're correct. There's been a lot written about us.

FROUG: Some of it good, some of it not, right? I've just about covered my questions, do you want to volunteer anything here?

HABER: Yeah, I'll tell you what I think writers should do as the key to their writing. I have two basic tenets about writing. I think that in order to write and be a writer, you have to write and not talk about it. I think the biggest weakness in young writers is that they talk about writing. They're writers who don't write. Writing is a lonely, difficult, hard, arduous chore—alone in a room, creating. You can't talk to people about it. You can't show people a first chapter of something and tell them you are writing the rest, because what you're looking for is affirmation that you're a writer and then you'll continue. What you have to do is write it and finish it, not talk about it. That's the first basic commandment of writing. The second one is, in my opinion, to succeed in this business today, never, ever give up. *Ever.* The secret to the business is tenacity. *Never give up.* If you want to be a writer, keep writing. I don't care if you have to write twenty scripts, if you believe in yourself. If you give up, we'll grind you down.

PERKINS: I totally agree with Bill's summation. The only thing I would like to add is, I've had more people come to me and say, "Gee, I think I'd like to be a writer. Do you think I should write?" I say, "If you have to ask the question, you probably shouldn't."

[As Bill and Rowland were exiting the conference room, Bill stopped and addressed me. "Tell them," he said, firmly, "if they're only writing for the money, they shouldn't bother."]